Urban

Recreation Planning

Urban
Recreation Planning

Seymour M. Gold, Ph.D.

Associate Professor of Environmental Planning
University of California, Davis

LEA & FEBIGER · **Philadelphia** · **1973**

Health Education,
Physical Education, and
Recreation Series

Ruth Abernathy, Ph.D., Editorial Adviser,
Professor, Physical and Health Education,
University of Washington, Seattle, Washington 98105

Library of Congress Cataloging in Publication Data

Gold, Seymour M.
  Urban Recreation Planning.

  (Health education, physical education, and
recreation series)
    Bibliography: p. x, 333
    1. Recreation—United States. 2. Leisure—
United States. I. Title.
  GV53.G64   301.5'7   73-1786
  ISBN 0-8121-0417-X

ISBN 0-8121-0417-X

Library of Congress Catalog Card Number 73–1786

Published in Great Britain
by Henry Kimpton Publishers, London

Printed in the United States of America

Preface

Urbanization is one important force which has rapidly changed this country from a rural nation to one composed of cities and suburbs. The majority of our population is now concentrated in metropolitan centers which exhibit a wide range of social, economic and political diversity. This diversity is both the cause and effect of a complex array of human problems and issues. One area of current concern is the inner and central city of metropolitan areas. The city's traditional role as a focus for government, commerce, culture and as a living environment is rapidly changing and this change coupled with diversity presents a number of challenging areas for park administrators, urban planners, behavioral scientists and environmentalists.

One relatively unexplored area is the residential environment's potential for providing leisure opportunities. Within a problem context, the area of outdoor recreation is conspicuous for its lack of sophistication or study of urban recreation planning. There is evidence to suggest that the residents of most cities have not been able to communicate their outdoor recreation preferences to the planner and decision-maker and when preferences have been expressed, there is no sensitive technique for translating them into opportunities.

This evidence argues that past and present planning efforts may be inadequate or ineffective in some respect, especially for coping with the recreational problems of the inner city. It suggests that some of the more traditional concepts of outdoor recreation planning may be unsound and that an alternative is needed and possible. To date, no agency or individual has detailed a national perspective on a needed alternative.

Whatever the past reasons for this lack of perspective, it is now critical for someone to attempt a review of the current situation in order to develop a possible alternative which can be applied and evaluated by others over time. If this book serves no other purpose than to challenge the current state of urban outdoor recreation planning with some measured observations from a review of the literature and professional practice, it has accomplished its intent. If it can go beyond to develop a constructive alternative to status quo, it has more than accomplished its study of the unknown and controversial.

This book was started in 1968 at the University of Michigan and completed in 1972 at the University of California, Davis. During the period of its development many events, people and places have influenced my thinking about cities and recreation.

My early contacts with Donald Michael, Richard Meier, Robert Hoover, Richard Duke, Charles Blessing and Herbert Gans were important in shaping my philosophy of urban planning and perspectives of the city. In the area of outdoor recreation the ideas, inspiration and support of Ann Satterwaite, Hugh Davis, Grant Sharpe, Arthur Wilcox, Leslie Reid, William Mott, Marion Clawson, Jack Knetsch, Douglas Sessoms, John Nesbitt and Diana Dunn were invaluable. I am indebted to Justin Leonard, John Bardach, William Stapp and Erik Svenson for their critical review of the original manuscript and their bold insights on research, leisure behavior, the environment and the future.

I am grateful to Sidney Lutzin of the National Recreation and Park Association and Roman Koenings of the Bureau of Outdoor Recreation who encouraged me to express these ideas in a book. Their advice, support and enthusiasm were most helpful. I also wish to thank Nancy Scybert for the heroic job of typing the manuscript and the many planning and recreation agencies, organizations and individuals who have made this book possible and whose data, experience, frustrations and hopes are the basis of this effort.

Finally, but foremost I appreciate the understanding of my wife Susan and sons Daniel, David and Robert. Susan's editing and my sons' patience will long be remembered.

Davis, California   Seymour M. Gold

Contents

I

Background
and
Concepts

I

Introduction

Urban recreation planning is a process that relates people to leisure time and space. It is a topic generally avoided by professionals because of a relative lack of concepts, techniques and substantiation. It is concerned with a host of intangible considerations and value judgments that are conjectural and need tesing over time. Because the nature of this topic is subject to a wide range of interpretation, it is necessary to clearly define the scope, problem, issues, objectives and organization of this book. The complexity and ambiguity characteristic of the planning process, outdoor recreation and the city prompt this detailed introduction.

SCOPE

This book relates an activity (outdoor recreation) to an area (the city) with a process (planning) and a measure or indicator in that process (space standards). Within these broad parameters, each element is described in terms of time, space and people to give the reader an illustrative focus and narrow the scope to five major dimensions.

National Perspective

A national perspective is used because there is nothing in the literature or practice to indicate a significant geographic difference in the problems or techniques commonly associated with urban recreation planning. There are also no significant regional or local distinctions in the magnitude and approaches to the problem. This book is concerned with Urban America or the 243 metropolitan areas of 50,000 or more population which are the living, working and leisure context for more than one half of this nation's population. Within each of these metropolitan areas, it is concerned primarily with the central and inner city because this represents the most dramatic example of the problems and potentials associated with recreation planning. However, the principles, methodology and approach to be described can also apply to suburban areas and small communities.

Present Time Horizon

The concern is present. As a reference in time, the summer of 1967 is considered a turning point separating the past from the present and urgent future of Urban America. The violence and issues dramatized during that summer represent a point of no return for recreation planning in cities. Although the historical roots of urban recreation planning will be described, the primary concern in this book is with the 1960's and 1970's. Projections to 1980 and the year 2000 are used to illustrate pronounced trends. However, in general, 1960 or 1970 data are employed and conditions in the central and inner city are described as they exist now.

Inner City Emphasis

A metropolitan area is commonly defined as an integrated economic and social unit with a large population. The formal designation is a Standard Metropolitan Statistical Area (SMSA) which contains at least one central city and adjacent communities.

A central city is the largest city of an SMSA and which gives the SMSA its name. The "core city" or "inner city" is a popular expression sometimes meaning the central business district and densely populated downtown neighborhoods of generally poorer residents.[1]

The inner city, as viewed in this book, is a densely populated area of generally low-income residents that is part of and usually surrounded by the central city and suburbs. In many instances, data

---

[1] National Advisory Commission on Civil Disorders, *Report of the National Advisory Commission on Civil Disorders* (New York: Bantam Books, 1968), **p.** 408.

are given for only the central city because much of the literature does not make a distinction between the central and the inner city. Wherever possible the data and substantiation to be used focus on the inner city. Figure 1 is a schematic illustration of a typical SMSA showing the geographic relationships of the exurbs, suburbs and central city to the inner city.

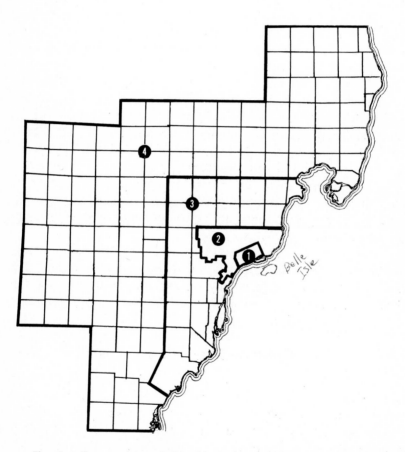

Fig. 1. Geographic relationships of a standard metropolitan statistical area: the Detroit region—1, Inner city; 2, central city; 3, suburbs; 4 exurbs.

Detailed characteristics of the inner city will be described in Chapter III. Most inner cities in America are characterized by the following general conditions: slums, poverty, crime, civil unrest, unemployment, traffic congestion, environmental pollution, racial or ethnic ghettos, declining property values, a lack of open space or opportunities for public outdoor recreation, high stress levels, litter and a low level of municipal services. There are many exceptions to these characteristics, and some authorities have a nostalgic response to them as a reaction to the relative sterility of suburbia. However, the facts clearly indicate that those who have the ability to leave the central city do, while those who have the option to return to the central city do not, given the opportunity. The flight to the suburbs is almost complete for most middle-income Americans. Only the rich and the very poor now live in the inner city.

The inner city has also been characterized by many writers as exciting, dynamic, colorful—the heart as well as the hope of Urban America. These values and opinions will not be debated. The residential environment will be described as it is, despite token efforts at urban renewal and some remaining pockets of high-income residents. Although there are many exceptions to any nationwide generalization, most authorities agree that the current physical and social problems of the inner city outweigh effective solutions and are growing worse.

This book is oriented toward the negative or problem aspects of the inner city. The intent is not to dismiss the hopeful dimensions, but to view things as they are and may well be in the future, given no dramatic changes in this country's existing priorities.

Outdoor Recreation Focus

Outdoor recreation as an activity is the focus. Its time, space and cultural aspects are described with reference to the planning for and use of a neighborhood park or playground. Public, tax-supported facilities dedicated to outdoor recreation in its traditional or innovative sense are of primary concern. Both the organized and unorganized aspects of outdoor recreation are considered. The neighborhood park or playground is analyzed from its traditional orientation toward children to its possible present and future role as a social and leisure focus.

Urban Planning Context

What planning is, or could be, and how it relates as a process to the allocation of resources for neighborhood recreational opportunities are the focus of this book. Planning is not presented as an end in itself or the solution to urban problems; to date no single process or profession has been able to cope effectively with the inner city. No pretense of being able to identify or discuss all of the relevant issues in planning or the complexities of urban living is made.

Outdoor recreation planning is viewed as part of the comprehensive planning process as described in the literature and demonstrated in professional practice. The planning process and the role of leisure planning are also viewed from the more innovative approaches now being discussed in the literature and demonstrated in practice. Both the conceptual and pragmatic potentials and limitations of each approach are examined in terms of their relevance to the inner city and the provision of neighborhood parks. The changing nature of both urban planning and outdoor recreation is described and related to a need for questioning the traditional approach to urban recreation planning.

THE PROBLEM

The fundamental question is: *How can the planning process be more responsive to the outdoor recreation objectives of an inner city neighborhood?* Its complexity is illustrated in the following sections which view the problem from four planes: description, relevance, relationships and research.

General Description

The prospect of mass leisure, or unemployment, its implications for outdoor recreation and the current need for a more systematic approach to recreation planning within the context of the comprehensive planning process prompt more basic and applied research in a wide range of problem areas.

One growing concern is the past, present and future role of recreation standards in the planning process. Their traditional role of allocating public land, facilities and programs is being challenged in light of new planning concepts, methodologies and techniques.

Current literature in the Recreation, Planning and Behavioral Science fields expresses concern over the use of arbitrary standards. Clawson states:

> Determination of desirable area of various kinds of open space in the past has depended primarily upon rather subjective considerations of planners and leading citizens as to what seemed enough. Very few objective studies and almost no experimentation have been made.[2]

It is common knowledge among many planners that uniform recreation standards, i.e., 10 acres/1,000 persons of open space in urban areas, cannot be rationalized except as guidelines. The arbitrary practice of enumerating so many facilities or areas per capita is a hazardous planning technique, yet it persists for lack of an alternative. Mounting evidence indicates that arbitrary recreation standards represent inadequate indicators of demand or needs and the capability of the public sector to produce the supply. Mueller and Gurin state:

> Standards expressed as so many acres per 1000 do not discriminate among communities in terms of varying propensities for recreation consumption. Differences among communities in terms of demographic and socioeconomic characteristics produce quite different patterns of recreation demand.[3]

Another discrepancy is the fact that supply usually creates demand, hence recreation standards have a self-fulfilling, if not self-exceeding, dimension which further complicates their effective use for recreation planning and resource allocation. One other shortcoming of standards is their insensitivity to a planning unit's available or projected fiscal resources. Communities vary in their tax base and consequently in their ability to acquire land and meet these recreation standards.[4]

A simplistic standards approach to recreation planning has become irrelevant because of a growing failure among single-function planners to relate to the comprehensive planning process. This is especially true at the metropolitan level where the complexity

---

[2] Marion Clawson, "A Positive Approach to Open Space Preservation," *Journal of the American Institute of Planners*, XXVIII (May, 1962), p. 126.

[3] Eva Mueller and G. Gurin, *Participation in Outdoor Recreation: Factors Affecting Demand among American Adults*. ORRRC Study Report 20. (Washington: Government Printing Office, 1962.)

[4] H. M. Levin, *Estimating the Municipal Demand for Public Recreation Land* (Washington: Brookings Institution, Oct., 1966).

of government demands increased rationality for allocating scarce resources to competing needs. Recreation planners, like other single-function planners, should seek methods to relate themselves to the comprehensive planning process with a better awareness of government objectives and resource restraints.

Other arguments against the arbitrary use of recreation standards reflect a "requirements approach" to resource allocation which is concerned with the trade-offs involved when an "optimum" output for outdoor recreation may involve serious opportunity costs for other public services such as education. Since all public goods or services compete for a jurisdiction's limited resources, any incremental expenditure for one denies that much for all the others.

A host of other questions about the past and present use and misuse of recreation standards have also been voiced by human ecologists, sociologists and political scientists. The indictment seems clear. However, alternatives have yet to be conceptualized and tested.

Despite these arguments, there is a new and more significant role which standards can assume in the planning process. The growing trend toward quantification of social values, a systems approach to planning and the "measurement explosion" generated by new techniques, such as Planning-Programming-Budgeting Systems (PPBS), project a revised and critical role for recreation standards in the planning process.

The problem is to determine how standards can be effectively used in a more sophisticated and responsive approach to recreation planning. It is *not* to determine what standards can be used or to establish any standards. Conceptually, the problem is to first understand the traditional approach to recreation planning and develop an alternative which is more adaptable to the demands of the present and future.

Although the differences between these planning approaches may seem unimportant, they will require many professionals to shift "methodological gears" in the middle of an ongoing process already strained by a lack of sophisticated methodology, data base, trained personnel, adequate budgets and an intuitive rather than a systematic approach to meeting objectives. The secondary effects of this disruption could be even greater than some of the problems outlined above. The challenge is to conceptualize the past, present and future role of urban recreation planning in the larger context shown in Figure 2.

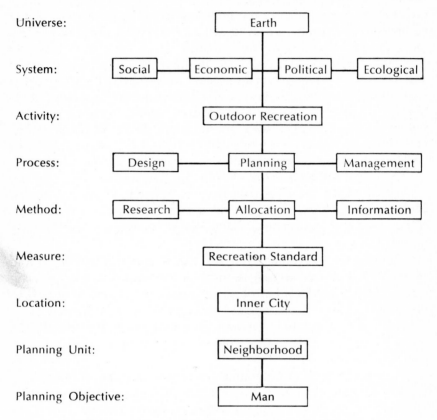

Fig. 2.   Context for urban recreation planning.

Relevance and Relationships

Many critical problems are related to this problem. They include: self-determination, discrimination, welfare economics, institutional change and environmental quality. All are more basic and urgent areas of concern than outdoor recreation. It seems more important to confront the fundamental issues of urban sociology, human ecology, resource allocation and environmental change now challenging the inner city's very existence, and then consider such questions as leisure or outdoor recreation. However, by the time these problems are solved, urban dwellers may have lost the desire to use, request or support recreation as a public service and will rely on other opportunities for their recreational needs. In some instances this may be inevitable and in the public interest, but the evidence makes a strong case for continuing to provide leisure services to the inner city.

Significant Issues

The problem generates a wide range of controversial questions which become issues when viewed by different publics. These issues are identified here because they will be used as benchmarks to evaluate selected planning concepts and techniques. They will also be used as "reality checks" to relate ideas to the real world of professional practice and urban living in the 1970's.

RESOURCE ALLOCATION

In a society of competing needs and relatively scarce resources, the questions of who gets what, when, where and why are important and controversial. The rules of a market economy apply to most commodities or services, but there are many aspects of leisure and outdoor recreation which defy conventional economic analysis. At the scale of a neighborhood park and the activities commonly associated with it, some economists suggest that it is impossible or irrelevant to attempt conventional economic analysis. The pressing issue of "welfare economics" or of the distribution of wealth in an affluent society has yet to be solved for most public services and private goods.

ADVOCACY PLANNING

The increasing tempo, scale and complexity of urban life and government have decreased citizen contact with the planning process; there is a growing credibility gap in the expertise of government. This combination of factors has alienated many people from centralized planning and their search for an alternative has prompted them to organize and employ consultants to help advocate and articulate their objectives. In many instances this initiative has put government on the defensive—it reacts only to pressure instead of anticipating needs.

In terms of leisure planning, the question of who can best do the planning for whom is becoming increasingly controversial. With respect to the inner city, serious questions, even open violence and a direct confrontation, are becoming more frequent in a small but militant movement against centralized planning and a desire for more self-determination through advocacy planning. If current trends continue, what may be at stake is the future of centralized recreation planning. This is a very real issue which both administrators and planners should anticipate, especially for the inner city.

ENVIRONMENTAL QUALITY

The current national emphasis on environmental quality has prompted a host of questions about the inner city and raised resident expectations for governmental action to the point of militancy. A growing number of authorities have begun to question the inner city as a place in which to live. Others are alarmed at how this affluent country can be indifferent to the environmental conditions of the inner city. They see a basic contradiction in national priorities that favors the suburbs of America.

Still others ask, "What good can the provision of recreational opportunities be in the area that has more urgent problems, e.g., chronic unemployment, inadequate housing, education and health services?" The issue is: What priority, if any, does recreation have in the inner city and who can best assume the responsibility for providing it in an effective manner?

QUALITY OF URBAN LIFE

The questions ultimately fall into two major areas: (1) individual capability to act protected by adequate standards in the physical and social environment, and (2) individual opportunity for variety, identity, range of choice and personal fulfillment. They imply a quality of urban life fast diminishing in Urban America, and ask, "Is the city really for people?"

When applied to recreation planning in the inner city, these issues are the source of increasing disappointment and suspicion by residents of centralized planning, local recreation agencies and urban government. Standards of recreation space are basic to the problem because they can be a way to measure things, e.g., area, facilities, or values and priorities.

Definition of Terms

The semantic jungle of planning, outdoor recreation and urban sociology prompts a definition of selected terms. Because these areas deal with controversial values, no specific definition can satisfy everyone or meet all needs. However, there seems to be a general acceptance[5] of the terms listed below in the Glossary:

Leisure – Any portion of an individual's time not occupied by gainful employment or in the pursuit of essential activities.

Recreation – Any leisure-time activity which is pursued for its own sake.

Outdoor Recreation – Leisure-time activities which utilize an outdoor area or facility.

Park – Any area of public land set aside for aesthetic, educational, recreational or cultural use.

Open Space – All land and water in an urban area not covered by buildings.

Standard – A measure for the allocation of resources to existing or potential needs as determined by stated objectives.

Plan – A course of action which can be implemented to achieve stated objectives and which someone intends to implement.

Planning – Designing a course of action to achieve ends, or a way of defining purposes and of choosing means for attaining them; or the systematic provision of information and alternatives to facilitate decision-making; or the anticipation of and preparation for the future; or the formulation of goals and designing means to achieve these goals.

Inner City – Those neighborhoods which usually surround the central business district of a metropolitan area and are considered within the geographic core of the central city.

Neighborhood – A residential area with a social and physical identity.

Ghetto – A residential area in which members of an ethnic or racial minority group live because of social, legal or economic pressure.

Slum – A highly congested residential area marked by deteriorated, unsanitary buildings, absentee landlords, poverty and social disorganization.

Strategy

Most books on recreation planning generally begin with answers and focus on effects instead of causes and upon details instead of concepts. This book proposes to begin with questions, focus on causes, and conceptualize a new approach and methodology for urban recreation planning. The primary objective is to develop a

---

[5] Charles Abrams, *The Language of Cities* (New York: Viking Press, 1971).

planning technique by which any neighborhood can engage in the planning process to help determine its recreational opportunities in terms of area and facilities. As this technique is refined over time for a relatively small planning unit (neighborhood) and narrow range of activities, it should be possible to adapt it to larger areas (city or region) and more diverse sets of activities and resources.

Approach and Viewpoint

The author's view is: (1) that of the professional urban planner, (2) that public parks are an indispensable element of urban form and function, provided they are well designed, properly located, adequately maintained and responsive to the needs or preferences of intended users, and (3) that standards for recreation space can and should have a sensitive role in the planning process. With these viewpoints the problem is approached in the following manner: An activity (outdoor recreation) takes place in an area (inner city). A process (planning) can be used to relate this activity to the area. A technique (space standards) is part of this process. This technique has different approaches (traditional and innovative) that can be applied to a situation (neighborhood park). The conceptual merits or shortcomings of each approach can be compared and evaluated with its respective present and future implications for Urban America.

The rationale for selecting a neighborhood as the planning unit and a park or playground as the recreational area for analysis is based on available data, the crucial role of each in the city and the premise: if one can develop a planning concept and technique for a small planning unit and limited set of activities, this concept can be generalized to larger planning units and a wider range of activities.

This rationale is also based on the premise: within a metropolitan area the larger the planning unit, the less adaptable it is to the implications of standards and the more subject it is to recreational ambiguity in terms of user groups, administrative responsibilities and user mobility. Both the neighborhood and its traditional park or playground are the smallest and best documented unit. They are also the areas with the widest range of individual diversity, most critical shortage of effective recreation opportunities, and probably the smallest unit for effective political representation.

The inner city neighborhood is selected because it provides a conspicuous illustration of the use or misuse of standards for recreation space. However, with a different set of variables, the same holds true for most central cities and suburbs. For brevity, the scope

TABLE 1
Recreation Planning Variables

Conceptual Orientation		Illustrative Variables		
General	Specific	A*	B	C
Standards	Type	Space	Development	Program
	Value level	Optimum	Average	Minimum
Location	Gov't level	Local	Regional	State
	Location	Inner city	City	Suburban
	Density	High	Medium	Low
Area	Orientation	User	Intermediate	Resource
	Responsibility	Public	Quasi-public	Private
	Type	Playground	Natural	Special
	Access	Pedestrian	Transit	Vehicular
	Planning unit	Neighborhood	Community	Citywide
Use	Activity type	Active	Passive	Special
	Intensity	Peak	Seasonal	Off-season
	Unit	Hours	Days	Year
User	Identity	Resident	Nonresident	Tourist
	Income	Low	Middle	High
	Mobility	Low	Medium	High
	Leisure	Low	Medium	High
Planning	Type	Advocate	Advisory	Central
	Responsibility	Group	Joint	Government
	Period	2 years	10 years	20 years

* Selected variables.

of this book is limited to the variables indicated in Table 1, Column A. If the reader is primarily concerned with the central city or suburban areas he can select a different set of variables. Any combination is possible, depending on the uniqueness of each situation.

Assumptions

Several assumptions are implicit in this book: (1) social research techniques can be used to obtain a representative indication of outdoor recreation preferences, (2) these preferences can be translated into dimensions of time, space and people, (3) these dimensions can be related to the demand for and supply of recreational opportunities to indicate need in terms of area, at a given time, for a specific activity or set of activities, (4) this need can be translated into a standard of acres/1,000 persons and a social indicator, which reflect the expressed preferences of residents, and (5) both the standard and social indicator can play an important role in the planning process.

The strategy of this book is to take one component (recreation standards) of a process (recreation planning/traditional approach) and adapt it to a different process (recreation planning/innovative approach) to develop a new technique which will then be applied and evaluated in an illustrative situation. The products will be: (1) a new concept and technique, and rationalization of both in terms of a user-oriented approach to recreation planning, (2) a formula for deriving what the standard of a given neighborhood could be, and (3) a social indicator or recreational opportunity index for program budgeting or program evaluation.

CHAPTER SYNOPSIS

This book is divided into two major parts. Part I (Chapters I–V) focuses primarily on definitions, description, historical background and a review of relevant literature on outdoor recreation, the inner city, the planning process and the recreation standard. Part II (Chapters VI–VIII) operationalizes this by a description and evaluation of the use of standards in the planning process. It offers an alternative to traditional planning techniques and applies this alternative to an inner city neighborhood.

Chapter II describes and analyzes the contemporary context of leisure in Urban America. Some historical beginnings are traced and selected cross-cultural factors are examined and related to a justification of urban open space. The emphasis is on the user. The focus is on the ideas and concepts which are now or have been the bases of the Recreation Movement.

Chapter III is devoted to a description of what the inner city is or could be, given some radical changes in American thinking. Some general characteristics, challenging potentials and significant alternatives are described. Also the neighborhood and its recreational characteristics are examined.

In Chapter IV, planning and the planning process are discussed to provide a context for problems related to urban recreation planning.

Chapter V concentrates on the outdoor recreation standard. A classification of standards, significant concepts, current usage and its implications are discussed. The purpose of this chapter is to illustrate the widespread and arbitrary use of standards in the planning process.

Chapter VI identifies the arguments for and against the use of space standards and develops these arguments into two approaches to urban recreation planning: the traditional and innovative. Emphasis is on comparison, rationalization and relevance to the problem. The need for an alternative is stressed and an innovative approach is developed.

In Chapter VII the innovative approach to urban outdoor recreation planning is applied to a typical situation. A creative solution to the shortcomings of the traditional approach is emphasized. Selected means of demonstrating this approach, the anticipated results and the relevance of both are discussed.

In Chapter VIII the potentials, shortcomings and implications of this approach on recreation in Urban America are summarized. Some suggested areas for research and action are outlined.

II

Recreation in Urban America

To date, no single source has developed a perspective on the time, space, use and development dimensions of recreation in America. DeGrazia's *Time, Work and Leisure*, Kaplan's *Leisure in America*, Neumeyer's *Leisure and Recreation*, Larrabee's *Mass Leisure and* Jensen's *Outdoor Recreation in America* offer a perspective on leisure, but all stop short of relating leisure to urban space and the planning process. Other references such as Butler's *Recreation Areas*, Hjelte and Shivers' *Planning Recreational Places*, Williams' *Recreation Places* and Rutledge's *Anatomy of a Park* have focused primarily on design apart from the behavioral and institutional context of recreation and urban planning as social services. This chapter integrates these ideas to provide a frame of reference for contemporary urban recreation planning.

HISTORICAL SETTING

A description of the historical development of recreation in this country is necessary to understand recreation's current context and future directions. Emphasis is on recreation as a movement primarily concerned with the provision of public recreation land, facilities and program in urban areas. The Recreation Movement is considered as one important aspect of the early Conservation and Social Reform Movements.

Colonial and Romantic Periods (1600-1900)

The earliest patterns of urban recreation behavior in America originated in 17th century England. The Puritans who first settled the American colonies disapproved of sports, games and amusement.[1] Despite their sanctions against recreation, they devoted much time to husking bees, tavern sports, hunting, fishing and county fairs. They were also instrumental in the establishment of the Boston Commons in 1634, this country's first urban public open space used for recreation.

The continued immigration of European settlers and the movement west began to diversify recreational activities. The frontier shooting-matches, house-raisings and weddings became recreational rituals for many. Religious revivals, dancing, horse racing, gambling and drinking were common lower-class activities. The upper classes, especially the owners of southern plantations, developed a gay and sophisticated social life centered around recreation. In urban areas, field sports, card playing, theatricals and concerts took place with increasing frequency in public and private outdoor settings.

In the early 1800's the growth of the industrial city and the decreasing work week began to exert several new influences on recreation patterns. Indoor sports became more common. The gymnasium, commercial theater, traveling circus and burlesque show became popular. Spectator sports such as boxing, foot races and boating began to attract considerable crowds. Excursion boats and swimming became accepted activities. Holidays were festive occasions for the lower and middle classes, while the wealthy left the city for summer homes and resorts.

During the latter half of the century, organized sports rose to prominence. Baseball became a national game. Bicycling, croquet, archery, tennis, roller-skating and football became common urban recreation activities. The small-town chatauqua, county fair and bingo game became American traditions. Many of these activities took place in what seemed to be a limitless expanse of open space or undeveloped areas in and around cities. But this was soon to change with the growth of an industrial society, large urban centers and residential slums. The transformation of open spaces into high-density residential areas without the amenities of open space began to alarm some individuals. Frederick Law Olmstead, the Father of Landscape Architecture in America, saw the need for:

---

[1] Martin H. Neumeyer and Ester S. Neumeyer, *Leisure and Recreation*, 3rd ed. (New York: The Roland Press Company, 1958), p. 59.

A promenading place for the upper classes, and a picnic and recreation area for the common working people of the city to complement the city, by providing an essentially rural landscape for tranquility and rest to the mind.[2]

His concept was translated into a design for Central Park in Manhattan, established in 1853 as America's first municipal park dedicated to outdoor recreation. Despite early political and economic opposition, Central Park was a tremendous success. It became the example of a large, well-designed municipal park and stimulated the building of hundreds of smaller ones which emulated its design concept.

Olmstead's aim for an area of "rural escape" from the intolerable residential conditions of this era was closely related to the social reform movement against urban slums. The American Playground Movement began in 1885, when the German idea of "sand gardens" was tried in a Boston slum. These gardens consisted of sand heaps, swings and other simple playthings. The first users participated in highly disciplined activities under the supervision of volunteer women, and the gardens were operated only in the summer. Their purpose was to "protect the children from the heat, danger, and dirt of the city, and the immorality of the city streets, and to protect the parents and neighbors in turn from being annoyed by children who were engaged in unsupervised play."[3] During this period a number of settlement houses began to develop model playgrounds to impress decision-makers with the need for the public provision of neighborhood parks and play space.

Early Twentieth Century (1900-1940)

Higher standards of living, increased leisure and new technologies had a direct influence on the Recreation Movement in this period. The five-day work week and two-week vacation with pay had a tremendous impact on leisure patterns. The development of public transit, the automobile and better roads drastically altered the pattern of user mobility to include regional, state and national parks. People could leave the city for open country and outdoor

[2] Frederick Law Olmstead, Public Parks and the Enlargement of Towns (Cambridge: Riverside Press, 1870), p. 23.
[3] Clarence E. Rainwater, The Play Movement in the United States (Chicago: University of Chicago Press, 1922), p. 22.

recreation as never before. Summer homes on the urban fringe became permanent suburban communities and commuting to the inner city became a way of life for the upper classes.

Large municipal park systems were established with major public investments in land acquisition, facilities and program during this period. The fledgling playground movement developed into the Recreation Movement, a municipal function and a profession. This period also heralded the beginnings of an emphasis on organized program and professional leadership, planning and management.

One notable trend of this period was an effort toward neighborhood organization reflected in "a new enthusiasm for local organizations." This was evident in the emphasis on decentralized control, school-centered activities and recreation centers. The movement spread widely, but never became effective because "the authoritative decisions came from central, city-wide administrative units rather than from local neighborhood organizations."[4]

During World War I the Recreation Movement focused its resources on providing diversions for soldiers. Rainwater summarizes nine ideological transitions of this period which began to change recreation from:

> (1) provision for little children to that for all ages, (2) facilities operated during the summer only to those maintained throughout the year, (3) outdoor equipment and activities only to both outdoor and indoor facilities and events, (4) congested urban districts to both urban and rural communities, (5) philanthropic to community support and control, (6) "free" play and miscellaneous activities to "directed" play with organized activities and correlated schedules, (7) a simple to a complex field of activities including manual, physical, aesthetic, social and civic projects, (8) the provision of facilities to the definition of standards for the use of leisure time, (9) individual interests to group and community activities.[5]

Hjelte adds five additional transitions characteristic of this period. They are a transition from:

> (1) "play movement" to the "recreation movement," (2) a local municipal movement only to a state and national movement, (3) programs detached from public education to programs integrated with public education curriculum and system, (4) organization limited to urban communities to that inclusive of rural areas as well, (5) an

---

4 Neumeyer and Neumeyer, *Leisure and Recreation*, p. 63.
5 Rainwater, *The Play Movement in the United States*, p. 192.

organization largely under quasi-public control with subsidies from public funds to full acceptance of recreation as a public function.[6]

The Depression of the 1930's, despite its negative social and economic impact on individuals, had many positive influences on the Recreation Movement. Economic hardship reduced attendance at commercial recreation attractions and created a soaring demand for available public facilities. Work relief programs employed thousands of persons to develop and expand recreational areas. The Recreation Movement seemed about to flourish after the Depression eased, but World War II intervened.

World War II Period (1941-1946)

This period emphasized "the values of recreation for the armed forces, industrial workers and civilian morale."[7] It witnessed the beginning of labor-union involvement in the movement and close association of organizations such as the YMCA, American Red Cross and USO to supply some of the programs and facilities the government could not because of manpower and equipment shortages. Other gains included:

(1) Demands for recreation services in normal communities similar to those experienced by service personnel on military posts and in communities adjacent to them, (2) Increased recognition of the need for professionally trained recreation personnel, (3) An increased recognition of the contribution of recreation to emotional balance and the basic needs of the individual, (4) A greater recognition of the place of the layman in recreation affairs, (5) A realization of the contributions of recreation to patient recovery.[8]

This period also saw the growth of industrial and therapeutic recreation and the beginning of federal aid to assist local communities in providing leisure services. It also showed some trends away from centralized management because many systems lacked professionals and had to rely on volunteers. Most important, it developed a pent-up demand of staggering proportions that was to erupt in the post-war period.

[6] George Hjelte, The Administration of Public Recreation (New York: Macmillan Co., 1940), p. 16.
[7] Charles E. Doell, A Brief History of Parks and Recreation in the United States (Chicago: The Athletic Institute, 1954), p. 62.
[8] Ibid.

The Post-war Period (1946-1960)

The post-war boom in urban development had a marked effect on recreation use patterns and development. The rapid expansion of schools, parks and all types of recreational areas was unprecedented and based on a drastic change in the population composition, mobility, amount of disposable income and increase in leisure time for large numbers of Americans. These conditions are dramatically summarized in the findings of the Outdoor Recreation Resources Review Commission:

> By the year 2000 our population will nearly double; and the overall demand for outdoor recreation will triple . . . the kinds of outdoor recreation most people take part in today are relatively simple . . . what people now do for outdoor recreation is not necessarily what they will do in the future . . . water is the focal point of outdoor recreation . . . the recreation problem is not one of number of acres, but of effective acres . . . people want outdoor recreation close to home and most people live in metropolitan areas . . . as mobility continues to increase, more people will travel farther to enjoy outstanding scenic, wildlife and wilderness areas . . . there are many overlooked outdoor recreation resources in urban areas.[9]

However, critical analysis of the legislation establishing the Commission and of the Commission's studies and published reports reveals a very limited emphasis on urban parks and primary emphasis on resource-oriented parks and users. This was not the fault of the Commission, but of Congress for passing a law which mandated: "Outdoor recreation resources shall *not* mean nor include recreation facilities, programs, and opportunities usually associated with urban development such as playgrounds, stadia, golf courses, city parks and zoos."[10] In essence, Congress stated that information about the recreation problems and potentials of cities was not needed; this is one cause of the problems characteristic of urban recreation today. By calculation or oversight, Congress can be held responsible for creating this turning point in the quality and quantity of urban recreation facilities. In retrospect, it seems paradoxical that a massive effort meant to improve the quantity and quality of resource-ori-

---

[9] Outdoor Recreation Resources Review Commission, *Outdoor Recreation for America* (Washington, D. C.: Government Printing Office, 1962). Summary hereafter cited as the *ORRRC Report;* individual studies will be identified by number, e.g., *ORRRC Study,* No. 22.

[10] U. S. Congress, Public Law 85-470, Sec. 2(3), June 28, 1958.

ented recreational opportunities may have caused their deterioration from overuse largely because of a lack of urban parks.

The emphasis of the *ORRRC Report* on resource-oriented recreation was reinforced by housing shortages which forced thousands of urban residents and returning veterans to move to the suburbs. Competing demands for other social services on urban and suburban budgets and a drastic increase in recreation use placed a strain on urban park systems. The strain began to show in the trend toward consolidation of park and recreation agencies, curtailment of programs and maintenance, and attempts to meet local needs with regional parks. It represented a turning point for the development of city parks and a reorientation of the Recreation Movement that was to become a problem and issue in the next period.

Space Age (1960-1970)

At the national level, the Bureau of Outdoor Recreation (BOR) was established to "serve as a focal point to implement federal outdoor recreation policies."[11] However, the Bureau's orientation was essentially the same as that of the Outdoor Recreation Resources Review Commission. Although the Bureau's stated concern was "with all types of outdoor recreation," in philosophy and practice the Bureau was involved "only secondarily with playground and community type recreation."[12]

Despite the Bureau's lack of emphasis on urban areas, a host of federal programs such as the Land and Water Conservation Fund and Open Space Program were enacted; these had a significant impact on urban parks. State and local agencies began to meet the requirements of these federal-aid programs. The emphasis was on unification of park and recreation departments and coordination of agencies with recreation responsibilities. In 1965, several recreation organizations consolidated into one, The National Recreation and Park Association (NRPA).

By any measure, the Recreation Movement would seem to have reached its historical zenith in this country. No one could dispute its widespread public support and massive potential to serve an affluent society's increasing appetite for recreation. However, a

---

[11] Clayne R. Jensen, *Outdoor Recreation in America* (Minneapolis: Burgess Publishing Company, 1970), p. 93.

[12] *Ibid.*, p. 94.

subtle change and decline became conspicuous in the quality and effectiveness of facilities and types of programs available to residents of the central city. In a relatively short span of years, the Recreation Movement had begun to turn away from many of the social values which were involved in its inception. A growing trend of user dissatisfaction and frustration with urban recreation facilities was identified as one of the important causes for the civil disorders in 1967. These disorders prompted a flurry of studies and renewed interest in the recreation problems of the inner city, but this interest quietly evaporated in the jungles of Viet Nam. National priorities and public interested shifted away from the civil rights and social issues of the 1960's toward the environmental issues of the 1970's.

CURRENT CONTEXT

Outdoor recreation in the larger context of American lifestyle and leisure is a composite of many elements. Most important to an understanding of the quantitative aspects of urban outdoor recreation are the: (1) dimensions of demand, (2) supply of opportunities, (3) scope of responsibilities, (4) state of organized program, and (5) status of organized research. A statistical perspective of each is given here to complement the conceptual treatment of these topics in all other chapters.

Because one of the objectives of this book is to contrast recreation in the inner city with other geographic areas, the data are national in scope and comparative wherever possible. These should: (1) help in later chapters to highlight geographic or demographic differences between the central city and other areas, and (2) point out the need for additional research where no data exist. These data are considered to be illustrative and should be carefully qualified because no central source or common technique yet exists for the information needed in these areas.

Dimensions of Demand

The traditional concept of demand for outdoor recreation is under serious question. At one extreme, many regard its quantitative aspects as a meaningful reflection of interest or participation in outdoor recreation. This school of thought is best expressed in Clawson's interpretation of "a schedule of volume in relation to a price"[13] and the Bureau of Outdoor Recreation's definition: "the amount and kinds of outdoor recreation opportunities or facilities the public desires."[14] At the other extreme many submit: "Demand as it is now defined and measured is consumption or irrelevant."[15] Regardless of which interpretation of "demand" one accepts, neither is any reflection of the quality of a recreational experience which may be the more important measure. With this qualification several aspects of "demand" are described here.

LEISURE

In a statistical sense, leisure provides the time dimension for outdoor recreation. It is discretionary time or that which is left after necessary obligations are met. Its use connotes purposefulness or choice, but does not exclude a decision to do nothing. Most definitions imply a freedom of time and attitude. In times past, leisure was the luxury of a few; today it is the privilege of many as Americans move toward a leisure-oriented lifestyle. This is not true for all sectors of American society and especially for the urban disadvantaged, but it is a characteristic of most people now living in urban America.

The amount of leisure time varies with each individual and his stage in life. For the "typical American adult," most estimates agree on "5 hours of leisure time" remaining after a "minimum level of existence and subsistence have been accomplished."[16] A recent national time-budget study indicates that the average married working man or the housewife spends "20 percent of every average working day in non-essential activities."[17] Clawson projects a figure of "34 percent by 2000." Clawson also estimates "Only about 3 or 4 percent of leisure time is used for outdoor recreation activity."[18] Time-budget studies indicate that the average working adult has 5.1

---

[13] Marion Clawson, *Economics of Outdoor Recreation* (Baltimore: Johns Hopkins Press, 1966), p. 41.

[14] U. S. Department of the Interior, Bureau of Outdoor Recreation, *Manual: Nationwide Plan* (Washington: Bureau of Outdoor Recreation, 1964).

[15] Jack L. Knetsch, "Assessing the Demands for Outdoor Recreation," in *Elements of Outdoor Recreation Planning*, B. L. Driver (Ed.), (Ann Arbor: University Microfilms, 1970), p. 132.

[16] Jensen, *Outdoor Recreation in America*, p. 2.

[17] Phillip E. Converse and John P. Robinson, *Summary of United States Time Use Survey* (Ann Arbor: The University of Michigan, Survey Research Center, 1966), Tables 1 and 5.

[18] Clawson, *Economics of Outdoor Recreation*, p. 22.

hours of free time per average day* and of this only 1.4 hours are spent in outdoor leisure.[19] The remaining 3.7 hours are used for watching television, conversation, reading and other leisure activities which often take place indoors or outside of parks. Of the 1.4 hours of free time spent in outdoor leisure, an estimated 0.1 hour is spent in local public parks with the remaining 1.3 hours spent for outdoor gardening, walking, reading and conversation.

Translating these blocks of individual time into a national estimate is difficult because of the lack of precise data. Table 2 gives estimates of the total time spent on certain outdoor recreation activities for which information is available. Note the possible duplications, i.e., fishing, boating and hunting. Also, many types of activities such as gardening and lawn care, which are possibly larger than any single item included, are excluded.

Table 3 gives a historical perspective on total time for all types of outdoor recreation activity since 1900. Although the totals are far from precise, they do suggest an enormous rise in the time spent

TABLE 2
Estimate of Leisure Time Spent in Selected
Recreation Activities 1960
(Million Man-Hours)

Travel for pleasure	5,330
Visits to public outdoor recreation areas[a]	11,047
Fishing in all areas	1,500
Hunting in all areas	1,125
Boating of all kinds	600
Bowling	660
Organized Sports[b]	600
Horse racing	150
Total	21,012

[a] National, state, county and municipal parks, national forests, federal wildlife refuges, Corps of Engineers and TVA reservoirs.

[b] Such as baseball, football, etc., but excluding golf and tennis. Spectator and participant time included.

From Marion Clawson, *Economics of Outdoor Recreation* (Baltimore: Johns Hopkins Press, 1966), p. 24.

[19] Converse and Robinson, *Summary of United States Time Use Survey*, Tables 1 and 5.

* An average day does not include vacations, holidays, or weekends. Free time is all nonobligated time.

TABLE 3
Time Spent on Outdoor Recreation 1900-1960
(Million Man-Hours)

1900	300
1910	650
1920	2,100
1930	5,300
1940	7,850
1950	12,200
1960	21,012
1970	50,000[a]

[a] Author's projection and estimate based on same criteria.
From Marion Clawson, *Economics of Outdoor Recreation* (Baltimore: Johns Hopkins Press, 1966), p. 25.

on outdoor recreation over the past two generations. They indicate at least 70 times as much time spent in outdoor recreation in 1960 as in 1900. Clawson does not hazard an estimate as to the future except to state:

> If the amount of leisure time devoted to outdoor recreation were to increase from between 3 and 4 percent in 1960 to 8 or 10 percent by 2000 . . . this would amount to 900-1,100 billion hours in outdoor recreation then, or 40 to 50 times the total time spent this way in 1960.[20]

POPULATION

The population of a planning area is the most important variable associated with recreation demand. Beyond the actual population figures, it is vital to identify age, sex, income, race, ethnic background, physical condition, geographic location, lifestyle, level of education, and a host of other demographic variables for sensitive recreation planning. Much of this information is available in the 1970 U. S. Census of Population and there is no need to duplicate it here. However, any national perspective on the changing dimensions of demand for urban recreation should acknowledge these salient facts:

> The U. S. has changed from a rural nation of 4 million people in 1790 to an urban one of approximately 204 million in 1970.

[20] Clawson, *Economics of Outdoor Recreation*, p. 26.

In 1970, over 70 percent of America lives on 10 percent of the land in 243 metropolitan areas. The approximate acres per person available within these areas is shown in Table 4.

Negroes comprise 11 percent (22 million) of the population . . . 60 percent live in the central cities . . . with a median income of about half the corresponding figure for white men.

TABLE 4
The Growth of City Living

Year	Urban People (1000's)	Urban Area (1000 Acres)	Acres per Person
1900	30,160	5,545	.184
1920	54,158	9,535	.176
1940	74,424	12,800	.172
1960	125,000	21,400	.171
1980	193,000	32,000	.164
2000	279,000	45,000	.160

From "Resources for the Future," *Resources Newsletter* (Washington, D. C.: Resources for the Future, September, 1963), p. 2. Also see *Statistical Abstract of the United States 1971.*

MOBILITY

Clawson and many others link population mobility with demand. They relate it in three general ways: (1) transportation determines relative travel time and the amount (time) of outdoor recreation that most people can enjoy, (2) transportation affects outdoor recreation in terms of monetary cost, and (3) transportation facilities influence the character of the recreation experience. Clawson estimates:

Per capita travel by all mechanical means averaged about 500 miles annually in 1900. By 1922 the automobile raised this to 1,600 miles. In 1941 this increased to 4,600 miles of which 86 percent was by automobile. By 1956 average annual travel per capita was up to 5,080 miles of which 87 percent was by auto. Further increases may increase this to perhaps 7,000 miles by 1980 and 9,000 miles in 2000.[21]

Not all travel is for recreation, but estimates suggest that at least 10 to 30 percent of all automobile travel may be for outdoor recreation or have significant recreational values. The ORRRC Report

---

[21] Clawson, *Economics of Outdoor Recreation*, pp. 97-98.

states: "61 percent of all adults participated in automobile driving for pleasure in 1960" and lists this as "America's most popular outdoor recreation activity."[22] The Bureau of Outdoor Recreation lists driving as "America's third most popular activity second only to walking for pleasure and swimming and indicates over 940 million occasions in 1965."[23] The most recent estimates of activity and type of recreational travel may already exceed travel by automobile in the total number of trips and importance. There is also a strong rationale for considering walking for pleasure as an element of urban recreation demand, but very little attention has been given to this prospect in most cities.

INCOME

The ability to afford or spend money on recreation is one measure of interest or demand. The amount of discretionary income is more important than actual income. Because many outdoor recreation activities have no direct user fees or charges, statistics should be viewed as only partial indicators of demand, especially for the range of activities found in most municipal or neighborhood parks. Table 5 lists the personal consumption expenditures for recreation in 1969.

In 1970 the Gross National Product in the United States was close to one trillion dollars. Of this, approximately one half or $500 billion can be considered as discretionary income. Approximately 10 percent or $50 billion of all discretionary income is spent annually on sports and outdoor recreation. For a 1970 population of 205 million, this would amount to an estimated $2,500 of discretionary income per capita or $250 devoted to outdoor recreation. All trends of personal, discretionary income are upward for the foreseeable future. Clawson projects:

> Real income to approximately double by 2000 . . . a greater proportion of this to be discretionary . . . a larger proportion to be spent for outdoor recreation . . . which could easily mean expenditures for outdoor recreation in 2000 will be eight times those of today (1966).[24]

---

22 *ORRRC Report,* p. 24.

23 U. S. Department of the Interior, Bureau of Outdoor Recreation, *Outdoor Recreation Trends* (Washington, D. C.: Government Printing Office, 1967), pp. 8 and 14.

24 Clawson, *Economics of Outdoor Recreation,* p. 111.

TABLE 5

Personal Consumption Expenditures for Recreation 1969

Type of Product or Service	1969
Total recreation expenditures	$ 36,305
Books and maps	3,226
Magazines, newspapers, and sheet music	3,778
Nondurable toys and sport supplies	5,213
Wheel goods, durable toys, sports equipment, boats, and pleasure aircraft	4,219
Radio and television receivers, records, and musical instruments	8,085
Radio and television repair	1,266
Flowers, seed, and potted plants	1,361
Admissions to specified spectator amusements	2,260
Motion picture theaters	1,097
Legitimate theaters and opera, and entertainments of nonprofit institutions (except athletics)	679
Spectator sports	487
Clubs and fraternal organizations[a]	1,108
Commercial participant amusements[b]	1,719
Pari-mutuel net receipts	952
Other[c]	3,118

[a] Gross receipts less cash benefits of fraternal, patriotic, and women's organizations except insurance; and dues and fees of athletic, social, and luncheon clubs, and school fraternities.

[b] Billiard parlors; bowling alleys; dancing, riding, shooting, skating, and swimming places; amusement devices and parks; daily fee golf greens fees; golf instruction, club rental, and caddy fees; sightseeing buses and guides; and private flying operations.

[c] Photo developing and printing, photographic studios, collectors' net acquisitions of stamps and coins, hunting-dog purchase and training, sports guide service, veterinary service, purchase of pets, camp fees, nonvending coin machine receipts minus payoff, and other commercial amusements.

From U. S. Department of Commerce, *Statistical Abstract* (Washington, D. C.: Government Printing Office, 1970), Table 317, p. 200.

Source: Dept. of Commerce, Office of Business Economics; *The National Income and Product Accounts of the United States, 1929-1965*, and *Survey of Current Business*, July issues. Prior to 1960, excludes Alaska and Hawaii. Represents market value of purchases of goods and services by individuals and nonprofit institutions. See also *Historical Statistics, Colonial Times to 1957*, series H 500-515.

PARTICIPATION

Demand (or consumption) is also expressed by actual participation in activities. Available data, though incomplete, do give some indication of measured use and preference by types of area, activity and age group. Selected aspects of national participation are listed in Appendix A.

Supply of Opportunities

The best available sources for statistics on the total supply of public and private opportunities for outdoor recreation have been prepared by the Bureau of Outdoor Recreation[25] and the National Park and Recreation Association.[26] Other sources of information are the *ORRRC Report* and the selected data in Appendix B. The following is an abstract of the *ORRRC Report* by Clawson:

> There are approximately 2.3 billion acres of land and water in the United States . . . about one-eighth of the nation's total land and water areas was included in non-urban publicly owned areas designated for some form of outdoor recreation use.
>
> Two-thirds of these areas were under 40 acres in size, but contained less than one-tenth of one percent of the total recreation acreage. . . . In contrast, slightly over 1 percent of the areas were greater than 100,000 acres, but together these totaled 88 percent of the total area.
>
> The federal government administers 84 percent of the total acreage . . . approximately 14 percent is administered by state agencies and the rest is administered by local agencies which are involved with urban recreation.
>
> The West with only 15 percent of the population . . . has 72 percent of the acreage . . . the Northeast with 25 percent of the people has only 4 percent of the acreage.
>
> About 70 percent of the total land is in National Forests which are not managed primarily for outdoor recreation and are remote from population centers.[27]

The problem is not one of number of acres, but of effective acres available to the public for a specific type of recreation. Its major implication is *imbalance*—vast areas are *unavailable* to the major concentrations of *urban* populations in both the eastern and western parts of this country. The problem is especially critical in the East where both user- and resource-oriented areas are lacking

---

[25] U. S. Department of the Interior, Bureau of Outdoor Recreation, *Selected Outdoor Recreation Statistics* (Washington: Government Printing Office, 1971).

[26] 1970 Local Agency and State Park Surveys, in *Parks and Recreation*, Volume VI, No. 8, August 1971.

[27] Clawson, *Economics of Outdoor Recreation*, pp. 182-204.

and residential densities are twice those of western metropolitan areas.

Scope of Responsibilities

The *ORRRC Report,* BOR and NRPA Surveys give a statistical summary of acreage, facilities, expenditures and personnel, but provide little information concerning the actual or intended scope of responsibilities in the area of outdoor recreation for different levels of government, the private sector and the individual. Historically the literature and practice tend to place most of the responsibility for outdoor recreation in the public sector where the facilities cannot or do not yield a profit. They tend to favor private initiative and responsibility where outdoor recreation can be provided as a commercial enterprise. The role of the individual and quasi-public institution, e.g., trade unions, universities, churches, has not been adequately defined.

State of Organized Program

The state of organized program is a nebulous and controversial area. Most authorities believe it to be the foundation and flower of the Recreation Movement. They praise the quality and quantity of most programs, believe that most are effective and suggest that more are necessary. For example, Meyer and Brightbill state: "Program provides the foundation for achieving objectives and creates a unity of purpose for the entire organization,"[28] while the Neumeyers believe: "The creation of the play spirit and getting people to enthusiastically participate in whatever leisure pursuits they may engage in are of greatest importance . . . Leadership is a means of guidance and instruction."[29] Other authorities do not share this view. They project a critical evaluation of the emphasis, content, direction and values evident in most recreation programs. Goodale believes:

> Recreation programs provide treatment for symptoms, but not the problem . . . the creative use of leisure . . . we have used programs to stuff a vacuum of time . . . to catch up to a demand which

---

[28] Harold D. Meyer and Charles K. Brightbill, *Community Recreation* (Boston: D. C. Heath and Company, 1948), p. 509.
[29] Neumeyer and Neumeyer, *Leisure and Recreation,* p. 359.

continues to outstrip us . . . programs provide visible evidence of a profession at work . . . because of a need to be visible, we frequently admonish ourselves to do something, even if it's wrong, or perhaps even if its value as a recreation opportunity is questionable.[30]

These critics suggest that "we have developed only our capacity to provide programs" and that "we have more difficulty determining the value of what we are doing . . . in terms of recreation value for the participant."[31] Despite 50 years of effort and the mass of facilities and leadership listed in Appendix B, there are a growing number of professionals concerned about the quality and meaning of most recreation programs for the majority of potential users.

Status of Recreation Research

No perspective on outdoor recreation would be complete without an examination of the current status of research defined by Clawson and Knetsch as "an organized search for new knowledge, including the new understanding that comes from a rearrangement of old facts and new ideas."[32] Clawson and Knetsch also carefully distinguish research from planning by stating:

Planning is primarily a means for putting known facts together, evaluating them, and coming up with a proposed line of action or lines. It may draw on research, but the moving purpose and often the scheme of analysis is different . . . each may influence the other . . . but there is a difference in the basic motivation and approach of the two . . . [33]

They characterize the *ORRRC Report* as planning, not research, and give several reasons for the relative lack of both basic and applied research in outdoor recreation. Among these are:

Recreation not being recognized as a serious field of inquiry by most professions. The intangible nature of recreation. A lack of trained personnel, funds and organized institutions . . . competing priorities in the natural and social sciences.[34]

---

[30] Thomas L. Goodale, "The Fallacy of Our Programs," *Parks and Recreation,* November 1967, p. 39.

[31] *Ibid.*

[32] Marion Clawson and Jack Knetsch, *Outdoor Recreation Research* (Washington, D. C.: Resources for the Future, Inc., Reprint #43, 1963), p. 250.

[33] *Ibid.*

[34] *Ibid.,* p. 251.

Clawson and Knetsch also identify several areas of needed outdoor recreation research to include: demand, resource allocation, economic impacts, pricing methods, financing and institutional organizations. They conclude:

> Research will be more important in the future than it has been in the past . . . usable results will flow rather slowly . . . the most important task is conceptualizing . . . once concepts are developed and tested there is a need to collect data on a much larger scale . . . several specialized research organizations are needed . . . and most of this research should be done by organizations with other interests as well as outdoor recreation . . . a need exists for a clearing house of recreation research.[35]

No estimate is available on the amount of funds or personnel committed to outdoor recreation research. This may be indicative of the relatively uncoordinated nature of efforts now underway or proposed. It is also a commentary on the effectiveness of the Bureau of Outdoor Recreation in accomplishing one of its established functions. A review of research catalogs still indicates that the majority of all completed or in-process research is oriented toward the resource rather than the user. More important, there is an alarming lack of basic or applied research on urban areas, the planning process or recreation behavior, and very little on inner city outdoor recreation.[36] These conditions are summarized in *A Program for Outdoor Recreation Research.*[37]

CROSS-CULTURAL OVERVIEW

Contradiction is common in most of the philosophical writing on leisure. Reasons for this divergence of ideas include: the differing professional backgrounds of each author, the author's time horizon and value judgments, a lack of empirical studies and the rapidly changing pattern of American life.

---

[35] *Ibid.,* pp. 274-275.

[36] U. S. Department of the Interior, Bureau of Outdoor Recreation, *Outdoor Recreation Research: A Reference Catalog* (Washington, D. C.: Government Printing Office, 1966-1972).

[37] National Academy of Sciences, *A Program for Outdoor Recreation Research* (Washington, D. C.: National Academy of Sciences, 1969).

Philosophy of Leisure

Most of the thought on leisure can be divided into two separate periods: (1) the Pre-industrial Period and life patterns associated with it, and (2) the Post-industrial Period and its evolving life patterns to include the future. Although this book is concerned with the present, one cannot begin to understand the current philosophical meaning of outdoor recreation in this country without some knowledge of its past meanings.

PRE-INDUSTRIAL CONCEPTS

Studies of the past and of other cultures suggest that in all societies some time during the day was devoted to leisure in one form or another. In pre-industrial societies, little formal distinction is made between work and leisure periods. There is evidence of leisure interspersed with work in the form of religious or sacred occasions and rituals. It was only with the development of agricultural surpluses, and the urban society which made this possible, that those who held power were able to devote some of their time to leisure.

Most anthropologists associate early concepts of leisure with ritual, play and enforced idleness because of weather, illness or age. The division of labor and consequent development of social classes gave certain individuals control over their resources and time. A distinction between work and non-work for at least the upper classes in the Egyptian, Grecian and Roman Civilizations and through the Renaissance to the Industrial Revolution is evident. Two major themes evolve during these periods. They are: (1) leisure as a way of life for the selected upper classes, and (2) leisure in limited amounts as a reward for the lower or working classes. Both of these themes had a considerable impact on outdoor recreation and much of the contradiction in the next period is based on them.

POST-INDUSTRIAL CONCEPTS

With the development of the factory, work activity was taken out of the home for a specific period of the day. The concentration of workers around their places of work increased densities and, in many instances, reduced the amount of available open space. These changes, in turn, created the need for institutionalized recreational opportunities. Miller and Robinson note two significant outcomes of the Industrial Revolution on leisure:

(1) The provision of leisure opportunities first by private entrepreneurs, and only recently by government, and (2) Man with machines
for the first time could produce material plenty for all and still have
leisure for all.[38]

This theme is restated by many authors who view man's new-
found leisure with either hope or despair. Douglas states the hopeful hypothesis:

> For the first time in human history leisure rather than work has
> become the dominant human factor which integrates life . . . to accept
> our leisure as seriously as we once did our work shifts a whole
> emphasis.[39]

Riesman found in the new leisure an opportunity for the development of more autonomy in the character of individuals, of more
capacity to be creative and free from over-conforming:

> Play (leisure) may prove to be the sphere in which there is still
> some room left for the would-be autonomous man to reclaim his
> individual character from the pervasive demands of his social char-
> acter.[40]

Overstreet states: "We have to an extent grown work wise. In
the future we shall grow leisure wise."[41] Like Veblen in *Theory of
the Leisure Class,* he decries the barbaric leisure of the ancient
privileged classes and argues for a leisure that expresses the art of
living gracefully, of going slowly enough to see and enjoy the beauty
of life. He quotes Whitman as saying, "I loaf and invite my soul,"
and reminds us that Aristotle said, "The end of labor is to gain
pleasure," and that even God is said to have rested from his labors.
Overstreet's words provoked considerable comment. His idea of
"civilized loafing" was supported by Bertrand Russell who points out:

> A great deal of harm is being done in the modern world by belief
> in the virtuousness of work, and that the road to happiness and pros-
> perity lies in an organized diminuation of work. . . . The work ethic

[38] Norman P. Miller and Duane M. Robinson, *The Leisure Age* (Belmont, California: Wadsworth Publishing Company, Inc., 1963), p. 71.
[39] Paul Douglas, "The Administration and Leisure for Living," *Bulletin of the
American Recreation Society,* XII, No. 3 (April, 1960), p. 11.
[40] David Riesman, *The Lonely Crowd* (New Haven: Yale University Press, 1950),
pp. 326-327.
[41] Harry Overstreet, *A Guide to Civilized Leisure* (New York: W. W. Norton
and Company, Inc., 1934), p. 9.

is an anomaly in the modern world . . . [and] must be replaced by a new morality, one which gives respect to leisure.[42]

The most articulate and recent philosophical statement on leisure comes from DeGrazia in his distinction between leisure and free time. DeGrazia consciously attempts to disassociate leisure from free time and identifies the problem not as the existence of too little free time, but as the threat of too much, and the difficulty as not of too much real leisure, but of too little.

> Leisure and free time live in two different worlds . . . nobody can have free time. Not everybody can have leisure. . . . Free time is a realizable ideal of democracy, while leisure is not. . . . Free time is a special way of calculating a special kind of time, while leisure refers to a state of being, a condition of man which few desire and fewer achieve.[43]

The theme of leisure time as a danger is also expressed by Nietzsche and Spengler who sought answers to the negative outcomes of leisure. Cutten advances the argument: "The coming of the machine before man was ready for it has forced leisure upon us. . . . The result is a calamity . . . every extra hour of leisure adds in geometrical progression to the danger."[44] He expresses the rigid, moralistic view of a number of authors shocked by the excesses of the 1920's and the release of new leisures. MacIver described the problem as one of "great emptiness for many people who find themselves released from the necessity of long hours of work."[45]

This negative side of leisure brought about by social and economic changes is regarded by many philosophers as a challenge. Burns argued in the 1930's: "we should value our space, time, take it seriously and make the most of its treasures.[46] Kaplan regards leisure "as the product of a consumer's revolution which requires new ways of studying and understanding."[47] He and DeGrazia stress

---

[42] Bertrand Russell, "In Praise of Idleness and Other Essays," in *Mass Leisure* by Eric Larrabee and Rolf Meyersohn (Glencoe, Ill.: The Free Press, 1958), p. 97.

[43] Sebastian DeGrazia, *Of Time, Work and Leisure* (Garden City, New York: Anchor Books, Doubleday and Company, 1964), p. 5.

[44] George Cutten, *The Threat of Leisure* (New Haven: Yale University Press, 1926), pp. 12 and 44.

[45] Robert MacIver, "The Pursuit of Happiness," in *Mass Leisure* by Eric Larrabee and Rolf Meyersohn (Glencoe, Ill.: The Free Press, 1958), pp. 118-122.

[46] DeLisle Burns, *Leisure in the Modern World* (New York: The Century Company, 1932), pp. 21-22.

[47] Max Kaplan, *Leisure in America* (New York: John Wiley and Sons, Inc., 1960), pp. 82-92.

the social and analytical challenges which must be faced to give more understanding and meaning to leisure. Another view is expressed by Pack who visualizes leisure as part of man's pioneering instinct. With the end of the frontier, he feels, man needs a new challenge and that leisure is able to meet this challenge by "furnishing legitimate and social outlets for the human creative instinct, which otherwise is so often diverted by our modern intensive civilization into channels that are essentially predatory."[48]

The literature is rich with many more examples of these positive and critical views of leisure in a Post-industrial Society. If there is any point of common agreement, it is that leisure will be either a significant social problem or positive potential, and the choice will depend on the development of a philosophy of the meaning and place of leisure in America.

Conventional Wisdom

Related to the prevalent philosophies of leisure are a number of popular ideas which should be acknowledged because they have been influential in determining the present and possible future directions of outdoor recreation in this country. These thoughts are labeled "conventional wisdom." They persist in the literature and professional practice.

For convenience and brevity, these ideas are categorized into several broad areas and listed in random order without reference to a single source. I do not agree or disagree with any statement. My intent is only to abstract what the literature notes as important. The positive or negative structure of each statement is a reflection of the general way this idea appears in the literature or is commonly held by many professionals.

DEMAND AND SUPPLY

Recreation and leisure cannot be easily defined and quantified, hence they present marginal fields for the application of the scientific method and serious research. . . . Demand is a function of four major factors: population, leisure, income and mobility. . . . Supply creates demand. . . . Outdoor recreation is a major leisure activity and it is growing in importance. . . . The demand is surging, whatever the measuring rod. . . . The simple activities are the most popular . . .

---

[48] Arthur Newton Pack, *The Challenge of Leisure* (New York: The Macmillan Co., 1936), p. 49.

and driving for pleasure is most popular of all. As the work week decreases, the need for outdoor recreation will increase—more leisure means more outdoor recreation.

PLANNING PROCESS

If recreational opportunities cannot be created in urban areas, place them on the urban fringe or elsewhere and people will use them for lack of any alternative. . . . The recreation space standard is only a guideline of community intent to provide a given measure of land, facilities or program. . . . Programs for the wise use of leisure are a public and governmental responsibility. . . . Citizen participation in the planning process is difficult, if not impossible, because of the complexity of the problem and relative lack of citizen awareness, motivation, ability and patience to effectively engage in it.

SOCIAL GOALS

Unstructured free time for the masses is the cause of social disorders. . . . There is a definite relationship between the number and type of recreation opportunities and social disorders such as crime, violence and mental disease. . . . Public open spaces in urban areas are unsafe, attract undesirable individuals and become the focus of vandalism. . . . The outdoors lies deep in the American tradition. It has had immeasurable impact on the Nation's character and on those who made its history. . . . When an American looks for the meaning of his past, he seeks it not in ancient ruins, but more likely in mountains and forests, by a river, or at the edge of the sea. . . . Today's challenge is to assure all Americans permanent access to their heritage.

RESOURCE ALLOCATION

Public parks are for those who cannot afford the cost of private areas. . . . More money is needed to solve most problems facing outdoor recreation and that this is higher in priority than imagination, planning and citizen participation. . . . Parks and recreation are legitimate objectives of social welfare; however, those who use them must pay the costs. . . . The provision of parks and open space in densely populated urban areas cannot be economically justified on a benefit cost basis with other public or private goods and services.

USER PREFERENCE

There is a direct relationship between the amount of use or participation in a given activity or area and user satisfaction. . . . User preference cannot be accurately sampled and effectively used to allocate resources because supply creates demand and demand creates an expression for more supply. . . . Recreation is for the young, healthy and active person. . . . The average American will not walk anywhere he can ride in his personal automobile. . . . The neighborhood playground is primarily for use by children. . . . There is a clear distinction between indoor and outdoor recreation in terms of values, user satisfaction and the resources required for each. . . . Americans are an outdoor people and, given the opportunity, will take advantage of most opportunities for outdoor recreation provided by either the public or private sector.

Many of these statements border on platitudes. They have never been substantiated, yet they are widely accepted in the literature. Some may have a basis in fact, but with such wide exception as to be meaningless in most situations. If there is anything consistent about outdoor recreation, both in theory and in practice, it is its *inconsistency.* A case will be made in subsequent chapters against the traditional use of arbitrary standards and the need for an innovative concept and technique for recreation planning, especially in the inner city.

URBAN OPEN SPACE

If open space* is desirable in an urban area, one should first know why, when, where and how to obtain it then become the means to an established end or objective. The questions of how much open space is necessary and its form and function should follow justification. This discussion summarizes some of the literature on open-space justification to establish a rationalization for neighborhood parks in urban areas and outlines some significant relationships and contradictions about public open space.

Basic Contradictions

There are two commonly held viewpoints about public open space in urban areas that are often used to qualify or contradict most justification. Each is summarized here to allow the reader to evaluate the relative merits based on available evidence.

---

* Public open space devoted to outdoor leisure use. Does not include other open spaces, e.g., freeway slopes, storage areas, cemeteries, airports, military installations, which generally deny public use. Use in a physical, onsite sense for activities normally associated with leisure and outdoor recreation to include: sports, games, play, picnicking, social interaction, arts and cultural programs. Use can also be visual or perceptual offsite use for aesthetics or imagibility.

LOSS OF TAXABLE PROPERTY

Public open space does not produce any taxable income or become taxable real property. However, it more than offsets this loss of tax base by increasing the values of adjacent properties. Statistics seem superfluous. One need only to observe the use of land adjacent to most public parks and contrast its assessed values with similar use of land not proximate to a public open space. The examples are visible, numerous and consistent in their disproof of the idea that public open space does not contribute to the urban tax base.

To argue the point by suggesting that public open space represents tax revenue opportunities foregone is to negate the incremental increase in the adjacent and surrounding properties because of this space. It also does not acknowledge the economic advantages of nondevelopment in terms of the public services needed to service this area, i.e., police, fire, schools, utilities. There is developing evidence to support this idea.[49]

CRIME AND VANDALISM

Crime and vandalism occur in public open spaces. However, there is no evidence that the frequency or magnitude of crime and vandalism is more concentrated in public open spaces than in any other portion of the urban area. For example, Detroit Police Department records reveal: "There appears to be no greater concentration or occurrence of reported crime and vandalism in Detroit public parks than any other area of the city."[50] Clearly, there is a dimension of fear in most cities and suburbs that now prompts many people to avoid public places in general,[51] and there has been an increase in crime in public parks as there has been everywhere in cities.[52]

Other research indicates a correlation between crime rates and the amount of area in public open space. Where public open space is well maintained, supervised, accessible and relatively abundant, the crime rate is relatively low as opposed to relatively high crime rates in areas lacking public open space. Socioeconomic distinctions and population-density differences between each area are major

[49] Livingston and Blaney Consultants, *Open Space in Palo Alto* (San Francisco: Livingston and Blaney Consultants, 1971).

[50] Detroit Police Department, *Annual Statistical Report*, 1960, p. 4.

[51] Life Magazine, "The Cities Lock Up," *Life*, 1971 (21):24-33.

[52] D. J. Muluhill and M. M. Tumin, *Crimes of Violence* (Washington, D. C.: Government Printing Office, 1969).

variables. However, they do not negate the potential of well-designed and well-located public open space to reduce rather than increase the crime rate in a given area. Even the staunchest critic of current urban open-space concepts, especially one of the neighborhood park, admits:

> Parks can and do add a great attraction to neighborhoods. The more successfully a city mingles everyday diversity of uses and users in its everyday streets, the more successfully its people thereby enliven and support well located parks that can thus give back grace and delight to their neigborhoods instead of vacuity.[53]

> Too much is expected of city parks. Far from transforming any essential quality in their surroundings, far from automatically uplifting their neighborhoods, neighborhood parks themselves are directly and drastically affected by the way the neighborhood acts upon them.
> City parks are not abstractions, or automatic repositories of virtue or uplift, anymore than sidewalks are abstractions. They mean nothing divorced from their practical, tangible uses and hence they mean nothing divorced from the tangible effects of them for good or for ill on the city districts and uses touching them.[54]

Poorly designed open spaces which do not accommodate a diversity of uses and social interaction can, and in most cases, will become a void for increased crime and vandalism. Design, location and supervision of the open space are the limiting factors, not the provision of the space itself. It seems unfair to blame public open space for the behavioral problems of society simply because it is easily identifiable. Urban life is a composite of reality where both "good" and "bad" behavior exist. The very least we should do before dismissing the values of public open spaces, because of their potential for crime, is to weigh their total public "good" against the bad. In this perspective, the total public good outweighs any shortcomings in almost every case.

Significant Relationships

The significant relationships between the city, man, leisure, outdoor recreation, open space and urban form have been the focus of much study in the fields of Urban Planning, Landscape

---

[53] Jane Jacobs, The Death and Life of Great American Cities (New York: Random House, 1961), p. 111.
[54] Ibid., p. 95.

Architecture, and Recreation. An abstract of these relationships is described here to establish a conceptual framework for a justification of urban open space.

MAN AND THE CITY

Man's current relationship to the urban area has become as vital to him as life itself. His reliance on the city for a livelihood, social interaction, food, shelter and services has made the urban area the focus of American life. "This does not say urban life is good, but rather that America as a nation has chosen it, for better or worse, as its habitat for some time to come."[55] People now meet their major needs and achieve the objects of their desires and ambitions in the urban area. Family life, employment, education, religion, standards of conduct, social controls and leisure activities all take place now in an urban setting.

Statistically, urbanization has affected every phase of American life. The fact "that between 1950 and 1955 97 percent of this nation's population growth took place in urban areas is startling as contrasted to the year 1800 when only 4 percent of the total population lived in cities of 8,000 or more."[56] There is every reason to believe that this trend will continue. By the year 2000, projections indicate that 90 percent of the total U. S. population will be living in urban areas.

Although history holds that man has flourished as have his cities, there is some question as to the degree of progress man can now achieve in the degenerate environment of most highly urbanized areas. This is not to say that urbanization is detrimental to man, for "his greatest advances have been in an urban environment."[57] Rather, it is an appeal for a better urban environment in which public open space is an integral and important part. "The question of whether man can master his self-imposed fate will be determined in large part by how well he solves the challenge of leisure and the public open space necessary to accommodate much of it."[58]

---

[55] Edward Higbee, *The Squeeze* (New York: William Morrow and Co., 1960), p. 19.

[56] American Institute of Park Executives, *The Crisis in Open Land* (East Lansing, Michigan: Michigan State University, 1959), p. 12.

[57] Higbee, *The Squeeze*, p. 26.

[58] William H. Whyte, Jr., *The Exploding Metropolis* (New York: Doubleday, 1958), p. 133.

MAN AND LEISURE

"Leisure is the raw material with which man may advance the level of mere existence."[59] Its availability and constructive use form one key to national strength. "Never has there been a period in the history of the world when leisure has been as widespread as it is now in America."[60] Labor and leisure are symbiotic, but the tone of a society is conditioned largely by the extent and use of its leisure. There is evidence to suggest that if a society engages in creative and constructive leisure, its culture will advance; if it indulges in useless and destructive activities, its social order generally deteriorates and progress ceases.

> Past civilizations have flourished and perished by how well people utilized their leisure. While work is necessary for subsistence and progress, and no country has ever been able to endure without it, a culture depends chiefly on leisure for its development.[61]

"Past relationships of man and leisure condemned idleness."[62] "Today most Americans work in order to be able to enjoy leisure which has become an end in itself and a status symbol of the first order."[63] Leisure currently assumes increasing proportions of every aspect of American life and encompasses every conceivable activity. "The average citizen now has more than 3,000 hours of leisure a year."[64] Both automation and technology have reduced the work week, while increased health standards have almost doubled life expectancies.

"Seventy-five years ago the average man spent 26 percent of his time working and had 7 percent remaining for leisure. Today he spends only 15 percent of his time working and 21 percent at leisure."[65] A projection to the year 1975 yields the following conservative estimates of the impact of leisure on our society.[66] As these vast amounts of leisure time accumulate, the need for an outlet becomes intense. One of the paradoxical problems of our age

---

[59] Neumeyer and Neumeyer, *Leisure and Recreation*, p. 8.

[60] Marion Clawson, *The Dynamics of Park Demand* (New York: Regional Plan Association, 1960), p. 6.

[61] Neumeyer and Neumeyer, *Leisure and Recreation*, p. 3.

[62] *Ibid.*, p. 56.

[63] Vance Packard, *The Status Seekers* (New York: David McKay Co., 1959, p. 41.

[64] Clawson, *The Dynamics of Park Demand*, p. 20.

[65] American Institute of Park Executives, *The Crisis in Open Land*, p. 9.

[66] "Place of Parks in Recreation," *Recreation*, Vol. 45, 1952, p. 456.

is how to utilize an abundance of leisure time effectively. How America copes with the question may well determine its future course as a major power.

Population	up 27%
Goods and services	up 100%
Income/capita	up 40%
People employed	down 20%
Average work week	down 15%
Paid holidays	up 60%
Paid vacations	50% longer
Automobile owners	up 100%

LEISURE AND RECREATION

Leisure and recreation, though closely related, are not synonymous. "The emphasis in leisure is on the element of time; recreation refers to one way leisure may be spent. One can spend leisure in many ways other than the pursuit of some forms of recreation, "Although in a broad sense most forms of recreation are free time activities and many leisure time pursuits have some recreational values."[67]

Some leisure may take the form of idleness. Recreation in a socially acceptable sense involves constructive activities for either the individual or community. "The common denominator in recreation is self expression."[68] The activities engaged in may be passive to active, extensive to intensive in scale or character. The essential element is not what the person does but the spirit in which he does it and the satisfaction derived. The urban dweller's need for a medium of self-expression in which he can take pride or derive security, exercise his physical self, release pent-up emotions, work off nervous energy, seek challenge and enrich his personality is proportionate to the increasing complexity of urban living.

OUTDOOR RECREATION AND OPEN SPACE

The need for outdoor recreation is directly proportional to the degree of urbanization. It is based primarily on: (1) man's biological need to retain some association with the outdoors, and (2) man's psychological need for contrast and change in spacial surroundings and activities.

---

[67] Neumeyer and Neumeyer, Leisure and Recreation, p. 17.
[68] Ibid., p. 184.

Man's need for association with the outdoors is part of his nature. Trevelyan said, "We are literally children of the earth and removed from her our spirit withers or runs to various forms of insanity."[69] This does not imply that man should not live in cities, but rather that, "Man is essentially an outdoor animal as far as his biological and physical needs are concerned."[70] In the past, this need was amply met by the rural life of virtually 90 percent of the population. Today urbanization has reversed this ratio.

Linked with man's need for a biological association with the outdoors is his need for a change in spacial surroundings and activity. Many people now have routine jobs. They live in relatively ugly, sterile and monotonous urban environments that generally lack physical and social diversity. These conditions generate a need for change in spacial surroundings and activities to provide a balance and contrast to urban development. This is not to condemn urban development, but rather to impose the dimension of open space on the urban environment in its proper place, scale, form and function.

OPEN SPACE AND URBAN FORM

Open space can be "the structural framework to which various forms and activities can relate to produce edges, foci, nodes, districts and ultimately regions of different size, scale and character."[71] The opportunity to experience an architectural element from the vantage point of open space and vice versa is a unique visual quality. Perhaps no single element can better shape and compliment urban form than well-placed open space. Its ability to differentiate, integrate or buffer various urban elements is unsurpassed. If there were ever an urban status symbol it is the amount and treatment of public open space. A prime example is Rome:

> Its physical facade is as perishable as that of any city, yet it is to be admired and preserved. . . . Twenty centuries of history greet the eye. . . . It is there in ruins and restorations. . . . It is in the gardens, boulevards, parks, and open spaces of all periods. It is in the fountains, cobblestones and plazas. . . . As a people most Romans are very poor, but no city is richer in public areas or happier in the pride of its citizens in their citizenship.[72]

---

[69] U. S. Department of the Interior, National Park Service, *Conservation Quotes* (Washington, D. C.: National Park Service, 1953), p. 31.

[70] Arthur T. Wilcox, *Introduction to Outdoor Recreation* (East Lansing, Michigan: Michigan State University, 1958), p. 4.

[71] Kevin Lynch, *The Image of the City* (Boston: Cambridge Press, 1960), p. 18.

[72] Higbee, *The Squeeze*, p. 229.

Sensitively designed public open space can also give the urban resident and visitor a sense of identity, association and direction. It can be one dramatic key to a viable urban environment. The greenbelt or wedge of open space on the fringe of sprawling urban areas can give definition to urban form and limit the physical size or shape of a city or neighborhood. It can provide one way of separating or integrating urban areas or neighborhoods from each other and the surrounding area.

JUSTIFICATION AND RELEVANCE

Public open space in urban areas has been justified in both romantic and rational ways. These justifications are illustrative of much of the romantic and rational thinking expressed in the literature and in professional practice. They are discussed in random order of importance.

SOCIAL

Man is by nature a gregarious, social animal. Most public open spaces can be justified for the social interaction matrix which they can provide if designed for this purpose. The suburban cyclone-fence relationship or a Sunday afternoon at the subdivision pool cannot replace the opportunities for social interaction available in most urban public open spaces. The stroll in the park, sandlot baseball game and evening band concert of the past are virtually non-existent in most urban areas where there is no public open space. People need an outdoor medium in which to interact or watch others. Most private open space cannot provide this for the general population at a cost that the population in the inner or central city can afford. Although most suburban backyards can adequately provide for primary social interaction, most people appreciate and will use an alternative if it meets their needs and objectives for both primary and secondary interaction.

The literature points to either a provision of safe and well-designed public open spaces now, or a decline in this country's sociooutdoor recreation patterns and a withdrawal into the limited confines of private open spaces which only the middle and upper classes will be able to afford. Evidence of this is indicated in the *U. S. Riot Commission Report* and by some of the demands for more parks expressed in almost every outbreak of racial violence in metropolitan areas. David Riesman in his analysis of the American character emphasizes: "People may some day learn how to buy not only packages of groceries or books, but the larger package of a neighborhood, a society, and a way of life."[73] He places the responsibility for giving the city some sociocultural definition (to include public open space) directly on the shoulders of the urban planner:

> City planners comprise perhaps the most important professional group to become reasonably weary of the cultural definitions that are systematically trotted out to rationalize the inadequacies of city life today, for the well-to-do as well as the poor. With their imagination, and bounteous approach they have become, to some extent, the guardians of our liberal and progressive political tradition. In their best work, we see expressed in physical form a view of life which is not narrowly job minded. It is a view of the city as a setting for leisure and amenity as well as for work.[74]

The urban planner in this sense becomes one of Riesman's "Avocational Counselors," charged with "filtering a variety of tastes, inclinations, social schemes and leisure into all that is a city both from a physical and social point of view."[75] This does not imply that a planner should impose his values on the city. Instead it suggests that he present alternatives which others can consider, approve, modify or reject.

ECONOMICS

"Parks are not to be placed on economic scales to be weighed against kilowatts, productive acreage, school buildings, housing developments, parking spaces and what not. They are not to be valued in money."[76] "The social and cultural benefits of public open spaces are widely recognized, but there are few who seem willing or able to commit themselves to a study of economic values."[77] Prewitt concluded: "There is no acceptable standard of evaluation that can be used to place a monetary value on parks and recreation that is not arbitrary."[78] However, despite all of the difficulties associated with an economic justification of open space, one approach

---

[73] Riesman, The Lonely Crowd, p. 349.

[74] Ibid., p. 348

[75] Ibid., pp. 341-342.

[76] American Institute of Park Executives, Open Land, p. 11.

[77] Planning Advisory Service, "Parks and Property Values," American Society of Planning Officials Newsletter (October, 1960), p. 92.

[78] Roy A. Prewitt, The Economics of Public Recreation (Washington, D. C.: National Park Service, 1949), p. 27.

has been used with some success. It is commonly called "the open space-property value relationship."[79] The effect of public open space on property values is supported by the National Association of Home Builders who state:

> Today's home buyer is looking for features beyond the confines of the house and lot. Proximity to school, park, and community recreation is high on his list of looked for items. . . . In the vicinity of park and recreation area, enhanced values of building sites up to 15-20 percent, with a high level of sustained value over the years are not an uncommon experience. . . . Where land is developed for park purposes, the highest increment of value is usually developed in properties immediately contiguous.[80]

The weight of example surrounding this statement can be seen everywhere. Olmsted's early study of the value of Central Park in New York City on adjacent properties revealed: "An increase of 183,000,000 dollars in property values over and above that prior to the establishment of Central Park."[81] The Federal Housing Administration states: "It is common practice throughout the United States to place a higher valuation on subdivided land if the development contains park land or if the subdivision is adjacent to or near a public park."[82]

No public improvement should be considered on the basis of immediate cost without also considering the long-term public benefit. Galbraith's call for a redress of the social balance emphasizes the current condition of "public poverty in the midst of private plenty" especially in public health, education and welfare to include public open space:

> The final problem of the productive society is what it produces. This manifests itself in an implacable tendency to provide an opulent supply of some things and a niggardly yield of others. This disparity carries to the point where it is a cause of social discomfort and social unhealth. There is a line which divides privately produced and marketed goods and services from publicly rendered services. Our wealth in the first is not only in startling contrast with the meagerness of the latter, but our wealth in privately produced goods is, to a marked degree, the cause of crisis in the supply of public services. For we

---

79 *ASPO Newsletter,* p. 92.
80 *Ibid.*
81 *Ibid.*
82 *Ibid.*

have failed to see the importance, indeed the urgent need, of maintaining a balance between the two.[83]

Open space in the economic sense becomes one of the public services Galbraith refers to as ". . . not carrying a price ticket to be paid for by the individual user such as postal service, but instead by their very nature they must be paid for by all and available to all."[84] Public open space in urban areas cannot be taken for granted when it can provide one of the significant economic and aesthetic balances to "private opulence and public squalor."[85] This is not to say that a redress of the social imbalance now plaguing Urban America can and will be solved by an injection of public open space into its cities; nor is it to condemn our national tendency "for public services to fall behind private production."[86] However, Galbraith favors an adequate provision of public open space in proportion with the entire array of public services to create a "social balance."[87]

RECREATIONAL

The recreational potentials of public parks are, in all likelihood, the most apparent sources for justification of public open spaces. Clawson writes:

> Recreation is a vital need in today's world. It is perhaps the greatest opportunity for self-expression, for doing what one really wants to do, not what one is forced to do to earn a living. The very phenomena which have brought leisure and income have also brought serious tensions for everyday life—both working and living take place hurriedly, under crowded and noisy conditions. Recreation under conditions of one's choosing is necessary to relieve these tensions. For many, the physical activity of outdoor recreation is vital in building and maintaining physical fitness and in discharging nervous energy. Recreation also has important values in reducing delinquency. . . . And perhaps most important, recreation is simply good fun. Man does not live for work alone; when he can play he does.[88]

---

[83] John Kenneth Galbraith, *The Affluent Society* (Boston: Houghton Mifflin Co., 1958), p. 251.

[84] *Ibid.*, p. 262.

[85] *Ibid.*, p. 257.

[86] *Ibid.*, p. 261.

[87] *Ibid.*, p. 265.

[88] Regional Plan Association, *The Race for Open Space* (New York: The Association, 1960), p. 20.

Outdoor recreation is also one means of maintaining and improving this nation's physical health. "The average urban American today is characterized by a relatively poor state of physical condition as compared to what it could be under his high standard of living."[89] Lack of outdoor exercise has been an important cause of this deficiency. More basically, a lack of adequate public open spaces in which to exercise is the problem. Overcrowded conditions and lack of public open space in most urban areas deny adequate opportunities for outdoor physical exercise. President John F. Kennedy said:

> There are an increasingly large number of young Americans who are neglecting their bodies—whose physical fitness is not what it should be—who are getting soft, and such softness on the part of the individual citizens can help to strip and destroy the vitality of a nation.[90]

Another recreational justification of public open space is the limit of private resources and effort that can economically be devoted to it. Hiking trails, running tracks, skating rinks, toboggan runs, bicycle paths, bridle trails, and even the common softball field generally cannot be rationalized in private ownership. Their extensive nature is beyond the income level of the average urban dweller without public subsidy. Even if the expense of said facilities could be borne by private means, the extravagant use of land involved in duplication of facilities would be contrary to urban form and function. It would seem that any major reliance on private open spaces for outdoor recreation would be the antithesis of the city and revert back to a rural scale of land use.

When aesthetics is related to outdoor recreation a more intangible, but nevertheless important, type of justification can be associated with some types of urban open space. "Woe unto them that join house to house, that lay field to field, till there be no place that they may be placed alone in the midst of the earth."[91] Open spaces are not merely places to visit, exercise in or learn from. They are areas in which one may encounter the aesthetic values of trees, sky and the feeling of enclosed space. "Man seeks a meaning

---

[89] *President's Commission on Physical Fitness, Final Report* (Washington, D. C.: Commission on Physical Fitness, 1960), p. 7.

[90] President John F. Kennedy, "Statement to American Recreational Congress," Washington, D. C., February 17, 1960.

[91] Isaiah 5:8, *Old Testament Bible.*

to life through God."[92] He constantly seeks to find expressions of God's creativeness in nature. In an urban area the character of some public open spaces can provide a limited contact with nature.

GOVERNMENTAL

Public open spaces offer one opportunity to implement the "democratic ideal." They should be of, by, and for the people. Where else can the people under potentially satisfying circumstances become acquainted with a governmental function? How else can a government better promote the unity of its citizens than through the integrating experience of informal outdoor recreation in public open space? There are questions which need study, but it seems reasonable to make these assertions. Deasy said: "There should be, in this town, and in every town some tracts of land adequate in size and beautiful in location dedicated and consecrated to the public where children may meet and play and imbibe lessons in liberty and Democracy."[93]

One vital justification for public open spaces is the preservation and enjoyment of significant historic sites. A city that forgets its past may jeopardize its future. Public open space containing historic features can help lend a more distinct character and diversity to many of this nation's sprawling, nondescript cities. The preservation of history is especially important in suburbs that lack the dimension of heritage.

Public open spaces can be an integration medium for a stratified society. Henry Van Dyke spoke for equality when he said, "There is no special directory in the wilderness [public parks]."[94] What better place can exemplify the American ideal for equality of opportunity than a public park where *all* men can come to enjoy themselves regardless of who or what they are? Open space makes no distinction between class or race. Parks in this respect are a "common ground" where a pluralistic society can assemble or interact if they wish.

Public open space can and should be one outward symbol of a community's pride in itself as well as a place where all of its citizens can come for leisure activities and inspiration, and to experience the fellowship of others. Few American cities are so poor that they

---

[92] William A. Spurrier, *Guide to the Christian Faith* (New York: Scribner's Sons, 1955), p. 67.

[93] National Park Service, *Conservation Quotes*, p. 8.

[94] *Ibid.*, p. 24.

cannot afford the blessings of public open space—and few so rich that they can afford to do without it.

PSYCHOLOGICAL

A psychological justification for public open space is based on the emotional needs which cause most urbanites to sometimes seek open space, open sky and solitude. These are normal behavioral instincts best explained by the "Multiple Causation Theory" of Sociology and man's need for self-actualization. They also relate to our sense of space and territoriality.

> Being crowded is the almost universal experience of today's urban dweller. His home grows smaller, his highways are congested, recreation places saturated and open landscape devoured as the squeeze for land in metropolitan America begins.[95]

The problem is as severe as it is simple: too many people in too little space. Senator Williams of New Jersey in presenting the Open Space Bill before Congress said:

> The urban life has great advantages—the thrill and excitement of vibrant activity, close contact, and endless cultural and commercial variety—but it is a   crowded existence and tensions inevitably run high, even to the point of group violence. We all sooner or later feel the need to escape to calmer surroundings. There is a certain psychic relief in open spaces that cannot be underestimated.[96]

The term "re-creation" denotes another basic psychological justification of open space. As stress has become an urban way of life, the pace of living has increased to a tempo capable of injuring the nervous system. John Burroughs said:

> We live, most of us, in a noisy world—a world full of hurrying to and fro, of rattling machinery, of clanging bells, of shrieking whistles, the world of business. In the midst of this tumult and confusion we lose our grip upon ourselves, and feel the strain so keenly that we realize we must break under it unless we find relief.[97]

Open spaces also offer the individual an opportunity for self-expression. "Below the conscious level of thought, everyone has

---

[95] Higbee, *The Squeeze*, p. xi of Introduction by Fairfield Osborne.

[96] U. S. *Congressional Record*, 87th Cong., 1st sess., 1961, Vol. 107, No. 24, February 9.

[97] National Park Service, *Conservation Quotes*, p. 34.

powerful psychological drives that seek expression."[98] Outdoor recreation in a public open space is one satisfying means of fulfilling this need.

A number of other references to the psychology of open space appear in the literature. They generally focus on the areas of environmental stress and proxemics which treat the spatial relations of human behavior. *The Hidden Dimension* by E. T. Hall, Carson and Driver's *An Environmental Approach to Human Stress and Well Being with Implications for Planning*, and Robert Sommer's books *Personal Space* and *Environmental Awareness* summarize the more significant concepts in these areas.

EDUCATIONAL

The potential of public open space in urban areas for educational purposes has been demonstrated by the establishment of outdoor education programs in many elementary and secondary schools. "The role of public open spaces in this educational effort is indispensable. As outdoor classrooms and laboratories, they can add a dimension of life and dynamism to the science curriculum to make studies more meaningful."[99]

Some open spaces are vital as control areas in which the student can study native flora and fauna in the city. Many educators feel that there are few better places to teach an urban child some of the basic relationships of urban life such as competition, survival or reproduction than natural surroundings. With proper development and interpretive methods, a visit to most public open spaces can be an educational experience.

CONSERVATION

The conservation aspects of public open space are not commonly associated with urban areas, but at least three have some justification: (1) retention of water supply and natural drainage, (2) alleviation of air pollution, and (3) provision of a limited habitat for natural flora and fauna. These do not commonly apply to open space at the scale of a neighborhood park, but should be considered

---

[98] William McDougall, *An Introduction to Social Psychology* (Boston: J. W. Luce and Co., 1923), p. 51.

[99] Verna Johnston, *Natural Areas for Schools* (Sacramento, California: Conservation Education Section, State Department of Natural Resources, 1959), p. 11.

in the justification of open space as a system. There is also a growing awareness that the best way to preserve wilderness and resource-oriented areas from overuse is to provide more recreational open space in cities.

The lack of public open space in urban areas has created some critical water supply and drainage problems. "Prior to urbanization of an area, 75 percent of the annual precipitation is absorbed by soil and vegetation with the remaining 25 percent is carried away via natural surface drainage."[100] Urban development dramatically reverses this ratio in addition to destroying crucial natural safety valves such as marshes and stream beds. Reservation of large public open spaces, especially wetlands, can be a low-cost, efficient, aesthetic and multiple-use solution for urbanizing areas unable to pay the high initial cost of developing sophisticated drainage to water-supply systems.

Air pollution is another problem of most urban areas which can be alleviated, to some degree, by more open space. "Open spaces allow pollutants to diffuse more readily and reduce, via a better circulation of air, the concentration of noxious particles which is the major source of trouble."[101] This does not imply that open space can solve the air pollution problem for this can be accomplished only through effective control and eventual elimination of the causes of pollution. Rather, it is to propose public open space as a means for psychologically and, sometimes, physically reducing the effects of air pollution.

Niering said, "Urban society cannot flourish without the support and balance of living things other than man."[102] The preservation of land in its natural, or near natural, condition is a most difficult, yet most necessary, justification for public open space in urban areas. "Conservationists, theologians and educators have long been aware of the link between man and the earth about him,"[103] but few urban planners have perceived this relationship. There is no substantial reason why an urban area cannot provide homes and employment for people, and a limited natural environment. There is also no valid reason why urban man should divest himself of the beauty, inspiration, education and contrast that some types of public open

---

[100] William A. Niering, *Nature in the Metropolis* (New York: Regional Plan Association, 1960), p. 57.

[101] *Ibid.*

[102] *Ibid.*, p. 7.

[103] Johnston, *Natural Areas for Schools*, p. 12.

spaces can provide in even the densest urban area. It is possible and rational to "design with nature."[104]

As a nation we should stop looking outside our cities for public open space. Instead, we should attempt to save or create public open spaces of appropriate size, scale, and character within the urban area. An urban area devoid of physical and natural diversity cannot provide the measure of environmental richness possible and necessary to the quality of life.

ENVIRONMENTAL CHANGE

Public open space also can be justified as a dramatic tool of environmental change, especially in the inner city. It can work as both a stabilizing and dynamic force to either maintain or radically change an urban environment. Its presence can consciously promote human scale, recreational activities, urban renewal and an awareness of the quality of life and environment still possible in cities.

As an element of change, it can be a focus for visual relief, social interaction and community identification. The provision of adequate and sensitively designed public open space can be a framework for the needed redevelopment or conservation of blighted areas. Perhaps no single force is more capable of bringing human scale back into the urban environment than an integration of public open space with all types of urban land use and activity.

Conversely, public open space can serve as a stabilizing force to slow and help to reverse the current rapid decline of the inner city. Next to a lack of adequate housing, jobs and schools, the most significant factor for the decline of the inner city is the lack of public open space and the suburban promise of "greener pastures." It is ironic that most people who flee the city in search of a suburban paradise soon find the open space they came for consumed by sprawl. It is late, but there is still hope that a relaxation of racial tensions followed by a dramatic infusion of public open space might yet save the inner city as a place to live.

SUMMARY JUSTIFICATION

No single statement can provide a summary justification of urban space; the problem is one of the needs and values of many. Richard Lieber said:

---

[104] Ian L. McHarg, *Design with Nature* (Garden City, N. Y.: Natural History Press, 1969).

Fortunately for all of us, open space has quite a different meaning which concerns itself, Antaeus-like, with the physical necessity of man to keep in touch with nature. It is that eon-old longing of the soul to find a haven of rest. No matter how much we do indirectly by way of sports and athletics for the body, the spiritual hunger and search for things hidden is the true answer to the question "Why open space?"[105]

The same idea has been summarized in a more tangible frame of reference:

The people in an urban area need open space for many different purposes: to conserve water and other natural resources; as a reserve for future needs, often unpredictable; to maintain special types of agriculture which must be near cities; to prevent building in undesirable locations in order to avoid flood hazard or a wasteful extension of services, to provide a rural environment for people who want to live that way; for pleasant views from urban areas, for a sense of urban identity; for buffers against noise and other nuisance; but above all, for recreation, which can be combined with many of the other uses."[106]

Open space is a fundamental element in an urban environment. The test of America's future is not only how well it can do in outer space, but also how it can meet the challenge of social services and environmental quality in urban areas. The provision, design and maintenance of public open spaces are vital factors in the environmental quality of cities.

---

[105] National Park Service, *Conservation Quotes*, p. 15.

[106] President's Commission on National Goals, *Goals for Americans* (Prentice-Hall, Inc., 1960), p. 239.

III

The Inner City

The city is a parade of paradoxes, a thousand promises. . . . It is a vast machine for living that purrs like a fat cat or rips the night with a scream. It is a gigantic file cabinet of human hopes that nobody can ever put in order.[1]

Worrying about cities has become the most fashionable form of self-torture. The certain truth about American city life is that it has moved beyond comprehension, that it is changing . . . nobody is in charge . . . anything can happen.[2]

It has come to this: Either we heal the ghetto or we will suffer urban civil war. . . . The fatal threat to the nation today is the alarming loss of faith among whites and blacks, rich and poor, in the ability of their political system to find answers to America's problems.[3]

No single domestic problem has received more attention in the past decade than the urban crisis. Most of the concern has focused on the central and inner city. This chapter will: (1) abstract and summarize some descriptions of the inner city as a place in which to live, (2) outline what appear to be the inner city's significant problems, potentials and alternatives, and (3) relate these to the neighborhood as a planning unit for outdoor recreation. The inner city is described for what it is. Its history and future are not as important

---

[1] *Life Magazine,* "Zoom in on the City," December 24, 1965, p. 24.

[2] Conrad Knickerbocker, "No One's in Charge," *Life Magazine,* December 24, 1965, p. 37.

[3] Ben H. Bagdikian, "It Has Come to This," *Saturday Evening Post,* 241:19-23 August 10, 1968, pp. 20-21.

as its present. Despite all the proposed programs and wishful thinking, there is now evidence to suggest that needed massive physical
and social changes will come slowly, if at all. For simplicity, the
terms "inner city," "ghetto" and "slum" are used interchangeably
because there is relatively little difference in their common use.
However, there is a semantic, physical and social difference in the
meaning of these words.

GENERAL CHARACTERISTICS

Terms and Concepts

Despite all that has been written and said about the inner city,
there is no concise and focused description of its general characteristics. Perhaps this is because its complexity defies generalization.
With this risk and the objective of brevity, the following terms and
concepts are most related to urban recreation planning.

Historically, the word and the physical image of a slum have
been in common use since the beginning of industrial society and
the rise of modern cities. Partridge notes that "the origin of the
word slum, although obscure, probably comes from 'slumber' since
slums were originally to the majority unknown, back streets or
alleys wrongly presumed to be sleepy and quiet."[4] In 1931, Webster's dictionary stated: "a slum is a foul back street of a city,
especially one with a slovenly and often vicious population." In
1953, a more charitable feeling prevailed, and a slum was defined as
"a thickly populated street or alley marked by squalor or wretched
living conditions."[5]

Literary classics such as *Oliver Twist* described the mood of the
London slum: "The street was very narrow and muddy, and the air
was impregnated with filthy odours."[6] Jacob Riis, in his book on the
tenement slums of New York, said:

> In the tenements all the influences make for evil; because they
> are the hotbeds of the epidemics that carry death to rich and poor
> alike. . . . That we have to own it, the child of our own wrong does

---

[4] Eric Partridge, *Origins, A Short Etymological Dictionary of Modern English*
(New York: The Macmillan Co., 1958), p. 31.

[5] *Webster's New World Dictionary* (New York: The World Publishing Company, 1950), p. 1375.

[6] Charles Dickens, *Oliver Twist* (New York: Dodd, Mead and Co., 1941), p. 74.

not excuse it. . . . What are you going to do about it is the question of today.[7]

James Ford's study of the 1930's concentrated on housing conditions and defined the slum "as a residential area in which the housing is so deteriorated, so substandard or so unwholesome as to be a menace to the health, safety, morality, or welfare of the occupants."[8] Other studies began to visualize the slum as a social phenomenon.

> . . . a distinctive area of disintegration and disorganization . . . not merely decaying houses . . . and poverty stricken adults . . . a social phenomenon in which the attitudes, ideas, ideals and practices play an important part.[9]

A growing awareness of the deterioration of American cities and the urban renewal programs of the 1950's gave rise to a number of euphemistic terms such as "blighted neighborhood," "deteriorated neighborhood," "low-income area," and "gray area." A number of authorities attempted to solve the problem by simply changing its name, while others spoke frankly. James B. Conant stated:

> In each [of the largest American cities] one can find neighborhoods composed of various minority groups . . . many of these areas are now designated "culturally different," but in my youth they would have been more simply designated "slums."[10]

Hunter adds a dimension of being "trapped" to the traditional definitions of a slum and calls them "new-world ghettos."[11] Historically, "ghetto" has meant an area in which a certain group was compelled to live. Today, different kinds of constraining forces have altered this definition. Racially, a ghetto is an area where members of a minority, particularly Negroes, are residentially restricted by social, economic and physical pressures from the rest of society. In this meaning, a ghetto can contain wealthy and middle-income

---

[7] Jacob Riis, How the Other Half Lives (New York: Sagamore Press, 1957), p. 2.

[8] James Ford, Slums and Housing: History, Conditions, Policy (Cambridge: Harvard University Press, 1936), p. 11.

[9] Conference on Home Building and Home Ownership, Washington, D. C., 1931 (Quoted in Ford, ibid., p. 8).

[10] James B. Conant, Slums and Suburbs (New York: McGraw-Hill Book Co., 1961), p. 7.

[11] David R. Hunter, The Slums: Challenge and Response (New York: The Free Press, 1964), p. 4.

residents as well as poor ones. Economically, a ghetto is an area where the poor are compelled to live because they cannot afford better accommodations. In this meaning, a ghetto is mainly inhabited by the poor, regardless of race or ethnic background.

Confusion arises from the failure to distinguish clearly between these different meanings of the word "ghetto." This book adopts both the racial and the poverty connotation because little general difference is observed between the economic and racial composition of most American inner-city neighborhoods. Hence the primary concern is with the inner city Negro ghetto of most American cities.

Herbert Gans, in *The Urban Villagers,* states: "There are two types of low rent neighborhoods, the entry area and the area populated by social rejects." In the entry area, newcomers to the city find their first places to live and begin to try to adapt their "nonurban institutions and cultures to the urban milieu." This is the "Urban Village."[12]

The area populated by "social rejects" is often called the "urban jungle."[13] This is often the type of area commonly associated with a wide range of social and pathological deviates to include: the sexual deviate, alcoholic, dope addict, prostitute, and a host of other personality "types" which society usually avoids or attempts to exclude from its residential areas. In general, these are considered people on their way down, while the "Urban Villagers" are considered on their way up the social scale.

Stokes divides slums into "slums of hope" and "slums of despair." He views the slum of hope as a way-station where a person may stay a long time believing that some day he will leave. He views the "slum of despair" as a place where residents have given up hope of moving up the social scale. He subdivides the "slums of hope" into those with people who are "employable and unemployable."[14] Harrington agrees with Stokes when he refers to ". . . the slum as a place to house failures from the old waves of immigrants, plus poor people of racial minorities who arrive in the slums when the economic opportunities that existed for the earlier immigrants simply are not there anymore."[15]

---

[12] Herbert Gans, *The Urban Villagers* (New York: The Free Press, 1962), pp. 17-22.

[13] Hunter, *The Slums,* p. 15.

[14] Charles Stokes, "A Theory of Slums," *Land Economics,* Vol. XLVII, No. 3 (August, 1962), pp. 187-197.

[15] Michael Harrington, *The Other America* (New York: The Macmillan Co., 1962), p. 2.

Seely expands this idea with a functional view of slums. He points out: "The slum is not just a dumping ground nor just a way station into the city. It is also a provider of goods and services that are demanded by the non-slum population. . . . In this respect it performs a permanent function in the urban complex."[16] Fried and Levin amplify this idea with their emphasis on the social function provided by a slum not only to the community, but to itself. They state:

> . . . these social functions become more critical as the rate or complexity of social change increases. This need can be optimally fulfilled in conditions of far better housing and less serious deprivation. But optimum fulfillment of the social functions of the working-class slum can be encouraged only if . . . the community is preserved . . . rather than slowly eliminated.[17]

Like Stokes, Seely divides slums into four basic types. To Seely, the slum population is characterized by two major differences: the difference between necessity and opportunity and the difference between permanence and change. For some, the slum represents a set of opportunities not available elsewhere. For others, it represents a set of necessities to which they have been reduced. Seely sees four major types of slum dwellers: the permanent necessitarians, the temporary necessitarians, the permanent opportunists, and the temporary opportunists.

Hunter characterizes these people: "Among the temporary necessitarians are the respectable poor. The permanent opportunists are fugitives and prostitutes. The temporary opportunists are beginners, climbers, and entrepreneurs."[18] He also describes the feel of the slum which he says is as important as any other single aspect: the attitude of the slum dweller toward the slum itself, toward the city of which the slum is a part, toward his own chances of getting out and toward the people who control things. He identifies these as elements of the slum problem:

> Poverty, run-down housing, crowding, concentration of lower class people, racial concentration, concentration of people of low educational achievement, low skill and cultural limitations, many welfare

---

[16] John R. Seely, "The Slum: Its Nature, Use and Users," *Journal of the American Institute of Planners*, Vol. XXV, No. 1 (February, 1959), p. 7.

[17] Marc Fried and Joan Levin, "Some Social Functions of the Urban Slum," in *Urban Planning and Social Policy*, ed. by Bernard J. Frieden and Robert Morris (New York: Basic Books, Inc., 1968), p. 79.

[18] Hunter, *The Slums*, p. 18.

cases, internal mobility, crime, health problems, broken families, relocation problems, inadequate community services, skid row, dirt, fire hazards, isolation and alienation, language problems and the slum atmosphere.[19]

Population: The Formation of Ghettos

Throughout the 20th century the Negro population of the United States has been moving steadily from rural to urban areas and from the South to the North. This migration resulted from an expectation of jobs in the North and the mechanization of farm labor in the South. Negro migration has been small compared to earlier waves of European immigrants; however, its concentration because of exclusion from white residential areas has created these basic trends:

> Almost all Negro population growth is occurring within metropolitan areas, primarily within the central city. . . . The majority of white population growth is occurring in suburban areas. As a result, the central cities are becoming more Negro while the suburban fringes around them remain almost entirely white.[20]

Within most central cities, Negroes have been excluded from white residential areas through discriminatory practices. Equally significant is the withdrawal of white families from, or their refusal to enter, neighborhoods where Negroes are moving or already residing. About 20 percent of the urban population of this country moves each year. The refusal of whites to move into changing areas when vacancies occur means that most vacancies eventually are occupied by Negroes and the result is continuing and increasing segregation.

In 1966 there were 12.5 million nonwhites living in all central cities of the United States; 12.1 million of these were Negroes.[21] Since the Negroes were highly segregated residentially, this number serves as a good estimate of the 1966 ghetto or inner city population in a racial sense. If an estimated eight million of the white population are added to this, one can visualize:

---

[19] *Ibid.*

[20] U. S. *Riot Commission Report,* pp. 12-13.

[21] Anthony Downs, "The Future of American Ghettos" (paper presented at the American Academy of Arts and Sciences Conference on Urbanism, Cambridge, Mass., Oct. 27-28, 1967), p. 2. By 1970 the number of Negroes in the central city increased to 13 million. See *Statistical Abstract of the U. S. 1971,* p. 16.

This underculture of the poor is 20 million people, white and black for whom the goals and aspirations of American society appear as one vast fraud. Each act of discrimination, each act of violence, each magic program that remains unfunded drives them tighter into their world.[22]

Approximately 29 percent of these racial ghetto residents had incomes below the poverty level of the equivalent of $3000 per year for a four-person household. Conversely, the total number of persons with 1966 incomes below the poverty level in the U. S. central cities was about 10.6 million.[23]

Approximately two thirds of these persons were white and one third nonwhite. Thus the ghetto in a purely economic sense contains about 3.6 million persons were ghetto residents in 1966; these were central city residents who were both poor and nonwhite. these were central city residents who were both poor and nonwhite. Hence, in its narrowest context, this book is concerned with about four million persons or approximately 2 percent of the population of the United States, and, in its broadest context, it is concerned with approximately 20 million persons or an estimated 10 percent of the total 1970 population.

Any planning concept designed to cope with the ghetto should recognize the fact that concentrations of Negro population in central cities are growing rapidly. The 1960 U. S. Census of Population indicates that in 1950 there were 6.3 million nonwhites in central cities. In 1960, there were 10.3 million. In 1966 there were over 12 million or an increase of approximately 75 percent or an average of 500,000 persons per year. In this same period (1950-1966) the white population of central cities went from 42 million to approximately 50 million, or an increase of 15 percent. However, in the largest central cities, the white population declined while the nonwhite population rose sharply. The 1970 U. S. Census of Population indicates no significant change in these trends.

All evidence points to the conclusion that future nonwhite population growth will continue to be concentrated in central cities unless there are major changes in national priorities for cities, local housing policies and the tolerance levels of people. Today "not one single significant program of any federal, state or local government is aimed at altering this tendency, or is likely to have the unintended

---

[22] James M. Gavin and Arthur Hadley, "The Crisis of the Cities: The Battle We Can Win," *Saturday Review*, February 24, 1968, p. 31.

[23] Downs, "The Future of American Ghettos," p. 2.

effect of doing so."[24] Moreover, because the fertility rates are considerably higher for nonwhites than for whites, the rate of growth in ghettos is likely to remain at fairly high levels to balance any possible decrease due to a decline in immigration.

Some tentative estimates by Downs indicate that the central city nonwhite population for the whole United States "could rise to 20.4 million by 1978."[25] Within individual cities, rapid expansion of ghetto areas will continue. Downs and others identify an average growth rate of 2.5 to 3.5 city blocks per week now shifting from white to nonwhite occupancy. If this trend continues, America's ten largest cities will have over 50 percent nonwhite populations by 1980 or sooner. Population estimates for 1970 indicate that several major cities have already reached this level and now project 75 percent or more nonwhite populations by 1975 or sooner.

Poverty: The American Paradox

In *The Affluent Society*, Galbraith describes America's standard of living relative to the rest of the world: "Poverty does survive in the United States. . . . We ignore it because we share with all societies at all times the capacity for not seeing what we do not wish to see."[26] The national facts on poverty are:

> 20 percent of all Americans live in poverty and another 20 percent live at a level that can be called deprived (below $6,000); in 1960 over 34 million people in 10.5 million families had incomes of less than $4,000 per year and 4 million unattached individuals earned less than $2,000.[27]

This totals 38 million people, or about one fifth of the total population. These figures generally hold true for 1970 and are reflected in the *1970 U. S. Census of Population*.

Housing and Overcrowding

In 1970 there were over three million urban substandard units which housed 12 million people calculated on an average of 3.3 per-

---

[24] *Ibid.*
[25] *Ibid.*
[26] John Kenneth Galbraith, *The Affluent Society* (Boston: Houghton Mifflin Co., 1958), p. 333.
[27] *U. S. Riot Commission Report*, p. 469.

sons per household.[28] Nationwide, 25 percent of all nonwhites living in central cities occupied substandard units. Most of these units are located in the inner city. The general trend, despite urban renewal efforts, is toward more substandard units concentrated in older portions of cities or, in most cases, the inner city.

Inadequate housing in central cities is not limited to Negroes. Nevertheless, the *U. S. Riot Commission Report states:* "The vast majority of people living in the poorest areas of most cities were Negroes, and . . . a high proportion lived in inadequate housing."[29] With reference to overcrowding or high densities, the *U. S. Riot Commission Report* and *U. S. Census of Population* give substantially higher densities for nonwhite units in the central city. In 1960, 25 percent of all nonwhite units were overcrowded. Moreover, 11 percent of all nonwhite-occupied units were seriously overcrowded compared with 2 percent for white-occupied units in ten metropolitan areas analyzed by the Commission. The same percentages hold true for 1970 and, in many cases, indicate higher densities and overcrowding.

Lower-Class People

All lower-class people do not live in slums, but practically all the people who live in the slums are lower class or at the lower end of a status-ranking continuum. Any discussion of social class is often distorted with emotionalism and conventional thinking. The traditional American response to class is: "while some people are better off than others, this is because of their initiative, drive and capacity . . . anybody has an equal chance to rise because ours is an open society."[30] However, a closer look reveals that this country does have social classes and that the majority of slum populations are in the lowest social scale.

Miller estimates that between 40 and 60 percent of the total population share or are significantly influenced by the major outlines of the lower-class cultural system, with 15 percent being the hardcore lower-class group.[31] He defines a series of concerns to identify

---

[28] U. S. Department of Commerce, Bureau of the Census, *1970 U. S. Census of Population* (Washington: Government Printing Office).

[29] *U. S. Riot Commission Report,* p. 469.

[30] Hunter, *The Slums,* p. 38.

[31] Walter B. Miller, *Cultural Features of an Urban Lower Class Community* (Washington, D. C.: Community Services Branch, National Institute of Health, 1959), p. 31.

lower class; these include: trouble, toughness, smartness, excitement, fate and autonomy. He also believes that low pay and unskilled, irregular employment essentially define the lower class. Gans, in *The Urban Villagers*, identifies these indicators of lower-class status:

> The display and defense of masculinity, search for excitement, central role of the peer group, subordinate role of children, lack of interest in children as individuals, separate social lives for men and women, detachment from the job, lack of trust in the outside world, a personalization of government and antagonism toward law and government.[32]

There are some concepts stated in the literature which cut across religious and ethnic groups with reference to lower-class people. Gans summarizes this concept with his definition: "classes are strata-with-subcultures that grow out of the structure of the national economy and society."[33] He also distinguishes between the working class and the lower class. He describes the working class as semi-skilled blue-collar workers who hold steady jobs. Their values differ from those of the middle class through a lesser concern for self-improvement, education and status. He points out that these differences are not problem-producing, but notes the lower-class characteristics which do produce problems, e.g., crime or emotional instability.

Warner, an anthropologist, discovered six classes in America: upper-upper, lower-upper, upper-middle, lower-middle, upper-lower and lower-lower.[34] These classes were based on people's perception of what class they were in and what classes other people were in. Kahl concluded that social classes in America could be identified by six criteria: "occupational prestige, style of life, interaction patterns, personal prestige, value orientations, and class consciousness."[35]

Education and Employment

Education and employment are linked in a pattern of hopelessness for many residents of the ghetto. Without an adequate education, employment is difficult in today's labor market. Without

---

[32] Gans, *The Urban Villagers*, p. 264.

[33] *Ibid.*

[34] W. L. Warner, Marcia Meeker, Kenneth Eells, *Social Class in America: The Evaluation of Status* (Chicago: Science Research Associates, 1949), *passim.*

[35] J. A. Kahl, *The American Class Structure* (New York: Holt, Rinehart and Winston, 1957), p. 31.

employment, most parents do not have the motivation to reach the educational potentials for themselves or their children. The result is a downward spiral which particularly affects children and young adults.

Most studies indicate a direct relationship between low income, low educational level, low job status and poor housing conditions. The high-school dropout rates for most inner cities range from 50 to 75 percent. Unemployment and under-employment rates are about 33 percent or almost nine times higher than the overall unemployment rate for all workers. Where education and employment could provide opportunities to move up the social scale, they often present overwhelming obstacles in a technological society which demands at least a high-school education for most jobs.

The low educational level of inner city residents and consequent low employability have a drastic impact on family structure, social life, and income levels in the ghetto. Men who are chronically unemployed or employed in the lowest-status jobs have a tendency to leave their families. The handicap of children growing up without fathers in an atmosphere of poverty and deprivation is increased as mothers are forced to work in order to provide support.

The culture of poverty that results from unemployment and family breakup generates a system of exploitative relationships within the ghetto, creating an environment characterized by personal insecurity and tension. "Children growing up under such conditions are likely participants in civil disorder"[36] and do not have a fair opportunity to progress up the social scale. *The Moynihan Report* states: "At the heart of the deterioration of the Negro society is the deterioration of the Negro family. . . .There is probably no single fact of Negro American life so little understood by whites."[37] Both employment and low educational levels are the causal agents of this deterioration.

Health and Welfare

The residents of most inner cities are significantly less healthy than most other Americans. They suffer from higher mortality rates, higher incidence of major diseases, and lower availability and utilization of medical services. These conditions are a result of poverty and characterized by: deficient diets, lack of medical care, inade-

---

[36] *U. S. Riot Commission Report*, p. 14.

[37] Lee Rainwater and William L. Yancy, *The Moynihan Report and the Politics of Controversy* (Cambridge: The M.I.T. Press, 1967), p. 34.

quate shelter and clothing, and, because of low educational levels, a lack of awareness of health needs or services.

> About 30 percent of all families with incomes less than $2,000 per year suffer from chronic health conditions as compared with less than 8 percent of the families with incomes of $7,000 or more. . . . Maternal mortality rates are four times as high for nonwhite mothers as white mothers. . . . In many areas where garbage collection is grossly inadequate, mostly in the poorer parts of large cities, rats proliferate. In 1965, there were over 14,000 cases of rat bite in the United States mostly in these neighborhoods.[38]

Environmental conditions in disadvantaged Negro neighborhoods create further reasons for poor health conditions. The level of sanitation is strikingly below most higher-income areas. "One simple reason is that residents lack proper storage facilities for food, adequate refrigerators . . . even garbage cans are sometimes stolen before landlords can replace them."[39] It also comes as no surprise that families who receive welfare assistance of one kind or another are concentrated in poor areas. Most studies indicate that an average of 75 percent of all families now in inner-city Negro ghettos are on welfare.

Crime and Insecurity

Shaw and McKay, in their pioneering study on crime in Urban America, conclude: "delinquency rates vary widely in different neighborhoods. The rates are generally highest near the center of the city and decrease with distance from the center. . . ."[40] Sutherland utilized this information in developing his thesis that "crime is a response to the general culture. . . ."[41] Other studies conclude: "in slums comprising approximately 20 percent of the average city's residential area occur 45 percent of the major crimes, 55 percent of the juvenile delinquency and 50 percent of the arrests."[42] The *U. S. Riot Commission Report* summarized crime in racial ghettos in this manner:

---

[38] *U. S. Riot Commission Report,* p. 269.

[39] *Ibid.,* p. 273.

[40] Clifford Shaw and Henry D. McKay, *Delinquency Areas* (Chicago: University of Chicago Press, 1929), p. 93.

[41] Edwin H. Sutherland, *Principles of Criminology* (Chicago: J. B. Lippincott Co., 1924), p. 62.

[42] Hunter, *The Slums,* p. 71.

Crime rates are consistently higher than in other areas . . . creating a pronounced sense of insecurity . . . one city had 35 times as many serious crimes against persons as a high-income white district. Unless drastic steps are taken, the crime problems in poverty areas are likely to continue to multiply as the growing youth and rapid urbanization of the population outstrip police resources.[43]

Hunter states: "This badness in the slums tends to drive out the good and speed the spread of slums."[44] The slums also discourage the establishment and growth of facilities and institutions which might help to stem the tide of further deterioration. The people who need help the most have the least available. In addition, the problems associated with high crime rates generate widespread hostility toward the police in the slums. This compounds the atmosphere of insecurity and fear and causes a continuing breakdown of communications between residents and police where it is most needed.

Inadequate Municipal Services

Even though slums cost cities more in direct expenditures for police protection, fire-fighting, garbage removal, welfare and health than do other areas, these services generally are inadequate to the need. A number of studies estimate that the slum costs about twice as much in services as a comparable non-slum area, and that it returns approximately only one half the amount in taxes as does the non-slum area. It is a well-established fact that slums are an economic drain on a city's financial resources.

However, what has generally not been established is why municipal services equal to the need cannot be provided, despite the imbalance in revenue from slums. There is no economic rule which states that municipal services are granted on the ability to pay or repay for the services with taxes. There is also no clear concept in most of the thinking on welfare economics which can show that an investment in human welfare is *not* in the *overall* public interest. Most studies show the contrary and indicate a significant multiplier effect for human investment.

The idea of matching the level of slum services to central-city or suburban service levels is also fallacious. From almost any aspect, e.g., density, lack of existing facilities, the slum needs considerably

---

[43] *U. S. Riot Commission Report*, p. 14.
[44] Hunter, *The Slums*, p. 73.

more services than do non-slum areas. More important, in an affluent nation there is little rationale for not reallocating or distributing
resources to where they are most needed in human terms. To hide
behind the cloak of benefit-cost economics in this instance is to
disassociate economics from one of its primary goals—social welfare.

SIGNIFICANT ALTERNATIVES

A survey of some selected alernatives either to improve or to
eliminate through national and local action is vital to an understanding of the planning concepts described in subsequent chapters. This
discussion is by no means a survey of all proposed alternatives, nor
does it imply any choice of a particular alternative. The objective
here is to outline what are the crucial policy questions and more
significant alternatives.

A Social Strategy

Most authors agree on a need to think about the inner city in
social rather than physical terms. The slum-clearance ideas of the
1950's and early 1960's now seem unacceptable because of their
proven ineffectiveness, the recent wave of riots in this country and,
more hopefully, because of a more enlightened view of man and
his relationship to society. Whatever the reason, there has been a
distinct change in the thinking about the inner city which now
focuses on development of social strategies.

The paradox of this new approach is that Americans typically
do not attempt to solve social problems by behavior patterns which
can be considered strategies. While the strategy concept implies a
comprehensive, long-range program to cope with significant social
problems, this country's approach to most social problems has been
through a process that Lindblom calls "disjointed incrementalism."[45]
Each decision-maker or actor makes whatever choices that seem to
him to be the most appropriate at that moment, in light of his interests and his own view of public welfare. He generally pays little
attention to the consequences of his action on others usually because
"(1) no one has the detailed knowledge and foresight necessary to
comprehend all those consequences and (2) no one has the time and

[45] Charles E. Lindblom and David Braybrooke, *The Strategy of Decision* (New York: The Free Press, 1963).

energy to negotiate in advance with all others likely to be affected by his actions. Instead he acts and waits for others to react."[46]

A process of mutual adjustment ensues. Those who are harmed by each decision recoup their losses by exercising whatever economic, moral or political powers are available to them. Those who benefit use their powers to encourage more of the same. Presiding over these actions are primarily "reactive" governments and institutions which keep altering the "rules of the game" and their own programs and behaviors to correct any grievous imbalances which appear.

There is no guarantee that the checks and balances built into this uncoordinated process will effectively counteract every negative condition emerging from it. It is becoming increasingly possible that each individual will be frustrated or motivated to take actions that could lead to collective civil disobedience and ultimately the destruction of life and property in cities and suburbs.

Thus far, the existing system has been remarkably effective at avoiding such outcomes. Part of this success results from society's ability to generate a set of basic values which exert an influence on individual decisions, and part from the ability of enough actors to perceive threatening trends in time to formulate and carry out ameliorating policies.

This means that the system should begin to forecast potentially positive and negative trends in society and devise policies and programs to meet these trends with alternatives. In some cases, where the trends that threaten society are entrenched in its institutional structure, some alternatives may not be possible without changes in institutions. These changes may only be possible if the power structure shares a feeling of the need for change and the objectives motivating it. It is at this point that a social strategy occurs and the development of alternatives becomes a prerequisite for action.

Some Alternative Strategies

The *U. S. Riot Commission Report* paints a grim future for the central city and especially for the inner city. This report and many other sources outline several significant strategies or alternatives. Most focus on both long and short-range answers to these two fundamental questions: "(1) should future Negro population growth be concentrated in central cities as in the last 20 years, and should

---

[46] *Ibid.*

Negro and white populations become even more residentially segregated? and (2) Should society provide greatly increased special assistance to Negroes and other relatively disadvantaged population groups?"[47]

Each of these questions is generally answered by a spectrum of extreme responses. For analysis, Downs reduces the alternatives to three sets listed in Table 6. He narrows the almost infinite combination of these alternatives into eight different groups and rules out three as inconsistent with integration concepts, political feasibility and time. His process of elimination leaves five basic alternative

TABLE 6
Significant Alternatives for the Negro Ghetto*

Alternatives	Action proposal
Degree of concentration	Continue to concentrate nonwhite population growth in either central cities or perhaps a few older suburbs next to central cities: Concentration
	Disperse nonwhite population growth widely throughout all parts of metropolitan areas: Dispersal
Degree of segregation	Continue to cluster whites and nonwhites in residentially segregated neighborhoods regardless of where they are within the metropolitan area: Segregation
	Scatter the nonwhite population, or at least a significant fraction of it, randomly among white residential areas to achieve at least partial integration: Integration
Degree of enrichment	Continue to provide relatively low-level welfare, education, job-training and other support to the most deprived groups in the population: Nonenrichment
	Greatly raise the level of support to welfare, education, housing, job-training and other programs for the most deprived groups largely through federally aided programs: Enrichment

* Table developed from paper by Anthony Downs, "The Future of American Ghettos," given at the American Academy of Arts and Sciences Conference on Urbanism, Cambridge, Massachusetts, October 27-28, 1967.

[47] *U. S. Riot Commission Report*, p. 395

strategies which are summarized as: "(1) Status Quo: concentra-tion-segregation-nonenrichment. (2) Ghetto Enrichment: concen-tration-segregation-enrichment. (3) Integrated Core: concentration-integration (in the center only)-enrichment. (5) Integrated Dispersal: dispersal-integration-enrichment."[48]

Downs analyzes each and concludes that a combination of the Ghetto Enrichment and Integrated Dispersal alternatives is the most realistic alternative for some American cities. However, he qualifies this with the need to try all of these alternatives or various combinations in individual cities, as appropriate. The *U. S. Riot Commission Report* distills these into: (1) The Present Policies Choice, (2) The Enrichment Choice, and (3) The Integration Choice.

PRESENT POLICIES CHOICE

Under this course of action the nation would maintain approximately the same share of resources now being allocated to programs of assistance for the poor, unemployed and disadvantaged. These programs might grow, but they will probably not grow fast enough to stop, or reverse, the already deteriorating quality of life in the central city. This choice is least recommended by the Commission because it could provoke the greatest amount of violent protest and civil disruption.

> Large scale and continuing violence could result, followed by white retaliation and ultimately the separation of the two communities into a garrison state. . . . To continue present policies is to make permanent the division of our society into two societies; one, largely Negro and poor, located in the central cities; the other predominantly white and affluent, located in the suburbs.[49]

This choice would do nothing to raise the hopes, absorb the energies, or constructively challenge the residents of the cities. It could reinforce the probability of serious violence and even open warfare between city and suburbs. It would also result in a severe polarization of races and an erosion of remaining private or institutional interests attempting to help the ghetto. What little industry and economic opportunities remain in the ghetto would probably leave. This would result in further tax loss and probably even less adequate municipal services to further frustrate and alienate residents toward more violence to achieve their ends.

---

[48] Downs, "The Future of American Ghettos," pp. 21-22.
[49] *U. S. Riot Commission Report,* p. 22.

ENRICHMENT CHOICE

The Present Policies Choice means a continuation of efforts like the "Model Cities" and the "War on Poverty." These are enrichment programs, designed to improve the quality of life in ghettos. However, because of their limited scope and funds, they constitute only very modest steps toward enrichment and would continue to do so even if these programs were expanded or supplemented.

The premise of the Enrichment Choice is performance. To adopt this choice would require a substantially greater share of the nation's resources in order to make a dramatic impact on life in the urban ghetto. Its second premise is that Negroes can achieve equality of opportunity with whites while living in complete separation.

The implication of the Enrichment Choice would probably have three immediate effects on civil disorders. The announcement of large-scale programs and the intent to carry them out might: (1) allay tensions or at least delay them, (2) stimulate expectations beyond the capability of society to deliver, increasing frustration and discontent, or (3) lessen the likelihood of civil disorders given the meaningful creation of productive jobs for large numbers of unemployed young people.

The third effect is unlikely with the growing number of Negro youth who are, and will be, increasingly unemployed or under-employed in a changing job market which demands a different set of skills than they have available. The first and second alternatives also have serious risks given the past performance of government to react in a constructive manner to an urgent problem. In the area of reducing civil disorder, it would appear that this alternative offers little hope of success.

The Enrichment Choice would support the Black Power view which asserts that "the American Negro population can assume its proper role in society and overcome its feelings of powerlessness and lack of self-respect only by exerting power over decisions which directly affects its own members."[50] This implies a separate but equal distribution of resources which, in the end, would result in separate black and white societies. The Commission feels that the country is now consciously or unconsciously making this choice and warns against it in this statement:

> It is a way of choosing a permanently divided country. Moreover, equality cannot be achieved under conditions of nearly complete

---

50 *Ibid.,* p. 404.

separation. In a country where the economy, and particularly the resources of employment are predominantly white, a policy of separation can only relegate Negroes to a permanently inferior economic status.[51]

INTEGRATION CHOICE

The Integration Choice would be aimed at reversing the movement of the country toward two societies, separate and unequal. Similar to the Enrichment Choice, it would call for large-scale improvement in the quality of ghetto life. But it would also involve both the creation of strong incentives for Negro movement out of central-city ghettos and the enlargement of freedom of choice concerning housing, employment and schools.

The result of this choice would fall considerably short of full integration. Past experience proves that some Negro households would be scattered into largely white residential areas, but the majority of both whites and Negroes would cluster in voluntary segregation. This choice would produce both integration and segregation, but the segregation would be voluntary. The Commission bases its recommendation of this choice on four major rationales: "(1) Future jobs are being created primarily in the suburbs, (2) Racial and social class integration is the best way of improving the education of ghetto children, (3) Developing an adequate housing supply for low and middle income Negroes will require out-movement and freedom of choice in housing areas, and (4) Integration is the only course which explicitly seeks to achieve a united nation rather than the present movement toward a dual society."[52]

The Commission feels this to be the *only* choice open to Urban America, if it is to begin reversing the divisive trend so evident in metropolitan areas. They feel that enrichment must be an important adjunct to integration; no matter how ambitious or energetic the program, few Negroes now living in the central city can be quickly integrated. In the meantime, large-scale improvement in the quality of ghetto life is possible and essential, but only an interim strategy. Programs should be developed which will permit substantial Negro movement out of the ghettos with the primary goal a single society where every citizen will be free to live and work according to his capabilities and desires, *not* his color. The Commission concludes: "the future of our cities is neither something

---

[51] *Ibid.*, p. 22.
[52] *Ibid.*, pp. 406-407.

which will 'just happen,' nor something which will be imposed upon us by destiny." They state:

> (1) The nation is rapidly moving toward two increasingly separate Americas, (2) Continuation and expansion of such a permanent division threatens us with the perils of sustained violence in our cities and a repudiation of the American ideals of dignity, freedom and equality of opportunity and, (3) We cannot escape responsibility for choosing the future of our metropolitan areas. . . . It is a responsibility so critical that even an unconscious choice to continue present policies has the gravest implications.[53]

RELATIONSHIP TO RECREATION PLANNING

All of the above alternatives have a direct relationship to urban outdoor recreation planning. The Present Policies Choice exemplifies, in almost every instance, what *not* to do. Illustrations will be given in later chapters which analyze the planning process, recreation-planning concepts and techniques associated with this choice. Both the Enrichment and Integration Choice should include an enlightened approach to urban recreation planning never before attempted on a massive scale. Rettie states:

> Recreation planning, even some of the best of it, has failed to be comprehensive, because it has failed to come adequately to grip with the urban realities of the United States in the late 1960's and beyond.[54]

The *U. S. Riot Commission Report* states: "Among the 20 cities that accounted for the 24 most serious disorders, grievances relating to recreation were found in 15 cities and were ranked of first importance in three, second in one, and third in four cities."[55] The Commission also identified those complaints which seemed most causal in the riots. Of the 12 most significant kinds of grievances, poor recreation facilities and programs ranked fifth behind police practices, unemployment, housing and education. Recreation was regarded as a more significant grievance than the ineffectiveness of the political structure, discriminatory administration of justice, inadequate municipal services and inadequate welfare programs. In several cases, dissatisfaction over recreational facilities was the stated cause of outbreaks of violence. Table 7 summarizes the place of recreation in the grievance scale.

---

[53] *Ibid.*, pp. 407-408.
[54] Dwight Rettie, "Plan Implementation, Coordination and Communication," in Driver, *Elements of Outdoor Recreation Planning*, p. 299.
[55] *U. S. Riot Commission Report*, p. 149.

TABLE 7
Weighted Comparison of Grievance Categories*

	1st Place (4 Points)		2nd Place (3 Points)		3rd Place (2 Points)		4th Place (1 Point)		Total[a]	
	Cities	Points	Cities	Points	Cities	Points	Cities	Points	Cities	Points
Police practices	8	31½	4	12	0	0	2	2	14	45½
Unemployment and under-employment	3	11	7	21	4	7	3	3	17	42
Inadequate housing	5	18½	2	6	5	9½	2	2	14	36
Inadequate education	2	8	2	6	2	4	3	3	9	21
Poor recreation facilities	3	11	1	2½	4	7½	0	0	8	21
Political structure and grievance mechanism	2	8	1	3	1	2	1	1	5	14
White attitudes	0	0	1	3	1	1½	2	2	4	6½
Administration of justice	0	0	0	0	2	3½	1	1	3	4½
Federal programs	0	0	1	2½	0	0	0	0	1	2½
Municipal services	0	0	0	0	1	2	0	0	1	2
Consumer and credit practices	0	0	0	0	0	0	2	2	2	2
Welfare	0	0	0	0	0	0	0	0	0	0

[a] The total of points for each category is the product of the number of cities times the number of points indicated at the top of each double column except where two grievances were judged equally serious. In these cases the total points for the two rankings involved were divided equally (e.g., in case two were judged equally suitable for the first priority, the total points for first and second were divided and each received 3½ points).

* From *U. S. Riot Commission Report*, p. 149.

THE NEIGHBORHOOD

The residential aspect of the inner city has more meaning if it is viewed as a series of residential planning units or neighborhoods. In this book these terms are considered synonymous. The primary purpose is to sketch a physical and social profile of the inner city neighborhood. A secondary purpose is to develop a recreational profile of the typical inner city neighborhood.

Physical Image

There are two distinct physical images of the inner city neighborhood. At one end of the scale is the planner's idealistic concept of what a neighborhood is or ought to be. At the other end is the resident's perception of what his living environment is or could be. There is a wide disparity between these extremes and considerable disagreement with each point of view. Lansing and Marans conclude: "A high quality environment as defined by the planner may not conform necessarily to that which conveys satisfaction to many citizens. This disparity in values has caused much of the resistance to planning proposals."[56]

Lansing and Marans base their conclusions on five measures of desirability: openness, pleasantness, interest, attractiveness and overall satisfaction. Any number of other variables might be measured in a similar manner, e.g., density, overcrowding, boundaries, landmarks, danger, and similar conclusions drawn. A number of studies have attempted to prove this. The point here is to acknowledge this difference as a continuing source of ambiguity among planners and residents.

PLANNER'S IMAGE

The planner's image of the neighborhood is generally colored by his middle-class values, educational background and traditional techniques. There is no agreement on the boundaries, densities, services, or function of a neighborhood, or even a consensus on their definition. Chapin divides the city into work, living and leisure-time areas. He views the residential areas as neighborhoods which should:

---

[56] John B. Lansing and Robert W. Marans, "Evaluation of Neighborhood Quality," *Journal of the American Institute of Planners,* Vol. 35, No. 3 (May 1969), p. 195.

. . . be located in convenient proximity to work and leisure time areas, large open spaces, and should include smaller open spaces . . . they should be located in areas protected from traffic and incompatible uses . . . and in areas where desirable residential densities with a range of choice can be assured.[57]

Chapin also states: "Planning districts of this type usually aim to recognize the service area of an elementary school . . . and the physical barriers present such as railroads, thoroughfares, watercourses and large areas of nonresidential use." He suggests: ". . . where no such delineations have been previously made, a somewhat arbitrary system of planning districts may be used or developed for analysis purposes. These may follow census tract boundaries or some other previously developed breakdown of the urban area into small statistical areas."[58] Local Planning Administration, another standard text for many planners, states:

> Residential areas may usually be divided into identifiable neighborhoods. . . . They emerge as the result of a variety of interacting physical, economic and social forces. The boundaries of neighborhoods are usually determined by traffic arteries or barriers such as railroads, water courses or open spaces.[59]

This source also lists "a number of well-recognized principles that apply to the identification and planning of neighborhood units," and lists these criteria for a neighborhood:

> (1) Convenient and safe walking distance from an elementary school, (2) Being bounded and not crossed by major streets, (3) Accessibility to a central recreation area, and (4) Ready access to a local shopping center at one edge of a neighborhood.[60]

Speiregen states: "A basic unit of urban design is the neighborhood."[61] Broady sums up much of the thinking on the neighborhood concept with this statement: "The concept originated simply as a means of relating physical amenities systematically to the distribution of population." He also relates the size of the planning

---

[57] F. Stewart Chapin, Jr., *Urban Land Use Planning* (Urbana: University of Illinois Press, 1965), p. 371.

[58] *Ibid.*, p. 365.

[59] International City Managers' Association, *Local Planning Administration* (Chicago: International City Managers' Association, 1948), pp. 196 and 200.

[60] *Ibid.*, p. 200.

[61] Paul D. Spreiregen, *Urban Design: The Architecture of Towns and Cities* (New York: McGraw-Hill Book Company, 1965), p. 73.

unit to an elementary school and suggests a population of 10,000 to support one elementary school. As a social unit, Broady believes that "the neighborhood plan and the allocation of facilities within it could also help to engender a sense of belonging and community spirit among the residents."[62]

The traditional or physical neighborhood concept is criticized by those planners conscious of its social potentials and problems. Two critics of the neighborhood concept seem to polarize most of the arguments and both of these individuals disagree to a great extent. Herbert Gans submits the physical concept of a neighborhood to be the basic need of the inner city.[63] Jane Jacobs maintains "the need for more sensitive planning to create a physical and social identity with a dimension of vitality that the resident can call a neighborhood."[64]

Jacobs argues that people want diversity that generates vitality and the focus of this is abundant street life. She argues against the insensitive high-rise building and large unused open space, and condemns the sterility of most current physical planning. Her position is based on these three assumptions: (1) diversity is ultimately what makes cities live, (2) the lack of it makes them die, and (3) buildings, streets and amenities can and do shape human behavior. She romanticizes the slum neighborhood and its vitality and makes an impassioned plea for a return to some of the positive social and physical amenities which they offer. Gans takes direct issue with most of Jacobs' ideas, especially with reference to the inner city. He states:

> The neighborhood with which she [Jacobs] is most concerned cannot serve as models for future planning, but the way in which she has observed them . . . can and ought to be adapted for use in planning. . . . Her book is a pathbreaking achievement, and because it is so often right, I am all the more disappointed by the fact that it is also so often wrong.[65]

---

[62] Maurice R. Broady, "The Social Aspects of Town Development," *Taming Megalopolis,* ed. by Wentworth Eldredge (New York: Doubleday, 1967), p. 943.

[63] Herbert J. Gans, "Social and Physical Planning for the Elimination of Urban Poverty," *Urban Planning and Social Policy,* ed. by Bernard J. Frieden and Robert Morris (New York: Basic Books, Inc., 1968), pp. 39-54.

[64] Jane Jacobs, *The Death and Life of Great American Cities* (New York: Random House, 1961), p. 117.

[65] Herbert J. Gans, "City Planning and Urban Realities," *Journal of the American Institute of Planners* (January, 1962), p. 132.

Gans refutes the assumptions of Jacobs by stating that "the first two of these assumptions are not entirely supported by facts"[66] and that "there is no evidence these two planning concepts are as important to low-income people as they are to planners."[67] The last assumption he asserts to be "a fallacy because it ignores the social, cultural and economic factors that contribute to vitality or dullness."[68] It is also irrelevant to the true causes of the inner city's problems.

Gans details a range of situations which disprove Jacob's central thesis of vitality. He submits that street life is a product of lower-class culture and has little application to planning except for some inner city ghettos. He also maintains that the future of the American city lies not with creating or maintaining neighborhood vitality, but with the solution of more fundamental social problems such as poverty, education and employment. His plea is for a social emphasis in planning which might ultimately alleviate some of the negative environmental conditions of the inner city. He dismisses any return to the romantic slum as naive and ineffective in helping to solve the problems of the inner city. He concludes:

> The standard neighborhood planning package [concept] cannot contribute significantly to the improvement of the lower-class milieu. The significant components of this milieu are other people, rather than environmental features, and until these other people are socially and economically secure . . . the milieu is not likely to improve sufficiently to prevent the perpetration of past deprivations on the young growing up within it.[69]

RESIDENT'S IMAGE

The resident's image of his living area is usually less structured and quite often different from the planner's idealistic view. The literature reveals no extensive research or national sample on how residents perceive their environment. However, several studies have made contributions in this area.

Svenson, in his study of an inner city residential area in Boston, concludes that people have a fair degree of consensus on the size,

---

[66] *Ibid.*

[67] Gans, "Social and Physical Planning for the Elimination of Urban Poverty" p. 42.

[68] Gans, "City Planning and Urban Realities," p. 132.

[69] Gans, "Social and Physical Planning for the Elimination of Urban Poverty," p. 48.

boundaries, landmarks, advantages and dangers of their neighborhood.[70] He demonstrates this with a questionnaire and has people sketch their perception of a neighborhood on a map. This approach to "behavioral mapping" has been used with reasonable success and is detailed in *Environmental Psychology*.[71]

Lansing and Hendricks found that the general resident image of a neighborhood "was the immediate vicinity of their homes," or, stated in visual terms, "what people could see from their homes."[72] To some extent, and especially with reference to the inner city, this agrees with Rainwater's thesis of "Fear and the House-as-Haven in the Lower Class" in which he views the house and immediate environment as the limits of an inner city neighborhood.[73]

Lansing and Hendricks examine this relationship for a number of factors to include social interaction, visual awareness and physical characteristics, and conclude: "People can evaluate neighborhoods and tend to take the quality of the neighborhood into account in deciding where to live."[74] They also discuss how the evaluations of professional planners tend to *agree* with the evaluations of residents on what is pleasant, but *disagree* on what is unpleasant (with the exception of college-educated residents).

Other insights into resident imagery of the neighborhood include Claude Brown's *Manchild in the Promised Land*,[75] Herbert Gans' *The Urban Villagers*[76] and William Whyte's *Street Corner Society*.[77] Each of these project a territorialism or image of a social and physical dimension which the residents refer to as their neighborhood. Each also describes how the resident relates only to this area and perceives little of life outside it. This is vividly summarized in Paul Jacobs' book, *Prelude to Riot:*

---

[70] Erik A. Svenson, "Differential Adaptation to Change in Urban Form" (unpublished Ph.D. dissertation, Massachusetts Institute of Technology, 1967).

[71] H. M. Prohansky et al., *Environmental Psychology* (New York: Holt, Rinehart and Winston, 1970).

[72] John B. Lansing and Gary Hendricks, *Living Patterns in the Detroit Region* (Detroit, Michigan: Detroit Regional Transportation and Land Use Study, 1967), p. 61.

[73] Lee Rainwater, "Fear and the House-as-Haven in the Lower Class," *Urban Planning and Social Policy*, pp. 85-95.

[74] Lansing and Hendricks, *Living Patterns in the Detroit Region*, p. 88.

[75] Claude Brown, *Manchild in the Promised Land* (New York: The Macmillan Co., 1965).

[76] Gans, *The Urban Villagers*.

[77] William Foote Whyte, *Street Corner Society* (Chicago: University of Chicago Press, 1955).

Their perception of the world is so limited that everything outside the narrow confines of their own lives have little or no significance for them. To get up in the morning . . . go to work, come home, work in the garden . . . learn to ski . . . these life patterns of the middle class . . are unknown to these generations of unemployed, underemployed, and low-paid workers.[78]

Conclusions from the research to date on resident perception of a neighborhood imply: (1) residents can and do have a sense of the neighborhood as a physical and social identity to which they relate, (2) in most instances this sense differs from the planner's image and is usually less idealistic and objective, and (3) the resident is more concerned with security and social relationships than with the spatial boundaries, densities, total population, amenities and physical features mentioned by most planners.

Political Leadership

The range of concepts concerning political leadership within the neighborhood is as divergent as that concerning the neighborhood's physical or social image. The more traditional views point to the inner city as an area lacking in both potential and actual effective leadership or citizen participation. Recent opinions refute these concepts and suggest that the neighborhood is not only capable of political leadership but should make a concerted effort at self-determination. Because there is so little agreement in this controversial area this book describes the positive and negative views expressed most often in the literature.

NEGATIVE VIEWPOINT

Bellush and Hansknecht state: "In our society effective political participation requires that an individual be a member of a group or organization."[79] They list the following prerequisites for participation in the political process: morale-cohesion, the capacity for organizational behavior, leadership, knowledge, and awareness. They believe that the morale of the Negro population in urban community tends to be so low that, even when a vital issue or opportunity presents itself, no initiative will be taken. They identify low

---

[78] Paul Jacobs, *Prelude to Riot* (New York: Random House, 1966), p. 102.

[79] Jewell Bellush and Murray Hansknecht, "Planning Participation and Urban Renewal," *Urban Renewal: People, Politics and Planning*, ed. by Bellush and Hansknecht (Garden City, N. Y.: Anchor Books, 1967), p. 279.

motivation, lack of effective political leadership, low levels of technical knowledge and poor communication, hence, a lack of awareness, as the causal agents and conclude: "Given the imperfect nature of the world a planner's experience with grass-roots democracy is apt to be a severely disillusioning one."[80] Gans supports this theme and states: " . . . some lower class people lack the motivation and skill needed to participate in a contemporary society."[81] Wilson reflects this same sentiment. He states:

> Such people are more likely to have a limited time perspective, a greater difficulty in abstracting from concrete experience . . . a preoccupation with the personal and immediate, and few attachments to organizations of any kind, with the possible exception of churches. . . . They are intimately bound up in the day-to-day struggle to sustain themselves and their families.[82]

Hunter points out that "people who are low on the scales of social and economic status do not participate in voting as much as people who are higher" and supports this with voting statistics. He concludes: "probably 60 to 80 percent of the lower class do not belong to any formal organization."[83] Harrington describes the world of the poor as a place where citizen participation is extremely difficult because slum people are "out" and they feel that they are out.[84] Hunter says, "The poor know that things are run by somebody else. They have no stake in the larger community . . . do not make its decisions, and most do not expect to get anywhere in it."[85] He gives four major reasons for nonparticipation.

First is residential mobility. People in the slums move from one place to another frequently. They may not move very far away, but the shifting about occurs quite often. Urban renewal contributes to this process, as does public housing. There is constant movement into the area, within it, and out of it. The latter is usually a response to improved economic conditions.

The second reason is that most efforts to organize the commu-

---

[80] *Ibid.*, p. 285.

[81] Gans, "Social and Physical Planning for the Elimination of Urban Poverty," p. 43.

[82] James Q. Wilson, "Planning and Politics: Citizen Participation in Urban Renewal," *Urban Planning and Social Policy*, p. 217.

[83] Hunter, *The Slums*, p. 172.

[84] Harrington, *The Other America*.

[85] Hunter, *The Slums*, p. 173.

nity or to stimulate greater citizen participation are staffed or pro-
moted by middle-class people. To the extent that lower-class
people feel that they are being dominated or used, they are likely
to remain distant or withdraw from any meaningful participation.

Self-defeating attitudes form the third barrier to citizen participation by slum residents. Lower-income groups tend to view life
pessimistically and resign themselves from the struggle. This defeat-
ism, resulting in a lack of participation, produces a loss of interest
in attempting to change their condition.

The fourth factor mitigating against citizen participation is intergroup tension. Where there is much to be hostile about, e.g.,
intergroup competition, environmental conditions, discrimination,
poverty, it is difficult to make a common effort or have an urgent
concern for the community.

Hunter identifies the self-defeating attitude as the strongest of
the above reasons. He describes it as "another way of saying that
there is a pervasive feeling of helplessness. Things are so big, and
far away, and the people who control them unreachable."[86] He
points out:

> In America, unlike Asia or Africa, the poor are in the minority,
> and the culture says all you need to get ahead is individual initiative
> and hard work. These two facts combined make it easy for anyone
> who is poor to convince himself that he is really no good and that
> this is why he is poor.[87]

POSITIVE VIEWPOINT

Recent events have caused growing numbers of authorities in
all fields to reexamine the negative viewpoints and speculate on
possible means of self-determination through the effective political
involvement of ghetto residents. The thrust of advocacy planning,
civil disobedience, militancy and violence as means to achieve
desired ends is so recent that researchers have had little time to
analyze and evaluate it. Nevertheless, it is something to be considered and does offer a possible alternative for citizen participation
at the neighborhood or citywide level.

The positive approach to citizen participation is best illustrated
in Alinsky's method of using conflict and political force to move

---

[86] *Ibid.*, p. 177.
[87] *Ibid.*, p. 178.

the system, but not to destroy it. He reasons that the holders of power are reluctant to share or relinquish that power, or even allow existing institutions to follow policies and carry out actions that will improve the conditions of the poor, unless they are forced to by hard-bargaining techniques.[88]

Alinsky feels that, in order to bargain effectively, both parties must have a foundation of power. No bargaining takes place when the negotiators are unequal in power; only imposed resolutions can come out of unequal power situations. In order for poor people to establish a power base, they must act in concert. To organize people in an atmosphere of hopelessness, issues and dormant conflicts must be dramatized so that the dispirited will have something to rally around. Opposition must be identified and singled out for attack. This provides a base against which all of the appropriate weapons in the arsenal of collective bargaining and political pressure are brought to bear, to include: voter registration, picketing, boycotts, adverse publicity, public meetings, threats and nonviolent demonstrations. This method is described by Alinsky:

> In the development of an organization for democratic citizen participation . . . resentments and dormant hostilities must be brought up to a visible surface where they can be transformed into problems. . . . A people do not break through their previous fatalism . . . until they have a mechanism . . . for effectively coping with these problems. . . . There can be no darker or more devastating tragedy than the death of a man's faith in himself, in his power to direct his future.[89]

Bayard Rustin, in his article "From Protest to Politics" states the belief that grass-roots participation is not only possible but also vital in bringing about changes in social and economic conditions at the neighborhood level. He supports direct action techniques as a way of dramatizing problems, issues and advocacy planning to achieve social objectives.[90] Jane Jacobs describes "neighborhoods as instruments of self-government" emphasizing that "there exists no substitute for localized self-government."[91]

---

[88] Saul Alinsky, *Reveille for Radicals* (Chicago: University of Chicago Press, 1946).

[89] Saul Alinsky, "Plan of Operations, Neighborhood Urban Extension" (Pittsburgh: ACTION Housing, Inc., 1963).

[90] Bayard Rustin, "From Protest to Politics: The Future of the Civil Rights Movement, "*Urban Planning and Social Policy*, pp. 334-345.

[91] Jacobs, *The Death and Life of Great American Cities*, p. 117.

Even Wilson, who holds a dismal view of citizen participation in lower-class areas, states:

> Although such people are not likely spontaneously to form organizations to define and carry out very general civic tasks, it is wrong to assume that they are not likely to organize or to allow themselves to be organized for any purpose. The important thing to remember is not that they are unorganizable, but that they can be organized only under special circumstances and for special purposes.[92]

Wilson describes how each person can and will act only if he sees individual short-term benefits and how these individual benefits can turn into collective protest with considerable effectiveness. This theme is repeated in much of the literature. A consensus that active citizen participation or advocacy in the ghetto is both possible and effective as one means to an end, previously obtained only by working with the system for a desired change, is the growing, possibly dominant, idea in Urban America. Whether this idea has substance remains to be tested and evaluated. However, it can be no less effective than traditional negative ideas of citizen involvement and might offer slum residents some hope for the future.

Recreational Profile

Within the inner city at the neighborhood scale, leisure, recreation and specifically outdoor recreation in what has traditionally been termed a neighborhood park or playground is the focus of most urban recreation planning. Although there is a wide range of leisure activities which take place in a system and hierarchy of different types of public and private spaces or facilities, the neighborhood playground is detailed here to provide an illustrative facility for the planning approach to be described in later chapters.

The neighborhood playground in its traditional role is not necessarily the only or best type of facility for an inner city neighborhood. Nor is it necessarily best adapted to the diversity, critical shortage of all types of open space, social problems, climate and a number of other factors characteristic of the inner city. But it does exist in some form in most inner city neighborhoods, has been studied by others, has some potentials for improvement and offers some insights into the nature of outdoor recreation for both children and adults in the inner city.

---

[92] Wilson, "Planning and Politics," p. 218.

Because of the relative lack of data on facilities other than the neighborhood playground, it is important to outline a broad perspective on the types of facilities, common programs, user characteristics, recreational use patterns and some significant problems and potentials in the inner city. Data on these topics are scarce because the traditional approach to recreation planning has been to aggregate the inner city with the central city and sometimes with the suburbs. This usually results in a superficial classification of "urban outdoor recreation" or one which seldom shows how deficient the inner city is in available and effective opportunities for outdoor recreation.

CONTRASTS BETWEEN INNER CITY AND SUBURB

Although there have been several recent studies of recreation in the inner city,[93] few have contrasted it with the suburb or other portions of the central city. Two notable exceptions are the studies of Kraus[94] on New York City and Lansing and Hendricks[95] on Detroit. The results of the studies are summarized in Tables 1 through 8 of Appendix C. Both studies indicate a substantial difference in recreation behavior between city and suburb. For example, Kraus reports:

> . . . a striking contrast between the reported recreational involvements of Negro and white participants . . . Negroes tend to dominate in certain sports e.g. track, swimming, basketball. By comparison Negroes participate at a much lower rate in . . . tennis, golf, archery . . . which have certain social-class connotations.[94]

Lansing and Hendricks make these observations about some significant differences between city and suburban recreation opportunities:

1. Of families with children under 16, more than one half make no use of public play space and, of these, most are in the suburbs, indicating what little public play space there is in the inner city is heavily used.

---

[93] Nesbitt, Brown and Murphy, *Recreation and Leisure Service for the Disadvantaged* 1970, National League of Cities, *Recreation in the Nation's Cities*, 1968 and State of California, *Recreation Problems in the Urban Impacted Areas of California*, 1970.

[94] Richard Kraus, "Negro Patterns of Participation in Recreation Activity," in *Recreation and Leisure Services for the Disadvantaged*, John A. Nesbitt et al. (ed.), pp. 324-325.

[95] Lansing and Hendricks, *Living Patterns in the Detroit Region*.

2. Nineteen percent of all families report that there is no public play space within walking distance and, among these families, most are in the inner city.

3. Of those who use public play space, most are well satisfied. However, of the two out of ten who say it is unsatisfactory, the number is ten times higher for inner city residents than for suburban dwellers.

4. Participation in most outdoor recreation activities is closely associated with income. Only 7 percent of adults with incomes below $2,000 went swimming compared to 53 percent with incomes over $15,000.

5. Inner city Negroes generally participate less than whites in outdoor recreation, even when they have the same income levels, which indicates a lack of opportunity in many situations, e.g., only 14 percent of inner city Negroes participate in outdoor swimming as compared to 44 percent of the whites surveyed.

6. Most suburban residents reported that they were satisfied with the attractiveness of their neighborhood, while less than one half of the inner city residents expressed this. Conversely, inner city residents expressed almost four times more dissatisfaction with their neighborhoods than did suburban residents.

These observations are not conclusive, but they do indicate: (1) a substantial difference between inner city and suburban recreation preferences, user satisfaction and opportunities, (2) that inner city populations tend to use those facilities provided, (3) a definite relationship between income, mobility, home ownership, lot size, education and race with respect to the frequency of participation and satisfaction for any given recreational experience, and (4) that most people consider outdoor recreation an important component of environmental quality.

The implications of these findings support the need for a different planning approach for each area and population. They also indicate the past and present allocation of recreation resources to be unequal or poorly distributed at the neighborhood scale. Most important, they clearly indicate that people consider outdoor recreation as a positive value in an urban environment and this can be measured and equated to what exists or is proposed.

FACILITIES AND PROGRAMS

The literature is filled with suggested examples, criteria and specifications about what a neighborhood playground should be, where it should be located and how it should be used. However, very little authoritative evaluation has been completed to link these guidelines with reality, and the types of facilities and programs common to the inner city.

Paradoxically some of the best insights into the nature of program and facilities within the inner city come from three books written by nonplanners or nonrecreationists: *No Place to Play*, by Tupper[96]; *The Death and Life of Great American Cities*, by Jacobs[97]; and *The Squeeze*, by Higbee.[98] Each author devotes a chapter to describing the dismal, unimaginative, unsafe and poorly maintained inner city park and playground.

Few good examples of inner city playground developments are evident except for some recent demonstration areas in St. Louis and New York City.[99] A recent report on outdoor recreation in New York City states that "of all the components in modern municipal recreation systems the neighborhood playground is the most important. In New York City it is the most neglected." [100] This report lists 11 of the largest cities in the country and details the total population served by playgrounds, number of playgrounds, their average size and the population per playground. These data are shown in Table 8.

Although these data are not necessarily representative of the inner city, by interpolation one might assume the size and population per playground indicated for New York City to approximate that in most metropolitan inner cities. A more conservative or realistic estimate might reduce these figures to a size of one acre and a service population of approximately 1,000 children (5 to 14 years of age).

There are little available data on the number and types of facilities or programs in the inner city playground or park other than the aggregate totals listed in Appendix D. Individual totals are available by city, but no breakdown exists for the inner city. There are no significant national data which evaluate the various types of equipment or programs in these playgrounds. However, several studies have isolated these observations about playground facilities and programs.

---

[96] Margo Tupper, *No Place to Play* (New York: Chilton Books, 1966).

[97] Jacobs, *The Death and Life of Great American Cities*.

[98] Edward Higbee, *The Squeeze* (New York: William Morrow and Co., 1960).

[99] Playgrounds designed by Paul Fredericks for the Pruitt Igo Public Housing Complex in St. Louis and the Jacob Riis Memorial Plaza in New York City. Several creative playgrounds are also being developed in San Francisco.

[100] National Recreation and Park Association, *A Study of New York Outdoor Recreation Needs* (New York: City Planning Commission, January, 1967), p. 146.

TABLE 8

Average Acreage and Population per Neighborhood
Playground 1966*

City[a]	Total Poulation (5-14 Years)[b]	Total Play-grounds	Average Size (Acres)	Population (5-14) per Playground
New York	1,175,079	1,395	1.26	842
Chicago	526,000	965	1.2	544
Los Angeles	374,331	580	3.0	646
Philadelphia	212,379	435	3.0	488
Detroit	252,191	223	2.1	1,130
Houston	141,271	415	6.0	340
Baltimore	141,792	45	. .	3,151
Cleveland	132,283	203	1.8	651
St. Louis	113,252	68	1.3	1,665
San Francisco	111,787	169	1.5	602
Boston	105,276	214	1.21	492

[a] Eleven largest cities in the United States.

[b] Population Figures, U. S. Census 1960.

* From National Recreation and Park Association, *A Study of New York Outdoor Recreation Needs* (New York: City Planning Commission, January, 1967), p. 146.

Facilities

Nading shows a correlation between the size of a playground and attendance. He suggests that "any relationship between larger playgrounds and greater use is statistically insignificant" and concludes that "density is more important than size itself because potential users may stay away from a small playground if it is overcrowded. . . ."[101]

Playground design plays a function here, especially in separating incompatible age groups. One report states: "attendance at municipal playgrounds has increased 400 percent since the city installed its new policy of segregating age-groups." This report

[101] Martin M. Nading, Jr., "The Relationships of Selected Program Variables to the Playgrounds of Fort Wayne, Indiana" (unpublished M. S. thesis, Indiana University, February, 1952), p. 125.

also states: "the function of the leader is not only in preventing discord, but in organizing the use of facilities in such a way to increase density of usage." [102] The concept of less land and more leadership could have some very effective applications in the inner city.

Despite interest in some of the more creative play equipment and a movement toward more innovative playground designs, the literature reveals no studies contrasting the effectiveness of creative versus traditional equipment for the same population at the same time. Although most authorities agree on the merits of creative play areas, it is still conjectural if they are really any more effective than traditional play areas or less effective than the "adventure play areas" described by Cooper.[103]

Program

Relatively little is known about this vital area. Butler cites an experiment with a community of 300,000 people to show the effect of trained leadership on use. He found "an unsupervised playground attracted 20 children. When a trained leader was hired, attendance rose to 448." [104] Nading supports this finding "with a rank order correlation of .42 between attendance and program quality and leadership." [105]

A Chicago study shows that "in four lower class neighborhoods, users tended to prefer unsupervised activities over supervised activities while in middle class neighborhoods the reverse was true."[106] However, this should be qualified with possible differences between the user's, the leader's and the supplier's goals rather than the user's goals employed to structure this survey.

---

[102] "Age-Group Playgrounds in Kalamazoo Please Child Patrons," *News Bulletin of the Public Administration Clearing House*, Release No. 5 (October 31, 1941).

[103] Clare C. Cooper, *The Adventure Playground: Creative Play in an Urban Setting* (Berkeley: Center for Planning and Development Research, University of California, 1970), and "Adventure Playgrounds" in *Landscape Architecture*, (October 1970), pp. 18-29 and (January 1971), pp. 88-91.

[104] George D. Butler, *Introduction to Community Recreation* (McGraw-Hill Book Co., 1967), p. 87.

[105] Nading, "The Relationship of Selected Program Variables to the Playgrounds of Fort Wayne, Indiana," p. 125.

[106] Chicago Recreation Commission, *Principles for Chicago's Recreation Plan* (Chicago: The Commission, May, 1954), p. 235.

Although it is clear that an increased emphasis on leadership generally achieves a number of supplier's goals, definitive research is needed to show how many and what kind of leaders would best achieve user's goals, or other goals held by the community. The literature shows little further research in this area where Gans identifices a substantial difference between user and supplier goals.[107]

RECREATION USE PATTERNS

The relative lack of information on use patterns and user's characteristics[108] makes analysis difficult, especially at the inner city neighborhood level. A number of pilot studies conclude that these areas need much more research. The findings of these studies are summarized below.

Extent of Use

The number of potential users in relation to a given population has been a subject of much speculation. Gans concludes that "the population using the playground is a minority, the number of children who use it at all, or sporadically is probably high, but the number of regular users is probably small."[109] He explains that this is often rationalized by a lack of facilities, but studies of leisure behavior among children suggest that alternative facilities receive as much, if not more, use.

A New York Census of Manhattan for a day in 1934 showed that, of all children studied, "8 per cent were found in playgrounds as compared to 92 per cent on the streets."[110] Nash reported "that 4.2 per cent of the school children within one quarter of a mile use the playground at any given appropriate time."[111] A similar study by York of a Mexican slum area in Los Angeles indicated an average daily playground attendance of 11 percent of the school enrollment.[112]

---

[107] Herbert Gans, "Recreation Planning for Leisure Behavior: A Goal Oriented Approach" (unpublished Ph.D. dissertation, University of Pennsylvania, 1957).

[108] National Academy of Sciences, *A Program for Outdoor Recreation Research*.

[109] Gans, "Recreation Planning for Leisure Behavior," p. 202.

[110] Halpern *et al.*, *The Slum and Crime* (New York: New York City Housing Authority, 1934), p. 156.

[111] Jay Nash, "Standards of Play and Recreation," *National Municipal Review* (July, 1931), p. 493.

[112] Ray D. York, "An Analysis of Playground Attendance and Activity" (unpublished M. S. thesis, University of Southern California, 1937), p. 21.

Similar patterns are described in other studies. San Francisco showed an average daily attendance of between 5 to 7 percent of the total population.[113] St. Paul indicated a high in its 1956 study which concludes "21 per cent of the possible users aged 6-17 used the playgrounds."[114]

These studies are not comparable or conclusive, but they lend support to the hypothesis that playgrounds attract only a minority of the potential users even where the facilities provided are considered adequate by the suppliers. This suggests a difference between user and supplier goals.

Age and Sex

The traditional playground is intended primarily for children, although recently some agencies have begun to stress it as a family area. What few studies have been done generalize: (1) elementary school-age children of both sexes make the major use of the playground, (2) the proportion of girls tends to decrease with age, and (3) the larger the playground, the fewer the number of elementary school-age children.[115]

Socioeconomic Level

Existing information is inconclusive, but does indicate some trends, especially if indoor recreation is used as a parallel to the playground. Many studies indicate a tendency for lower-income groups to utilize recreation centers less frequently than higher-income groups and suggest that the recreation center (or playground) appeals most to the upwardly mobile strata in both classes. They indicate that participation varies inversely with the socioeconomic level of the area. Whyte, in *Street Corner Society*, writes:

> The primary function of the settlement house is to stimulate social mobility, to hold out middle class standards and rewards to lower class people. . . . The settlement house is constantly dealing

---

[113] Community Chest of San Francisco, *Recreation in San Francisco* (San Francisco: The Community Chest, 1950), Appendix Tables II and III.

[114] Amherst Wilder Foundation, *Participation in Leisure-Time Activities, 1955-56* (St. Paul: The Foundation, October, 1956), p. ix.

[115] Martin M. Nading, Jr., "The Relationship of Selected Program Variables," (unpublished M. S. thesis, Indiana University, Fort Wayne, February 1952).

with people who are on their way out of Cornerville. It does not win the loyalty of the great majority of people . . .[116]

Gans supports this concept with his thesis that the playground attracts children who themselves seek one or more of the goals which the suppliers have formulated for them. This suggests that children of the working class oriented to the middle-class bias and self-improvement goals of the Recreation Movement would be more likely to come to the playground in which an appropriate leader is stationed.

Frequency of Use

In order to evaluate the importance of the playground it is meaningful to know whether it is patronized by regular or occasional users. A study of Puerto Rican children in New York City revealed that "33 percent of the children said they used the playground frequently, and 48 percent occasionally."[117] Most studies indicate frequency of use as a function of user preference which means that use will vary with different activities or kinds of playgrounds as well as with the leadership associated with each. If a community wishes to attract regular users to a playground, it should provide activities, program and leadership consistent with this objective. Nading's findings support this by showing a relationship between a high average number of visits, the acreage of the playground, and the quality of leadership and activity.[118]

Service Area

Most recreation standards suggest a service radius for the neighborhood playground of ¼ to ½ mile and favor the former figure in high-density areas such as the inner city. Most studies indicate that the majority of users come from within a ¼-mile radius. The distance traveled increases with the user's age, and is higher for boys and men than for girls and women. It also increases for a variety of activities and the more desired and less common activities draw from a larger area. No studies which differentiate between all types of activities and their individual service areas are available.

---

[116] Whyte, Street Corner Society, p. 104.

[117] Catholic Youth Organization, The Leisure-Time Problems of Puerto Rican Youth in New York City (New York: Archdiocese of New York, 1953), p. 30.

[118] Nading, "The Relationship of Selected Program Variables," p. 120.

Brewer's early study of several cities determined that among 25,000 children between 2 and 15 years of age, 50 percent traveled ¼ mile or less; 24 percent, ½ mile or less; 12 percent, between ½ and ¾ mile; 7 percent, between ¾ and 1 mile; and 7 percent, 1 mile or more.[119]

A Chicago study indicates that 96 percent of the users came from homes within ⅜ mile of the playground.[120] This is primarily a reflection of the large percentage of young users. Developing evidence now indicates the optimum service radius to be approximately 500 feet from a user's home.

No data are available on the use–distance relationships as affected by social class differences. It is assumed that children in lower-class families would travel a longer distance to a playground than those of middle-class families because of the generally more self-reliant nature of lower-class children. Other elements such as resistance to or familiarization with environmental dangers such as busy streets could also have a marked influence on distance–class relationships, but no information concerning this is available.

Population Density and Distance

There is evidence to support the assumption that, in densely populated areas, playgrounds should be provided within a ¼- rather than ½-mile service radius. Brewer found, in Minneapolis–St. Paul, that less than 35 percent of the children traveled ¼ mile or less, whereas in Detroit the proportion was 52 percent. He concludes that "in larger [denser] cities . . . playgrounds must be closer together than has been the custom in the past."[121] Similarly two residential areas studied indicate:

> In the dense area 59 percent of the users came from within the first ¼ mile, 25 percent came from the next ¼ mile and 16 percent came from beyond ½ mile. In the less dense area, only 48 percent came from the first ¼ mile, 37 percent from the next ¼ mile and 14 percent from beyond the ½ mile.[122]

---

[119] C. E. Brewer, "The Influence of Zoning on the Design of Public Recreation Facilities," *Proceedings of the American Society of Engineers* (Chicago, February, 1925), Table 2, p. 245.

[120] Chicago Recreation Commission, *Plan,* Appendix A, p. 6.

[121] C. E. Brewer, "The Influence of Zoning on the Design of Public Recreation Facilities," p. 4.

[122] Eugene T. Lies, *A Study of the Leisure-Time Problem and Recreation Facilities in Cincinnati and Vicinity* (Cincinnati: Bureau of Government Research, 1935), pp. 132-143.

Other surveys in California show "the higher the population density of a residential area, the shorter the effective service distance of the neighborhood recreation center."[123] Unfortunately, since most studies do not distinguish between the factors producing these relationships, it is not possible to determine whether the relationship is due to user behavior or to the fact that, in a denser area, the playground is more intensively used, and thus more likely to discourage those living farther away. There is no *a priori* reason for believing that density affects user attitudes and behavior with respect to the maximum distances the users would walk to one or another facility, given the absence of social or physical barriers.

NONUSE OF NEIGHBORHOOD PARKS

Most studies indicate that: (1) only a *fraction* of the potential users frequent neighborhood parks or playgrounds and (2) although most people have more leisure time they are spending proportionately *less* of it in neighborhood parks. Most definitions of leisure or recreation imply a freedom of time, attitude and personal choice. Where and when *choice* is available, it is no accident that "today many city parks are almost empty . . . and the very word park raises in most minds the image of a formal area nearly empty or partly filled with disreputable characters, and adorned by walks, benches, and 'keep-off-the-grass' signs."[124] In many instances the lack of choice is the only generator of park use in some areas rather than the positive attractions of a given park.

People should not be expected to spend all of their leisure, or especially their outdoor leisure, in public parks. However, there would seem to be a much greater use potential for neighborhood parks if they were more convenient, attractive and interesting places to visit. Measures of leisure activity outside of parks can be interpreted as an indicator of nonuse, if one assumes that a public park which is conveniently located, well designed and properly managed would attract at least some of those adults who are now part of the silent majority of nonusers. The same parallel can be drawn for the *majority* of children and teenagers who do

---

[123] California Committee on Planning for Park, Recreation Areas and Facilities, *Guide for Planning Recreation Parks in California* (Sacramento: State Recreation Commission, 1956), p. 71.

[124] Roger Revelle, "Outdoor Recreation in a Hyper-productive Society," *Daedulus: Journal of the American Academy of the Arts and Sciences*, Fall, 1967, p. 1174.

not commonly use the neighborhood parks for socializing, challenge or creative play, nature study and other possible activities to include active sports, i.e., baseball or football. In this context the problem is one of seeking the level of *quality* necessary to attract and hold potential users who are nonusers by *choice* rather than lack of opportunity.

Even under optimum conditions of excellent weather, convenient access, close proximity and good development, maintenance, or program, observations indicate relatively *low* use levels for neighborhood parks where it seems relatively *high* or at least moderate use levels could be expected based on the population in the potential service area. Most use levels seldom exceed 10 percent of the total possible users at peak use periods and average between 1 to 5 percent during normal use periods. These percentages hold constant for both inner city and suburb and show little deviation with regard to the total supply of recreational opportunities available, family income, age, sex, race or national origin. There is also no significant difference between different portions of the country. A review of selected recreation plans and of the best available data[125] supports these observations. Estimates of peak use visitation seldom exceed 10 percent of the service area population and normal use is seldom expected to exceed 5 percent of the potential users within a given service area.

Based on a synthesis of the literature and observations, it is reasonable to conclude that: (1) public parks accommodate only a *small* proportion of the total population at any given time or with any degree of regularity, (2) peak use levels seldom exceed 10 percent of the service area population, (3) public parks now accommodate an *insignificant* portion of the average adult's and child's leisure time, and (4) both the number of users and amount of time spent in public parks are *decreasing* relative to the total number, length and frequency of recreation visits to resource and intermediate oriented non-urban public parks or private recreation opportunities.

If only a fraction of potential users frequent neighborhood parks, it is important to understand why. There are at least three fundamental explanations: (1) the users may have some significant physical, mental or cultural differences from nonusers, (2) the park

---

[125] Lansing, Marans and Zehner, *Planned Residential Environments;* and Mueller and Gurin, *ORRRC Study Report 20.*

does not coincide with the leisure preferences and satisfactions*
of the majority of potential users, and (3) there are some physical,
environmental or institutional restraints that encourage nonuse.
These explanations can be translated into major causes and categorized as: (1) behavioral, (2) environmental, and (3) institutional.
Table 9 lists the primary causes for each category and selects the
two most significant items for illustration.

TABLE 9
Major Causes of Nonuse in Neighborhood Parks

Behavorial	Environmental	Institutional
User orientation*	Convenient access*	Goal differences*
Social restraints*	Site characteristics*	Personal safety*
Previous conditioning	Weather and climate	Relevant program
Competing activities	Physical location	Management practices
User satisfaction	Facilities and development	Maintenance levels

* Most significant in each category relative to all factors.

User Orientation

Gans offers this insight:

Perhaps the most fundamental reason for nonuse is much of the
leisure programs offered by public recreation is self-oriented, whereas
the leisure that is preferred is largely fantasy oriented . . . The public
recreation movement attempts to provide activities which encourage
self-improvement, self-expression or interaction while individual leisure preferences tend towards involvement of the person in vicarious
role playing and various sorts of fantasy, that result in a different orientation towards the self.[126]

The fantasy-orientation referred to by Gans is usually provided by private suppliers in our society, e.g., movies, television,
spectator sports. Fantasy-oriented recreation is usually more exciting than self-oriented activities, and most young people, especially teenagers, seem to prefer *challenge* and *excitement* in their
leisure. Much of this excitement focuses around sexual and romantic situations which are not condoned in public parks.

---

* *User preference* is the voluntary choice of an activity to fulfill a leisure desire
or need, e.g., self-actualization. *User satisfaction* is the fulfillment of a leisure desire
or need and preference. Satisfaction is related to the preconceived and actual recreation experience.

[126] Gans, "Recreation Planning for Leisure Behavior" p. 312.

This type of excitement also commonly worships status symbols, e.g., motorcycles or folk heroes, which are not generally held in high esteem, understood or accepted by many recreation planners or administrators as what is or could be the creative, constructive or wholesome use of leisure time in public places. In terms of providing excitement, the neighborhood playground usually competes with the street. This observation has been recorded in several studies over the past 40 years beginning with Sage who describes 34 street activities which compete with the playground and concludes: "The lure of the street is definite . . . children have a good time there. This competition with the playground is recognized and the only means of overcoming it is with good design and program.[127]

The tendency for children to desert the playground for the street is notable in suburban developments where the street is usually the greater source of excitement and more heavily used for recreational activities than adjacent parks or playgrounds. This same tendency is also evident in cities and is the central idea of Jane Jacobs' plea for "street neighborhoods."[128] The correlation between street or sidewalk excitement has been noted in several studies[129] Although the idea of making play areas exciting is not a new one in this country[130] or in Europe,[131] it has yet to receive large-scale acceptance because of an unfounded concern for the aesthetics and liability associated with the adventure play area.[132]

The distinction between self- and fantasy-orientation is a broad one, but begins to have validity if one examines the differences between two physically similar facilities—the playground and the amusement park. Both are essential outdoor areas and have various kinds of equipment for physical activity, sociability and free play. But in the amusement park there are opportunities for interaction, excitement and challenge often lacking in most public playgrounds. There are also diversity, sense of adventure, identity, movement and interest that are usually not characteristic of most neighborhood

---

[127] J. Sage in *Public Recreation Survey of New York* by Lee Hammer et al. (New York: Committee on the Regional Plan, 1928), Appendix, p. 2.

[128] Jacobs, *The Death and Life of Great American Cities*, pp. 113–140.

[129] See references in Bibliography to: Appleyard, 1970; Lynch, 1970; Friedberg, 1970 and Bengtsson, 1970.

[130] W. R. Williams, *Recreation Places* (New York: Reinhold, 1958).

[131] Lady Allen of Hurtwood, *Planning for Play* (Cambridge, Mass.: MIT Press, 1968).

[132] Cooper, *The Adventure Playground*, passim.

parks or playgrounds. The gap between these areas might be closed by the development of more creative or adventure type of playgrounds which combine the fantasy-oriented themes of the amusement park with the good design that these areas so often lack.

Social Restraints

Another possible reason for the nonuse of neighborhood parks and playgrounds might be their lack of a familiar and comfortable social context. Most Americans spend their leisure time in primary, informal relationships with familiar people. Most of this interaction takes place in private where people who share each other's values can interact without being self-conscious. The Puritan Ethic which frowns on a public display of pleasure still runs strong in the American tradition. Evidence the relative lack of outdoor restaurants or drinking places in public parks and the reluctance of many Americans to use sidewalk cafes when provided in conspicuous areas.

Public recreation activities often attempt to duplicate this informal relationship in organized programs which may involve people who do not share a previous acquaintance or values. This chance for social interaction may be important from the supplier's point of view; however, most people are not likely to relax in this situation. While reticence often declines after a short period of informal interaction or organized group activity, it is equally likely that many people attempt to avoid these situations; this may be a reason for the nonuse of neighborhood parks. The design or management characteristics of many parks can compound this problem by creating real or imagined obstacles to social interaction, e.g., immovable park benches, "keep-off-the-grass" signs, narrow sidewalks, or prohibition of alcoholic beverages and dancing or music.

Convenient Access

Most studies indicate that the majority of users of neighborhood parks come from a radius of ¼ mile or less. The distance traveled increases with the user's age, and is greater for boys and men than for girls and women. It also increases for a variety of activities; the more desired and less common activities draw from a larger service area. One recent study concludes that a maximum 400-foot service distance is the optimum for the neighborhood park and suggests that the center focus and recommended service radius of ¼ mile may be a significant cause of nonuse.[133] This condition is now commonly used as one rationale for cluster subdivisions.[134]

Site Characteristics

Site characteristics, such as topography; landscaping; lighting; water; shade; shelter from the winds, rain or sun; quiet areas; privacy; identity and diversity, are generally lacking or are token efforts in many neighborhood parks. Examples of these conditions are conspicuous in the majority of neighborhood playgrounds described by most authorities. Tupper states:

> City playgrounds are in desperate need of upgrading. All too often they are places the children stay away from. Lack of money and imagination has resulted in a proliferation of drab squares of concrete or asphalt with a few swings, a slide or two, and perhaps a basketball standard.[135]

Tupper makes a strong plea to provide playgrounds with children's wants and needs in mind rather than the typical low-cost, low-maintenance, no-risk approach to playground design. She feels that "a playground should be constructed so children will want to go there and will be reluctant to leave, because it offers them more fun than they can find elsewhere." She stresses the need for "more creative types of equipment and challenge experiences instead of the general emphasis on safety and sterility.[136]

Jane Jacobs refers to "dozens of dispirited city vacuums called parks eaten around with decay, little used, unloved." She believes that too much is expected of city parks. "Far from transforming any essential quality in their surroundings . . . parks themselves are directly and drastically affected by the way the neighborhood acts upon them."[137] These thoughts are supported by a number of other critics.

With a few notable exceptions[138] we have yet to seriously plan or manage our areas with emphasis toward minimizing site charac-

---

[133] H. P. Bangs and S. Mahler, "Users of Local Parks," *Journal of the American Institute of Planners,* Vol. 36, No. 5 (September 1970), pp. 330-334.

[134] W. H. Whyte, *The Last Landscape* (Garden City, N. Y.: Doubleday and Company, 1968).

[135] Tupper, *No Place to Play,* p. 252.

[136] *Ibid.,* p. 253.

[137] Jacobs, *The Death and Life of Great American Cities,* pp. 90 and 253.

[138] See: Williams, 1958; Bengtsson, 1970; Friedberg, 1970 and Lady Allen of Hurtwood, 1968, for examples.

teristics as conspicuous and contributing causes of nonuse. It would seem that good park design is more a matter of administrative commitment and professional values than lack of money, expertise, development technology and user satisfaction.

Goal Differences

The goal and value differences between the supplier and user are demonstrated in a number of ways which may contribute to nonuse. Much American leisure behavior is now marked by spontaneity, choice and diversity. Although the Recreation Movement commonly gives lip service to the idea of spontaneity in leisure, it continues to emphasize organization, program leadership and scheduling of activities.

The concept of organized recreation programs may be at odds with the leisure behavior patterns of most Americans. It also seems that the Recreation Movement is oriented to a concept of competitive sports or vigorous outdoor physical activity which may be outdated or more than the average American is willing to accept. There is growing evidence that Americans may have rejected the traditional moral and physical justifications of outdoor recreation to spend their leisure in comfort and convenience—indoors.

Beyond these apparent differences, several studies indicate a growing gap between user and supplier objectives. This condition is usually compounded by the suppliers and decision-makers who often have a different set of objectives from the park user. Table 10 summarizes these differences. Other visible differences between park users, suppliers and decision-makers include age, sex, racial and ethnic background and professional education. Most neighborhood parks are a tragic monument to these differences because they usually reflect the objectives, values and conditioning of the suppliers or decision-makers instead of the users.

The population dynamics of cities and growing mobility of Americans compound the goal differences between users and suppliers. Many cities and some suburbs are now experiencing a change in racial or ethnic populations that can be measured in blocks per month. The park designed for the white, middle-class patrons of the inner city in 1900 may no longer be relevant to current populations. Likewise, a park designed for the 1970 population of a suburban neighborhood may not be relevant to 1990 populations. The planning assumptions of neighborhood stability and the provision of specialized, permanent types of recreational opportunities

TABLE 10
Goals and Objectives of Selected Reference Groups[a]

Reference Group	Expressed Goals or Objectives[e]
Community decision-makers[b]	Pride and status Cohesion and social betterment Reduction in juvenile delinquency Increase in economic development Increase in public health and safety Beautification or aesthetic betterment Increase in culture and education Community improvement
Suppliers of public recreation[c]	Happiness or enjoyment Personal growth Physical and mental health Personal safety and welfare Integrative sociability Citizenship and democratic values
Users of public recreation[d]	Group interaction and sociability Relief from roles or surroundings Status, identity, recognition Competition and self-evaluation Variety, excitement, challenge

[a] Herbert Gans, "Recreation Planning for Leisure Behavior: A Goal Oriented Approach" (unpublished Ph.D. dissertation, University of Pennsylvania, 1957), pp. 1-739, passim.

[b] Ibid., pp. 318-324.

[c] Ibid., pp. 115-135.

[d] Ibid., pp. 301-310.

[e] As abstracted from a review of the literature by Gans, supplemented and developed into a table by this author.

may be obsolete and romantic. Parks that do not reflect or anticipate the social dynamics of a neighborhood invite nonuse.

Personal Safety

The recent increase in crime may be an important developing cause of nonuse of public parks. Although available data indicate most neighborhood parks to be no less safe than an individual's working or living environment there is now a dimension of fear in most cities and suburbs that prompts many people to avoid public places in general. This combined with what some cities and suppliers have traditionally labeled as "deviant behavior"* in public parks to include vandalism, drinking, narcotics, nudity and civil disorder has reduced the levels of normal use in many neighborhood parks.

Contrary to conventional wisdom, crime as an apparent cause of nonuse may not be as important as many would believe. A recent national study of "Crime in Parks" concludes "there is far less violent crime or even anti-social behavior in parks than on streets and much less than in the home."[139] A survey of users and nonusers (balanced for age, sex and race) found these reactions:

> Most people consider parks as important or more important than other city services. . . . About a third are confirmed nonusers, and nothing will bring them to parks. . . . The remainder simply prefer forms of recreation not found in parks. . . . The biggest issue that bothers users is the deficiencies of physical facilities. . . . One of the least significant is crime.[140]

When crime is related to the environment and user attitudes this study found that the "most feared neighborhood parks are those used for a single purpose . . . planning, design and construction do not now provide for real or perceived risks of criminal attack . . . lighting, communication, and other physical security features are grossly inadequate."[141] The conclusions of this study combined with systematic observations and interviews of users in parks they consider to be "safe" clearly indicate sustained use as the most important factor in reducing or preventing crime in parks.

Some Implications of Nonuse

The implications of nonuse raise serious questions about the existing and future value of neighborhood parks in urban areas. These questions challenge the traditional rationale[142] for the establishment

---

* "Deviant" means that it may not conform to the traditional values of the majority of users or public officials for a given time or place, but may not be interpreted as illegal or immoral by the courts, e.g., certain types of dress, social behavior, etc. 2See Simons (1969) for description of deviants and deviant behavior.

[139] Harold L. Malt, "An Analysis of Public Safety as Related to the Incidence of Crime in Park and Recreation Areas in Central Cities," by Harold Lewis Malt Associates for U. S. Department of Housing and Urban Development. (Unpublished government report, January 1972, scheduled for publication by USGPO in June 1973.)

[140] Ibid.

[141] Ibid.

[142] Typically described in: Meyer, Brightbill and Sessoms (1969); Doell (1963); Shivers and Hjelte (1971).

of new parks or redevelopment of existing parks. If the majority of potential users or taxpayers should decide* to no longer support the neighborhood park concept, it is not conjectural to project the demise of public park systems in many cities and suburbs because these parks are both the actual and symbolic bases of these systems.

This scenario may be inevitable and in the public interest where these parks are no longer serving their original purpose or potential users. However, viable alternatives to the neighborhood public park have yet to be developed for those few who may still wish to use these parks as well as the many who, by choice, do not use them.

The fundamental questions are: (1) Do urban populations really need public neighborhood parks if they cannot be located, designed and managed to attract potential users and accommodate their recreational needs? (2) Can the recreational needs of urban populations be accommodated better in private, regional and national parks or other forms of leisure and recreational activities that generally take place outside of neighborhood parks?

There is nothing sacred about the neighborhood park concept. Despite the possible merits of this concept,[143] it may be passe or an irrelevant vestige of the "City Beautiful Movement."[144] The romantic origins of this concept may no longer fit the leisure patterns and lifestyle of a "hyper-productive Society."[145] However, before the concept is discarded, especially in the inner city, it would seem appropriate to analyze more carefully and attempt to correct the causes of nonuse. For example, through research, demonstration and practice:

1. Have we made an attempt to understand the recreation experience, why people come to neighborhood parks, where they go once there, what they do, their preferences and satisfactions, anxieties or disappointments?

2. If we understand the behavioral aspects of the recreation experience, have we made a sincere attempt to apply this knowledge in the planning and design of neighborhood parks?

3. If we have applied this knowledge in the planning and de-

---

* In a projected era of scarce resources and competing needs for all public services with a policy emphasis of government providing only essential services that the electorate are willing and able to support.

[143] As typically described in Doell, 1963 or Shivers and Hjelte, 1971.

[144] M. Scott, *American City Planning* (Berkeley: University of California Press, 1969).

[145] Revelle, *Daedalus.*

sign of neighborhood parks, has this been complemented with effective management?

In a professional or institutional context these questions suggest a new approach to urban recreation planning and what may be a last opportunity to cope with the problems or realize the potentials of neighborhood parks before they are completely abandoned in some cities by potential users and taxpayers. A new and needed approach to urban recreation planning for neighborhood parks suggests at least the following areas for additional research and action:

1. Citizen involvement on a sustained basis in all phases of the planning, design and management or decision-making process. Advocacy and pluralism in the planning process are possible and should be encouraged.

2. Understanding and greater tolerance of some forms of leisure behavior often labeled "deviant" in neighborhood parks such as: drinking, music and dancing. Parks are one reflection of reality in a plastic world. They may be an appropriate place for people to see themselves and others. What was considered in "good taste" or appropriate leisure behavior 50 years ago when many neighborhood parks were established may no longer be valid.

3. Goals, objectives, policies, practices and standards that relate to each planning area and the potential users living in that area instead of the usual abstractions established to represent the entire urban population, but may represent none.

4. Rationalization and evaluation of the form and function of existing and proposed areas based on user objectives executed by either the users or objective researchers instead of the suppliers.

5. Renewal or relocation of existing parks that do not meet user objectives. Design for rapidly changing neighborhoods instead of emphasizing the permanence of facilities or past orientation of a given park. It is irrational to design facilities for 50 years where some neighborhoods in cities or suburbs can expect more than a 50 percent change in population in 5 years.

6. Rationalize the benefits and costs of existing parks in measurable terms that can be used for programs budgeting. Parks should be placed on the same scale as other social services for analysis. It is possible to develop "social indicators" for urban parks.

7. Encourage advocacy planning for self-generated parks, voluntary program leadership and self-maintenance whenever and wherever possible. The concept of a public agency assuming complete responsibility for the planning, design, construction, management and maintenance of neighborhood parks may be irrelevant and expensive.

8. Concentrate on how good instead of how much in the design, development and management of neighborhood parks. Substitute a minimum-standard approach to park design with what is feasible, needed and wanted by potential users. Emphasize multiple use, flexibility, innovation and demonstration as a planning technique to find out what is the most effective array of opportunities for users.

9. Encourage the development of appropriate concession facilities in all parks or locate new parks in or adjacent to complementary private developments. There is no reason why a neighborhood park must be an island surrounded by a cyclone fence, separated from or excluding appropriate private developments and eating or drinking facilities. It may be possible and logical to locate neighborhood parks in association with other utilities such as day-care centers, restaurants, medical or office centers, motels and churches.

10. Make special provisions in neighborhood parks for the disadvantaged to include the poor, physically and mentally handicapped, senior citizens, and ethnic minorities. The idea of designing neighborhood parks for some mythical average population is absurd and does not recognize the heterogeneous composition of urban populations.

This approach to urban recreation planning will require a degree of professional competence beyond what has been normally expected of most park and recreation planners and designers. It will also require the patience and humility to experiment with new ideas, admit failure when it occurs and try again. If we cannot or will not make this effort in the 1970's, it will make little difference in the 1980's or certainly by 2,000, because public neighborhood parks in most cities will be history or unusable monuments to indifference.

The stakes are extremely high. They include all that neighborhood parks can be as a focus for social interaction, urban beautification and the provision of convenient opportunities for the meaningful use of leisure time. Effective neighborhood parks may also be one way to keep people from overusing or misusing resource-oriented areas to accommodate their user-oriented recreation desires. In this perspective, more and better local parks may be one solution to the overuse of national parks and wilderness areas.

The record indicates that we may have, through neglect or indifference to user objectives, overlooked or avoided the phenomenon of nonuse. The implications of nonuse on the continued support of local park and recreation systems and the possible demise of these systems could have a serious impact on urban form and function that demands more research and action.

IV

Urban Planning

In this chapter the current planning context of Urban America is described to establish a framework for recreation planning. The focus is on what planning is, or could be, and how it relates to the problem. Substantiation is minimized in order to abstract the thoughts of many others. Planning is viewed not as an end in itself, but as one positive force capable of helping to improve the quality of life and environment in Urban America.

NATURE OF PLANNING

Past and Present

The nature of planning in America is subject to many interpretations, a wide range of differing opinions and a lack of clear definition and purpose. In a pluralistic society, everyone has his own idea of what planning is, how it should be done, where, when and for whom; and these ideas change with time. Despite these ambiguities it is possible to abstract the nature of planning here to establish a conceptual base for the following chapters.

HISTORICAL PERSPECTIVE

Throughout history, most cities have developed in response to human needs that were best met by people living together. The

113

origin of most early cities can be traced to their location on an easily defendable site or a trade route, or close to a combination of natural resources which provided the population with raw materials to sustain life and which could be transformed into marketable products.

City planning is as old as recorded civilization, dating back to 2,000 B.C. when the first cities known to man were founded by the Egyptians. The Greek Civilization was responsible for an emphasis on civic design, site planning and citizen participation. The Greeks developed the earliest concepts of the city as an ecosystem, optimum size, living in harmony with nature and new communities. The Romans excelled in civil engineering, efficiency and the development of community facilities such as water, sewage and transportation systems. Their cities were monumental, did not respect the natural landscape and were often plagued with environmental problems.

Medieval times witnessed the development of walled cities for defense. This period produced the highly planned cities of Europe which began to stress the pedestrian and more effective land use because of the dense concentration of population and activities. The Renaissance focused primarily on civil art, architecture and the development of technology to solve urban problems. French and English cities of this period were characterized by impressive public buildings, broad avenues and large open spaces landscaped with elaborate fountains and formal gardens. These cities developed the concept of a formal urban pattern that later became the dominant influence on planning in Colonial America.

While European cities were planned over a period of centuries, American city planning has had a relatively brief history. In 1682, Philadelphia was the first American city to be laid out in the familiar gridiron pattern. In 1781, Pierre L'Enfant designed a radial street pattern for Washington, D. C. Modern city planning in America began with the social reform movement of the 19th century. Significant portions of many large cities of this period were characterized by unplanned growth, land speculation, flourishing slums, mixed land use, traffic congestion and a lack of community facilities such as adequate schools, parks and sewage treatment. These conditions prompted many community leaders and individuals to seek an alternative to their deteriorating urban environment.

The Chicago World's Fair of 1893 provided what seemed to be the needed alternative. Its example of an orderly arrangement of monumental buildings, parks and wide avenues stimulated many citizens to compare what they saw at the Fair with their own communities and to begin to do something to bring about a change.

Within a short time the "City Beautiful" movement was born. Throughout the country, planning commissions were established, monumental civic center plans were adopted and many large parks were acquired. Civic art or "urban beautification" became a desirable objective. Perhaps the most visible accomplishment of this period was Daniel Burnham's plan for the Chicago waterfront in which he made his famous challenge:

> Make no little plans; they have no magic to stir men's blood and probably themselves will not be realized. Make big plans; aim high in hope and work . . . remember that our sons and grandsons are going to do things that would stagger us. Let your watchword be order and your beacon beauty.

The period between 1915 and the early 1930's saw a change in emphasis from the "City Beautiful" to the "City Practical." The focus shifted to public improvements and services, zoning, and, especially, circulation and transportation as America began to experience the impact of the automobile on its lifestyle, economy and physical character. It was also during this period that the idea of planning as a separate public function to be carried out by a specific government agency and the concept of a master plan first developed in most communities. In the 1930's, planning began to shift from a physical toward a social focus to cope with the economic problems of the depression years. This decade was highlighted by an enlarging Federal role in urban affairs, most notable in the areas of public housing, slum clearance and recreation development.

World War II had little direct effect on planning except to increase the backlog of deficiencies. However the post-war boom of the late 1940's and early 1950's gave planning and urban development its greatest challenge. The demand for housing, community facilities and roads created a new complex of problems that are as yet unsolved. One social problem created by the war was the influx of large numbers of low-income workers from rural to urban areas where the defense factories provided employment. These people had little time or opportunity to adapt to urban living. Their social problems, combined with the deteriorating physical environment of the inner city, created a series of social and physical conditions which led to the National Housing Act of 1949. This Act was the beginning of substantial Federal involvement in urban areas through urban renewal programs. The Housing Act of 1954 extended this concept to include rehabilitation as well as clearance of substandard housing. At this same time a host of other Federal programs in the areas of transportation, recreation and pollution were established to cope with the growing needs and problems of Urban America.

The early 1960's witnessed a needed expansion of the Federal role in urban areas and planning by the establishment of a cabinet-level Department of Housing and Urban Development and a wide range of demonstration and aid programs in the areas of housing, transportation, community facilities and beautification. The most recent program is the Model Cities Act of 1967 and several subsequent revisions which propose to demonstrate what a future Urban America can be like given the necessary resources.

URBANIZATION AND TECHNOLOGICAL CHANGE

"Perhaps the most significant dimensions of the 20th Century are world urbanization and technological change at a scale and pace often difficult to comprehend in human terms."[1] Mass urbanization and uncontrolled technology are the primary cause of most social and environmental problems. These problems are the result of the relationship between man and his environment, which can be simply explained as "man makes environment, environment makes man." Dubos states:

> Irrespective of genetic endowment, a child who grows up in a city slum will differ as an adult from one who has spent his life within the sheltering cocoon of a modern apartment house. . . . Environmental factors obviously condition all aspects of human life, but nobody really knows which factors are influential or how they work.[2]

The scale and character of this urbanization involves a degree of social interaction and technological complexity never experienced by man. The implications of unplanned or poorly planned growth are already evident in polluted air and water; strained transportation systems; the lack of adequate housing, schools or open spaces; social tensions; open violence; and a deterioration of the natural and man-made landscape in and around cities. These problems considered separately are not necessarily new to civilization. However, if

---

[1] Kingsley Davis, "The Urbanization of the Human Population," in *Cities,* editors of *Scientific American* (New York: Alfred A. Knopf, 1966), pp. 4-7.

[2] Rene Jules Dubos, "Man Adapting: His Limitations and Potentials," in *Environment for Man,* ed. by William R. Ewald (Bloomington, Indiana: Indiana University Press, 1967), p. 20.

their complexity and concentration continue without solution, they may signal the decline of the city—and with it the civilization it serves.

COMPLEXITY AND CONFLICT

Beyond mass urbanization and uncontrolled technology, any perspective of our present and future should acknowledge complexity, turmoil and scarcity as a realistic part of urban living in the 1970's. At the core of most urban problems is the critical issue of who should make the value judgments to cope with social and technological change, and how, when and why they should be made. Because these issues are so related and complex they often result in conflict; a solution which appears to serve everyone may serve no one, and one which benefits a certain group may disadvantage another.

These conflicts are especially evident in and around cities where the concentration of population, technology and the institutions that use or depend on each other usually have different values and objectives in regard to the "public interest." Although most will agree on such ends as "survival and quality of the environment," each individual or institution may have different means of reaching those ends. This creates the conflicts generally associated with the planning process.

In a pluralistic society with a democratic form of government, progress is often slow and incremental because of these conflicts. Where reason, excellence and idealism might be expected, compromise, mediocrity and pragmatism frequently prevail. Expedience, personalities and short-range considerations often dictate long-range decisions. Such is the imperfect nature of "individual freedom," and it is within this context that planning assumes its role in the political process. An aware and enlightened society should be able to determine the limits of "individual freedom" on any given issue. Here the planning process can be used as one effective way of translating public policy into alternatives that can be systematically considered in order to minimize conflict.

ENVIRONMENTAL PROBLEMS

Planning is a continuous process of change, challenge and response to man's goals, values and needs. As a process it can provide society with a sensitive and imaginative approach for problem-solving and a creative or analytical tool for studying man's relationship to his surroundings. Above all, planning is or should be a humanitarian effort justified by society's will to survive in harmony with nature, adapt to change, and experience a richer life. This justification can be translated in terms of human needs, values or priorities which are reflected in these major problems now facing America:

> A diminishing choice of living, working and leisure opportunities. . . . A growing lack of privacy, individual identity and sense of place within the urban environment. . . . A lack of sensitive and positive controls over the use of land. . . . A growing shortage of adequate community facilities such as schools, parks, and playgrounds to meet existing and future needs. . . . A trend toward social stratification by race and income. . . . A diminishing local tax base and lack of adequate fiscal resources to accommodate the growing needs for public facilities and services. . . . An inefficient circulation system incapable of safely and effectively moving all types of traffic. . . . A lack of adequate public transportation systems. . . . A lack of expressed goals, objectives and alternatives. . . . A lack of institutions to deal with change. . . . An uneven allocation of resources in a geographical basis. . . . A lack of effective means for citizen participation in the planning process. . . . The lack of an "ecological conscience" for urban areas. . . . A growing conflict over the allocation of limited natural and human resources for present and future needs. . . . A lack of effective communication and cooperation between all concerned with the urban environment.[3]

These urgent problems present an opportunity for the collaboration and cooperation of individuals, professionals, institutions, businesses, industry and government. There is no realistic alternative to the effort if both survival and the quality of life possible in this country are serious goals. Past civilizations might have been able to solve these problems by individual efforts. However, man's will to survive and cope with the complexities of the 20th century now prompt him toward a unified approach to solving environmental problems. Perhaps the most "basic environmental problem" is not one of substance, but of *values*, communication and understanding of ideas. Here, of all our resources, the most precious becomes human awareness; for in the use of our human and natural resources most of the barriers are no longer technological—they are in our minds.

---

[3] Seymour M. Gold, "Environmental Planning," in *Environment and the Citizen: Opportunities for Effective Action*, William B. Stapp (Ed.), (New York: Holt, Rinehart and Winston, 1973), p. 106.

Aspects of Planning

Despite semantic difficulties, the literature and practice generally agree that planning: (1) deals with the future and (2) develops alternatives for more rational decisions. Most authors and professional planners feel that planning should be representative of what people want, imaginative in projecting what might be, and realistic in recognizing what is possible. They regard planning as a process and a means of anticipating, or reacting to, change.

PURPOSE AND OBJECTIVES

There is general agreement by most authorities that the primary purpose of planning is to: (1) meet events that man expects to happen, (2) accomplish things that he wants to happen, and (3) avoid or prevent things that he does not want to happen. Change, and the problems associated with it, are the essence of modern urban living. If the city is to be a desirable place in which to live, work or visit, it must develop a unified course of rational action toward solving its current and future problems.

Planning is one means of obtaining a perspective on these problems, developing some realistic alternatives, and helping to formulate a series of goals, policies and recommendations which can be used as one basis of public and private decisions and community action. City planning can be justified if it brings the major issues into focus to stimulate informed public discussion, consensus and the beginning of constructive efforts toward a realistic solution of common problems. If planning can go beyond this and serve as an accepted guide for decisions, coordination of effort and innovation or the development of new ideas, it has more than justified its purpose.

The broad objective of planning is to help create "an optimum environment with man as the measure."[4] This might be expressed in such sub-goals as quality of the environment, quality of life, and harmony between man and his environment. A traditional way of stating these goals has been to maximize human welfare by helping to create a better, more healthful, efficient and attractive urban environment. Some of the more commonly accepted objectives of planning include its being used to:

1. Improve the physical environment of the community to make the

---

[4] Dubos, "Man Adapting," p. 3.

community more functional, beautiful, safe, interesting, exciting and efficient.

2. Promote the "public interest."

3. Inject longe-range considerations into the determination of short-range decisions.

4. Bring professional and technical knowledge to bear on the political decisions concerning the social, economic and physical development of the community.

5. Prompt and facilitate effective cooperation and coordination between all concerned with community development.

6. Identify problems and indicate possible alternative solutions.

7. Identify major opportunities and potentials.

8. Stimulate citizen participation in the planning process.

9. Develop and interpret social and economic indicators which can help measure change.

10. Help formulate alternative goals and objectives which can become the basis of action-oriented proposals.

> Three things are needed to produce sound, effective decisions on urban growth and change: (1) facts, accurately developed and soundly analyzed that define problems and provide a basis for their solution, (2) criteria and *standards* that point the way toward consistent policy and alternative solutions, and (3) community discussion, understanding and support that assures adherence to democratic principles and action.[5]

To meet these needs, urban and regional planning has developed as an art, science, activity and profession. Although conceptually related in purpose, in practice it is useful to differentiate each:

Planning: "A Science." The scientific method is the basis for much city-planning activity, especially when and where planning involves the use of quantitative techniques such as statistical surveys, projections, systems analysis and simulation.*

Planning: "An Art." The design process is the basis of many planning efforts especially in the more physical and qualitative aspects of relating a city's form to its function.

Planning: "An Activity." A wide range of all segments of society engage in various aspects of planning and have a role equal to, if not greater than, that of the professional planner. This is especially

---

[5] Frederick T. Aschman, *The ABC's of Community Planning* (Chicago: Community Planning Division of Sears, Roebuck and Co., 1962), p. 11 (Emphasis added.)
* See Glossary and Charles Abrams, *The Language of Cities*, for definitions.

true of the mass media, business, industry, the church, unions and other community institutions and organizations.

Planning: "A Profession." With over 70 universities offering graduate degrees in planning, it has become a recognized field of professional study.†

LEGAL FRAMEWORK

Planning as a recognized function of government has its basic concepts, authority and responsibilities grounded in law. A familiarity with this framework is necessary to understand the scope, purpose and limitations of planning.

Public Interest

In the planning process, the "public interest" generally refers to the health, safety and general welfare of the population. The traditional emphasis has been a negative one with a concern for constraints to prevent conditions hazardous to the physical well-being of people. Recently the "general welfare" has been broadened to include such items as "convenience," "economy" and "amenity," and the emphasis has shifted to a positive concern for mental and emotional well-being. Thinking has begun to center more on what is "optimum or desirable," than on what is "minimum or adequate."

Protection against accident hazards, excessive noise, atmospheric pollution and moral hazards and the provision of adequate privacy and aesthetics now have legal precedent. Many items that were formerly considered under the law as "amenities" are now considered as "essential" to the public health, safety and welfare. The success of any planning effort depends on a sensitive definition of the "public interest" which can be visibly expressed through a community's social, economic and physical goals, the electoral process, or in community attitude surveys.

---

† A graduate degree in Urban and Regional Planning or a closely related field and membership in the American Institute of Planners (AIP) are becoming prerequisites for most responsible planning positions. In 1970 there were over 8,000 professional planners in the United States. Most have qualified for membership in the American Institute of Planners by a national examination and/or a combination of academic training from an accredited university teaching planning and four years of acceptable professional planning experience. There are also many related professionals in other fields, i.e., landscape architecture, architecture, civil engineering, geography, ecology, economics, law, environmental health, design, sociology, psychology and other fields now actively engaged in various aspects of planning.

Individual Freedom

Historically the word "planning" has suggested control and has often been viewed as an intrusion on individual freedom. This interpretation can be generally traced to the use of the word by kings, dictators or utopian thinkers to rationalize their efforts. In America, planning is one visible process of a representative government in which decisions are made by elected or appointed officials—not planners. The planner advises the decision-maker, but makes no policy decisions. The final plan is determined by the political process within the legal framework of government.

> The function of planning is not to destroy individual freedom. It is to protect and preserve the individual's property and interests by limiting those activities of individuals that encroach on the liberties or welfare of others, and by providing through community effort opportunities for the individual that he would be incapable of providing for himself.[6]

Planning should be used to enlarge choice or protect individual rights. Planners should not dictate values. They may personally hold a different set of values from those held by the community, but must place their values aside for the expressed goals and values of the community. It is when the community's values are not expressed that planners often make inept recommendations and individual freedom is threatened.

Private Responsibility

In this country, each citizen is guaranteed his constitutional rights by law. With these rights come certain moral responsibilities to respect law and order and to show a concern for human dignity. It is here that many of the values of planning are found and so often contested by those who might seek excessive personal gain at the expense of others. It is also here that many of these values have been defined by legal precedent, local custom, practice and the marketplace.

Most plans consider private responsibility as important as public purpose in attempting to formulate objectives and alternative means of reaching them. Although the market mechanism has usually been a constraint on private initiative, there is a developing trend toward placing a value on environment, and to hold the individual or organ-

---

[6] International City Managers' Association, *Local Planning Administration*, p. 13.

ization responsible for actions detrimental to the public interest. The development of a "private conscience" for the environment is one of this nation's most critical resource problems, for no amount of public effort can cope effectively with these problems and still maintain our current measure of individual freedom.

TYPES OF PLANNING

The wide range of planning activities or programs at all levels of government and the private sector can be classified by their primary objectives into these general types:

Resource planning. Programs for the allocation and development of natural resources such as soil conservation, wildlife propagation and reforestation.

Urban and regional planning. Programs primarily concerned with the arrangement of and relationships between all types of land use, housing, transportation, education, leisure and other systems.

Facility planning. Specialized programs for the provision, design and management of facilities such as highways, schools, parks, airports and utilities.

Environmental health planning. Programs for public health and safety, air and water pollution abatement, noise abatement, disease prevention, pest control, and stress reduction.

Social planning. Programs for the establishment of new institutions and the development of existing ones to carry out community goals. At the municipal level, this can include family, educational or leisure planning and "advocacy planning" to meet the objectives of an organized group.

Planning can also be classified by the "client" it serves or the types of plans prepared. Generally it is simply "public" or "private," but it can also include specialized clients such as the military, trade unions and churches. "Public planning" should be used to define and implement the objectives of all residents in a given planning unit which is usually identified as the "community," hence the term "community planning." However, the community should *not* be considered as a whole. Instead it should be viewed as a series of groups with different values and needs which make up the whole. It is within the different groups of a city and its "communities" that "advocacy planning" can be most effective. Simply defined, "advocacy planning" is an organized planning effort to attain the objectives of an organization, planning unit or individual. It is based on this concept:

Planning is a means for determining policy. The right course of action is always a matter of choice, not of fact. Planners should engage in the political process as advocates of the interests of government and other groups. Plural plans rather than single agency plans should be presented to the public and the scope of planning should be broadened to include all areas of interest to the public.[7]

Beyond public and advocacy planning is a sphere of private planning which seeks to attain the ends of the organization or individual doing the planning. This is best represented by corporate types of planning in which the public interest is usually secondary to private objectives because of the profit motive. This differs from public planning in which the "public interest" should be foremost, and the planning is not done by the people who will directly benefit from the effort. In this sense, corporate planning is advocacy planning for the private sector, just as public planning is advocacy planning for the public sector.

TYPES OF PLANS

A plan is a course of action which can be implemented to accomplish stated objectives and which someone intends to implement. It is different from a concept, idea or recommendation. A plan implies action, a commitment of resources and the responsibility to implement, review and revise that plan. According to this definition, many of the things we call "plans" are not plans. They are studies, reports or wishful thinking.

Plans can be classified by their scope, geographic area or content. "A plan which is comprehensive in scope indicates the principal acts by which all of the most important ends are to be attained."[8] This contrasts with a *single-purpose* plan which has a single objective such as the provision of a road or dam. *Policy plans* provide a framework for decision-making, but generally lack the implementation dimension of a comprehensive plan and the more rigid dimension of a single-purpose plan. The comprehensive plan is:

> An official document adopted by a local government setting forth its general policies regarding the long-term physical development of a

---

[7] Paul Davidoff, "Advocacy and Pluralism in Planning," *Journal of the American Institute of Planners,* November, 1965, p. 331.

[8] Martin Meyerson and Edward Banfield, *Politics, Planning and the Public Interest* (Glencoe, Ill.: The Free Press, 1955), p. 31.

city or other area. The plan should be broad enough to include all aspects of a development or redevelopment program.[9]

In terms of the geography or planning unit, most plans can be classified as to the national, state, regional, metropolitan or local area which they represent. "Generally each higher geographical unit should reflect the consensus of the lower units it encompasses. However, in practice this is seldom possible in a pluralistic society."[10]

THE HUMAN ELEMENT

The human element of planning is often overlooked in the pressing issues, sophisticated methodology and administrative detail of modern urban government. Planning should be one important means of self-determination in a participatory democracy. This brief description of the human elements in planning is important to an understanding of the planning process.

Professional Planners

The professional responsibilities of planners are outlined in the legal framework of government and their code of conduct.[11] Planners are responsible to the public who will directly benefit or suffer from their efforts. In general they do not make policy decisions in a democracy. Instead, they study the problem, identify alternatives and recommend possible solutions to decision-makers. The comprehensive planner's usual role is to consider the whole rather than the parts. At the operational level of government, he generally does not initiate, coordinate or administer anything or any one, despite popular opinion.

Decision-Makers

Planning as a function of society is the domain of a wide range of public and private decision-makers. These individuals may have a variety of backgrounds and objectives, but they all have the capacity to formulate, act on or modify policies which can be crucial to the success or failure of any planning effort. A city is the total of thousands of decisions made by individuals, institutions, business and government over a period of time.

---

[9] Abrams, *The Language of Cities*, p. 67

[10] Meyerson and Banfield, *Politics, Planning and the Public Interest*, p. 31.

[11] American Institute of Planners, *Handbook and Roster/1968* (Washington, D. C.: American Institute of Planners), pp. 30-35. Also in 1970 and 1972 version.

The process of urban development is most visible in the public sector where the law charges the planning official with the responsibility of making planning decisions. The law expects no special knowledge or skills of the planning official, only the conscientious application of his best judgment based upon the facts and their relationships, ramifications and implications. His judgment can be no better than the facts supplied to him. Since he is not expected to obtain the facts, but only to act on them, the planning official or decision-maker is dependent on the specialized knowledge and skill of the planner and other professionals.

The planner should be held responsible for his professional efforts by the decision-maker. If he is incompetent, he should be replaced. There should be a system of checks and balances between the planner and the decision-maker. The decision-maker needs the planner's information and alternatives in order to make rational policy decisions, and the planner needs the decision-maker to formulate policy which can be implemented over time by public and private efforts.

Individuals

The individual's interest in planning is considerably different from both the planner's and the decision-maker's. While the planner is usually concerned with methods, techniques and alternatives, and the decision-maker is preoccupied with issues, values and political constraints, the average citizen is most generally concerned with self-interest, a specific objective and results. The time horizons of each are also different. The planner is prone to long-range considerations, the decision-maker to short-range political expediency and the citizen to immediate action.

Concerned and constructive citizen involvement in the planning process will demand a more rational and representative role for the decision-maker. There is, however, some question of how much time and energy the average citizen is able to devote to his own cause—or if he even cares enough about his urban future to actively do something about it before he feels threatened in some way.

Effective planning cannot be done in a vacuum. The power of constructive citizen participation, aroused public opinion and the informed voter cannot be overstated. Plans cannot realistically reflect human needs without these types of involvement and, lacking them, will probably never be implemented. Any plan can be no better than the citizen values put into it and no worse than the decisiveness, imagination and foresight it may lack. The individual citizen can and should play a decisive role in the planning process. His direct and sustained involvement should be the measure of an effective planning effort.

CRITICAL ISSUES

The sweep and speed of urbanization have raised many questions for which there are no simple answers—if there are answers at all. Questions such as:

> Who will live where? Where will jobs be located? How do people get from home to work and back again? Where should open space and recreation areas be located and how should they be designed and for whom? What environmental criteria or amenities are desirable for urban living? Who should pay for urban services, where, when and why? Is human resource planning a concern of government? Can a physical and social environment be planned to accommodate people's needs? What are the goals and objectives of America? Is planning for people?[12]

Within a planning context these questions ask: (1) how much planning in the public sector can we tolerate without endangering our traditional freedoms, and (2) how much unplanned development can we risk without destroying freedom of choice and the quality of the environment? Within a problem context these questions can be classified into these major areas:

1. Attitudes—A public indifference and complacency to both the negative and positive forces of environmental change.

2. Housing—A growing lack of alternatives for individuals to choose from in deciding how and where to live.

3. Transportation—An increasing volume and density of traffic in conflicting patterns with relatively little coordination, and relationship to the urban form, function and human needs.

4. Controls—A number of conflicting and often unenforceable or ineffective restraints which exert a negative influence on the environment, and a relative lack of positive incentives.

5. Conservation—A growing conflict over the allocation of limited natural and human resources for present and future needs.

---

[12] Bureau of Government Research, *The Local Planning Process in New Jersey* (New Brunswick, N. J.: Rutgers University Press, 1967), p. 187.

6. Privacy—A growing sense of individual frustration over uncontroll-able intrusions on his personal life.

7. Variety—A trend toward more social stratification, monotony in our physical environment and mediocrity in our institutions, products and goals.

8. Ecology—A lack of awareness and knowledge of man's relationship to nature and the possible implication of his acts in human and natural terms.

These problems have become pressing issues in most communities. Many are now within the realm of environmental planning. Some of these issues will require new institutions to cope with their unique dimensions. Some may forever remain unsolved. Planning cannot be realistic or relevant if it avoids the essence of the issues which should be clearly reflected in a community's stated goals and objectives and a vital part of any comprehensive plan. To avoid these critical issues is to effectively sidestep the nature of planning and its relationship to people and their environment.

THE PLANNING PROCESS

Planning is a process by which a community perceives the future, articulates its objectives, and considers alternatives. In the United States community planning is now regarded as a continuous process because of advancing technology and changing citizen and consumer preferences are continuously altering opportunities for community development.[13]

Most people and practitioners view planning as a continuous and incremental process composed of a series of evolutionary and rationally organized steps which develop guidelines for urban growth, development or renewal. The product of this process is usually called a "plan," which is generally regarded as a starting point for decisions and revisions to adapt to a community's changing needs, priorities and resources.

Two Approaches

There is general agreement that the planning process involves a number of steps which are usually organized into five stages: (1)

---

[13] Weaver, The Urban Complex, p. 143.

survey and analysis, (2) goal formulation, (3) development of alternatives, (4) implementation, and (5) review and revision. Although these five stages are common to most planning efforts there is a considerable difference in concept and method between the "traditional" and "innovative" approach to planning. The "traditional" approach is usually associated with the professional values, concepts, methods and technology characteristic of the pre-1965 period; while the more "innovative" or new approach to planning has evolved since 1965 and remains to be tested in the 1970's.

TRADITIONAL APPROACH

The traditional approach to planning emphasizes these general concepts: (1) quantity over quality, (2) physical over social objectives, (3) form over function, (4) exploitation over conservation of human and natural resources,* and (5) the community rather than the individual. These concepts are usually reflected in the more traditional methods which focus on: (1) single product plans, (2) a terminal planning process, (3) a centralized planning function, and (4) rigid planning units usually related to political or physical boundaries.

INNOVATIVE APPROACH

The new approach to planning emphasizes a different set of values which ranks: (1) quality over quantity, (2) social over physical and economic considerations, (3) function over form, (4) conservation over exploitation of human and natural resources,[14] and (5) the individual over the community. These concepts are reflected in methods which generally focus on: (1) alternative or policy types of plans, (2) a continuous planning and review process, (3) a decentralized planning function, and (4) flexible planning units based on natural and human resources, activities, functions or relationships.

The new approach relies primarily on the development of sophisticated models, gaming simulation, advocacy planners and systems analysis to develop policy alternatives and evaluate objectives in light of stated goals. It is considerably more quantitative in method and more qualitative in its objectives than the traditional

---

* Exploitation in a negative sense, i.e., overuse, destruction, neglect of resources; conservation in a positive sense, i.e., economy, wise use, protection of human and natural resources.

[14] *Ibid.*

approach. While the traditional approach might have been adequate for dealing with the problems of the past, it appears to be increasingly inadequate to cope with the problems of the present and future. It would seem that planning is in a transition between accepted methods of the past and yet untested methods of the future.

Stages in the Planning Process

Each of the five stages in the planning process and the steps, methods or studies involved can be explained in terms of the preparation of a comprehensive plan. Because planning is a continuous process and each community has its unique requirements, each stage may not follow in the order outlined above. However, under normal circumstances this is how most comprehensive plans are prepared today. Because this book is primarily concerned with a goal-oriented approach to leisure planning, only goal formulation will be discussed, assuming that the reader can find adequate treatment of the other stages in other sources.[15]

GOAL FORMULATION

All too often any attempt to formulate local goals and objectives is omitted from most planning efforts. In the haste to cope with urgent problems, there is a tendency to plunge into the planning process at the program or project level without any realistic knowledge of community values or aspirations. This usually results in conflict and duplication of effort, and most programs will not accomplish their intended purpose. Goals, objectives, policies, practices and programs, each defined, related and applied, can be effective aids to the preparation and implementation of a comprehensive plan. Most attempts at goal formation are confronted with semantic problems. The following definitions are suggested by Young:

> A "goal" is an end to which a design trends. . . . It provides society a direction not a location. In this sense a goal is an ideal and should be expressed in abstract terms. . . . It is a value to be sought after, not an object to be achieved. . . . An "objective" is capable of both attainment and measurement. . . . Its purpose is implicit rather

---

[15] William I. Goodman (Ed.), *Principles and Practice of Urban Planning* (Washington, D. C.: International City Managers Association, 1968).

than explicit. . . . It is an aim or end of action, a point to be reached. Nothing needs to be said about why or how the point should be reached.[16]

"In general, goals are universal and lasting while objectives change under varying circumstances."[17] "Goals are a statement of highly desirable conditions toward which society should be directed, as opposed to objectives which are the stated purposes of an organization or an individual capable of planning and taking action to gain intended ends."[18]

GOALS AND THE PLANNING PROCESS

"To have meaning plans should be formulated in terms of goals and objectives."[19] The formulation of goals and objectives involves five distinct steps: "(1) establishment of the perimeter of concern, (2) establishment of the range of choice, (3) examination of the relationships of goals, (4) relative evaluation of goals or sets of goals, and (5) establishment of goals as policy."[20] Planning may be defined as the process of determining goals and designing means by which these goals may be achieved. The planning process generally begins with goal formulation and continues by analyzing alternative methods of reaching them.

In this context, planning may be defined as a process of helping to formulate goals and objectives and suggesting means by which they may be achieved. Where the necessary data are already available the planning process can begin with goal and objective formulation and continue with the development of alternatives to achieve these objectives. Goal-oriented planning is a continuous process which responds to felt needs as opposed to the traditional strategy of data gathering, analysis, and the preparation of inflexible plans. "The planning process involves four basic steps: (1) goal formation, (2) establishment of measures or standards, (3) application of standards to these goals to convert them into objectives, (4) designing alternative means by which these objectives might be realized."[21]

---

[16] Robert C. Young, "Goals and Goal Setting," *Journal of the American Institute of Planners,* XXXII, No. 2 (March, 1966), p. 78.

[17] *Ibid.*

[18] Committee for Economic Development, *Budgeting for National Objectives* (New York: Committee for Economic Development, 1966), p. 25.

[19] *Ibid.*

[20] Young, "Goals and Goal Setting," pp. 82-83.

[21] *Ibid.,* p. 78.

Once goals are established, they must be converted to objectives. "Where standards are applicable they can be utilized to the point where specifications emerge. The standard defines the loose terminology of the goal and the objective becomes the attainment of the standard."[22] For example, if the goal were "Quality of Life" and the objective to have leisure opportunities to meet present and future needs, standards could express this objective in terms of acres and facility specifications, program leadership or recommended locations, i.e., within walking distance of each resident.

The final step in the planning process is developing a course of action to implement these objectives. This involves a series of "practices," i.e., location determinations, site planning, engineering studies, promotional campaigns and proposals for financing, operation and maintenance. This is where a wide range of alternatives should be considered. Computers can be used to apply techniques such as program budgeting and systems analysis to analyze the possible costs and benefits of alternatives.

These practices usually take the form of "programs which are time phased plans for the allocation of resources, i.e., land, labor, capital."[23] The program, i.e., beautification, urban renewal, street-widening, represents a broad classification for applying a wide range of practices which work toward a specific objective, i.e., public safety, economic opportunity, identity, convenience.

"Viewed in this manner goals are not merely a list of platitudes to be adopted in a plan as a means to justify the subjective conclusions of planners or decision makers. They become a vital force that determines not only action proposals, but the entire course of research."[24] More important, they become a way to convert vague ambitions to detailed directions, i.e., policies, programs, standards, that can serve as specifications in the research and implementation of a plan to guide community development. Without some overriding goal or series of goals, any city runs the risk of competition or conflict between many well-meant programs, i.e., mass transit versus parking structures, or parkland acquisition versus freeway encroachment on existing parklands.

Goals are conditioned by values which the members of a community, individually and collectively, hold to be important. These values are expressed in the marketplace, the voting booth and by

---

[22] *Ibid.*

[23] Committee for Economic Development, *Budgeting for National Objectives,* p. 25.

[24] Young, "Goals and Goal Setting," p. 79.

citizen interest. Social research methods can be used to measure and analyze many of these values and test possible goals and objectives for community support. Political prudence and our representative form of government suggest at least a public opinion sample prior to goal formation. However, if this is not expedient, one alternative is to develop preliminary goals by intuition or judgment and subject them to public discussion and acceptance. The time involved and inherent political risks of this alternative prompt most communities to sample public opinion first and then develop goals.

GOALS AND PLANS

"A plan is meant to carry us toward a goal, but is not a goal in itself. A goal is not a plan, but something to be planned for."[25] Goals are not achieved just because they are stated. They must be supported by policies and a realistic program of implementation. "Sound planning should be based on an accepted social purpose and the determination of such a purpose becomes an important step in the planning process."[26] Planning is the opposite of improvising. In simple terms it may be described as organized foresight plus corrective hindsight. Conceived as a process, it needs realistic goals to create a common ground for concensus, cooperation and action.

Once determined, goals can serve as research targets in the preparation of a plan, which in turn can provide a blueprint for achieving the goals. The usefulness of the plan will depend on a general understanding and acceptance of the goals and objectives by all concerned. If establishing goals at an early stage in the planning process does not represent the effort of all concerned, any plan is likely to fail. People not involved in the goal-formulation process at the beginning cannot be expected to understand or support the products of the planning process.

Most physical plans display serious shortcomings in terms of implementation because they lack the catalyst of policy to move between ends and means in a consistent manner. Policy is "any governing principle or course of action."[27] It becomes the broad

---

[25] American Society of Planning Officials, "What is Expected of a Planning Program," *ASPO Newsletter* (May, 1964), p. 42.

[26] Frederick J. Adams, *Urban Planning Education in the United States* (Cincinnati: Bettman Foundation, 1954), p. 1.

[27] Donald H. Webster, *Urban Planning and Municipal Public Policy* (New York: Harper and Bros., 1958), p. 39.

framework for guiding governmental action. Policies can take ideas from the level of abstraction and express them in visible statements of intent and action. The dramatic growth of most cities prompts the high degree of administrative flexibility inherent in policy plans. At the same time it dictates a series of reasonable limits for political actions totally inconsistent with an established policy, or forces visible modification of that policy.

The merits of policy planning for dealing with rapid change have already relegated "physical planning" to the area of site planning and engineering studies. The national trend is toward policy plans instead of the traditional land use or zoning type of plan. For any city to not adopt this approach to planning would make its current and future task of coping with rapid change even more difficult. A recent study notes:

> Perhaps the major arguments against physical plans are the legal difficulties of adopting and implementing them. . . . Policy plans, on the other hand, can and do provide a variety of guides to community development without the restrictions associated with physical plans or maps intended to do the same things. . . . For purposes of guiding decision makers the written word is a more effective, adaptable and comprehensive means of communication than a map.[28]

A policy is also more explicit and descriptive than a map for reflecting social priorities, conditions or problems. This is not to suggest the elimination of maps in a comprehensive plan. What is suggested is a policy dimension to physical plans that can be adopted and implemented where the map usually cannot. Policy plans do have limitations. They cannot cover every situation. They require a high degree of consensus from community leaders and citizens. This does not negate the value of the policy plan, but it does prompt public participation in the planning process to a much *greater* degree than the physical plan requires. At the very least, it requires a systematic sample of public opinion, an informed electorate and effective communication.

If the purpose of a city's capital budget is to reflect rational policy decisions, serve as a tool of effective management, and help determine how scarce resources can be allocated among competing needs, the virtues of a flexible policy plan as contrasted to the less flexible physical plan are evident.

---

[28] American Society of Planning Officials, *Policy Statements: Guides to Decision Making,* Report #152, November, 1961, p. 2.

ILLUSTRATIVE GOALS

Based on these concepts, a series of hypothetical goals are listed here to illustrate their possible application in the planning process. For example, a city might formulate these possible goals: (1) quality of the environment, (2) quality of life, (3) harmony of man with his environment.

In terms of priority these goals might be approached in the order listed. This does not imply that all of these goals should receive the same level of effort. It simply projects that effort directed toward reaching goal #1 will move the community toward goal #2, and that both goals #1 and #2 would be prerequisite to realistically moving toward goal #3.

Illustrative objectives to reach these goals could include: health, safety, beauty, knowledge, efficiency, convenience, vitality, identification, opportunity and choice. Without realistic accomplishment of these objectives the city could not achieve its goals. Beyond these objectives, alternative sets of policies and practices (standards, techniques, principles, or criteria) could be developed to outline different ways to achieve these objectives.

The complexity of choice can pyramid to computer scale and linear programming techniques. It is here that quantitative techniques such as PPBS, PERT, Gaming Simulation and CPM* can be used to facilitate decisions. This choice implies maximum political flexibility and prompts much greater public participation in the planning process than is generally the case in the traditional physical approach to planning.

Each set of alternative policies and practices can be combined into a program (e.g., beautification, off-street parking) in which a strategy for action, economic analysis or priorities can be developed, and responsibilities can be assigned for implementation. This is where program, planning, and budgeting systems can be used to equate the costs and benefits of competing alternatives in light of objectives, policies, or practices directed toward a goal or series of goals.

If planning is to be effective, it must be guided by clearly stated objectives. The link between these objectives and the administrative procedures or programs necessary to reach them should also be clear. The more explicit objectives are, the more easily policies and plans can be developed to attain them. Formulating objectives is a

---

* See Glossary.

never-ending process of refinement and review to keep up with the changing nature of community values, technology and local or national events. It is the most vital and frustrating part of the planning process—and critical to the success of any planning effort.

THE FUTURE AND THE PLANNING PROCESS

Any attempt to speculate on the future and how it relates to Urban America and planning should acknowledge at least three areas: (1) developing trends in society, (2) uncertainty and prediction and (3) the new dimensions of planning.

Developing Trends

Among the many developing trends in society, three are viewed as most likely to have the greatest impact on planning and urban life. They will also have an impact on the approach and techniques of urban recreation planning.

RATIONALIZATION

The future will witness a much greater effort and application of scientific techniques to help formulate goals and to organize men so that these goals can be attained by the most efficient means. This approach to applying the most efficient means for determining and realizing ends is called "rationalization." It is only a technique and does not imply wisdom or reason because it can be used for positive or negative ends, e.g., war or peace.

Rationalization can also be used to lead many into thinking that they are being reasonable, if not wise, in the pursuit of their goals. It is a double-edged sword which can lead to enlightenment or deception. It should be used with discretion, and the results seriously questioned in terms of what is really important. For example, by a sophisticated application of scientific techniques one might "rationalize" more freeways in an urban area, but is this the best and only way to move people?

SOCIAL WELFARE

Many of our current problems are the result of a past emphasis on things rather than people. The future projects a trend toward the "City Humane" from the "City Beautiful" and "City Functional" eras of the past and present. This implies a new emphasis on the "quality of life" and "quality of the environment."

It will require the development of a wide range of "social indicators" to help society evaluate its social progress in the same manner as it now measures economic progress. This trend will not be an easy one for society to accept. It will require a reallocation of resources, reorientation of our growth ethic, and personal sacrifice. But the long-term potential as an investment in "human welfare" should have important social and economic advantages for society.

CITIZEN ACTIVISM

The pronounced trend toward constructive as well as militant citizen involvement in self-determination is already a fact. Advocacy planning is already being practiced in most large communities in response to the mistakes of the past and promise of the future. The thrust of students, the underprivileged and organized groups of all types seeking a better representation and articulation of their objectives is already evident throughout the country. This is a healthy indication of awareness, motivation and a determination to make the democratic system more representative and responsive.

There is little question that the immediate consequences of a high level of citizen activism will cause anxieties, conflict and even open violence if the system cannot or will not react in a constructive way to demands of the people it is supposed to represent. There is also little question that the constructive value of this trend is, or will be, an important dimension of American government and planning, if both are to succeed.

Uncertainty and Prediction

Urban society and the times are characterized by a dimension of change, challenge and response never experienced by man. The increasing tempo and complexity of urban living have been triggered by explosions in the areas of knowledge, wealth, population and leisure. Separately, each has had a significant impact on society. When combined, these explosions create conditions and implications difficult to cope with in the present and almost impossible to accurately predict for the future because of the uncertainty of man and events.

CHANGE

If changes or conditions were to take place with equal force or speed, they might allow projection or prediction. But, in reality, change is uneven, dramatic, and sometimes chaotic. While, in the past, progress has usually been incremental, it is now subject to great forward leaps. A breakthrough in one area can have a profound influence on other areas.

Who anticipated the automobile, space flights, income taxes, air conditioning, frozen food, computers, penicillin, the hydrogen bomb, television, automation, collective bargaining, nuclear power, civil rights, social security, skyscrapers, satellites, electronic snooping devices, vending machines, mobile homes, supermarkets, jet transports, detergents, tranquilizers, federal aid, shopping centers, teaching machines, suburbia and a host of other items we now take for granted?[29]

Each innovation has had a significant influence on American life; in combination they have created a need for man to adapt which could lead to civil disorders and chaos. Some already believe the situation to be beyond control. The problems of human adaptation to an urban environment are so complex that it is beyond most to even identify what they are, much less to attempt solutions to some of the disorders now facing Urban America.

DISORDERS

Some of the disorders facing America are already familiar in urban areas. They include: juvenile delinquency, traffic congestion, water and air pollution, urban blight, suburban sprawl, narcotic addiction, technological unemployment, vandalism, depressed areas, inflation, ghettoes, poverty, diminishing open spaces, forced relocation, crime, suicide, flight to the suburbs, water shortages, inadequate schools, bankrupt local governments, slums, landscape deterioration, environmental stress, youth alienation, and riots.

These problems are already difficult, if not impossible, to solve. They become even more complex when a solution designed to solve one problem often produces another or several others of even greater magnitude. A more systematic approach to long-range planning may begin to offer some ways to at least help to identify problems in light of expressed national goals and objectives.

---

[29] Ernest Erber, "New Directions in Planning," *The Local Planning Process* (New Brunswick, N. J.: Bureau of Government Research, Rutgers State University, 1967), p. 180.

INNOVATION

Beyond the present is an uncertain future in which innovation and technology used to solve present problems may create still others. Who is considering the future impact on society and the environment of lasers, pesticides, brain implants, increased lifespan, disease eradication, undersea mining, psychedelic drugs, interplanetary space travel, hydroponic farming, supersonic transports, weather control, cybernation, genetic manipulation, the elimination of poverty . . . and world peace?

There is a growing awareness that planning should begin to concern itself with these types of questions by extending its time horizons and scope, for there are few professions in this society charged with the future. Such truly comprehensive and futuristic planning does not exist anywhere at present because it is difficult to define a client other than "Spaceship Earth."[30] But there is ample evidence that it is one of the "new directions" toward which planning is steadily moving.[31]

New Dimensions of Planning

Three areas which seem paramount in the "new dimensions" of planning are: (1) an emphasis on human values, (2) the use of applied technology in the planning process, and (3) the creation of new institutions to cope with particular problems. Each of these dimensions is summarized below.

HUMAN VALUES

Although much has already been said and written by others on the vital subject of human values, it cannot be overemphasized: if planning and the city are truly for people, it is incumbent on all concerned to know the values, behavior patterns and characteristics of those people who will be affected by a policy decision or action.

Intuitive or arbitrary assumptions can no longer be made about human welfare as a basis for preparing plans. People should be studied by using the tools and techniques of the Behavioral Sciences. Human needs and reactions to proposals should be made known

[30] Kenneth E. Boulding, "Economics of the Coming Spaceship Earth," in *The Environmental Handbook,* Garrett DeBell (Ed.), (New York: Ballantine Books, 1970).

[31] Donald W. Michael, *The Unprepared Society* (New York: Harper and Row, 1970).

through all of the formal and informal channels of communication already available or possible in the planning process. A new emphasis on the quality of life, quality of the environment and a harmony between man and his environment can or should replace planning's traditional emphasis on physical order, objects and expression.

TECHNOLOGY

The use of technology in the planning process has, for the first time, given the planner some significant tools equal to the task of handling large amounts of information, complex problems and coping with uncertainty. Quantitative methods such as systems analysis, operations research, program-planning and budgeting, program-evaluation review technique, critical path method and gaming simulation* with the electronic computer as a tool have opened new avenues, in the areas of data collection, analysis, goal formulation, budget preparation and program scheduling.

These methods are probably the only way the professional planner can begin to deal with the variables and complexity of a metropolis. They have also become a way of translating abstract values such as "beauty" into more tangible sets of human wants or needs. Another significant advantage of these new technologies is our current capacity to simulate and test alternatives before implementation. By developing a model of a system which can be programmed on a computer to compress time, change the variables or make judgments in terms of established criteria, the planner now has a powerful analytical tool. The advantages of this technique have barely been realized.

All of these approaches make use of systems analysis which is simply a quantitative method to determine the relative worth and/ or the relationships between components of that system. The applications to something so complex as a city are obvious. For the first time they give the planner a way of dealing with complexity that has defied traditional techniques. However, these techniques should not be thought of as a substitute for the human imagination, perception and commitment necessary to solve urban problems.

INSTITUTIONAL CHANGE

Perhaps the most fertile area for needed innovation to meet the demands of the future is the establishment of new institutions

---

* See Glossary.

or the revision of existing ones. The complexity of planning, cities and social issues no longer allows the alternative of solving problems independent of each other. This "frontier philosophy" will be replaced by a "team effort" which requires a level of collaboration, cooperation or coordination generally beyond the will or ability of most existing institutions and individuals.

If institutions such as government, industry, unions, universities, schools and the church do not review their traditional approach toward urban problems, new institutions may develop to replace them in part or whole. Most institutions will have to change their traditional approach of dealing primarily with effects to an enlightened approach of treating causes. The effort required will not be without conflict, for institutions generally react slowly to change because of their established single-purpose objectives. But they can and will adapt if they wish to survive and continue.

The future will not only prompt institutional change, it will create it in a wide range of new institutions such as public authorities for housing, education and leisure; private corporations for human development; and personal commitments to organizations promoting change. The important point to acknowledge is that institutional change is as vital to effective planning as any of the developing trends and applied technologies. It should be viewed as a possible product of planning as well as a way of changing planning to be more responsive to people's needs.

An Overview

It is not possible to summarize all that planning is or should be because *change* is what planning is all about. There are and always will be as many viewpoints on planning as there are people. This chapter has provided one view that should give the reader a conceptual context for urban recreation planning.

Today America stands on the threshold of an urban age never before known to man. Its potential to cope with challenges and capitalize on opportunities is limited only by the measure of foresight, imagination and effort of all concerned. The luxury of delay is gone. If this nation is to take the necessary action to insure a future environment for man, it should begin *now* by recognizing the central city for what it is and could be. A massive effort should be mounted to attack the problems of the central city and to prevent the perpetuation of similar problems in existing suburbs and new developments. We should begin to ask not only how much, but how good and for whom, what and why? Is less more? What is really important? Is it possible to replace our Gross National Product with a "Great National Product?" To defer these questions is to forego the opportunity; there is no better time to shape our future than now. With reference to urban open space Whyte makes this dramatic appeal:

> Let's be on with the job as though there were little time left . . . use the tools we have now, and not worry so much over what will be right for A.D. 2000. . . . Vigorous action now will not preclude future choice; it will give more choice. . . . Our options are expiring. . . . We have no luxury of choice. We must make our commitments now and look to this landscape as the last one. For us, it will be.[32]

Planning is no longer a subject of academic debate. It is one essential to survival and living in cities. The planning done *now* will shape the urban environment for future generations. Future generations will not be able to create a humane environment in their own time because it will be too late. Many of the problems in cities will be beyond solution or irreversible. What is at stake is much more than sheer survival. It is the quality of life and environment still possible in Urban America. We owe these future generations no less than we have inherited and hopefully more.

---

[32] Whyte, *The Last Landscape*, pp. 401-402.

V

The Recreation Standard

No single concept or measure has had a more significant impact on the urban recreation experience than the recreation standard. The widespread application of standards is so central to contemporary recreation planning that this chapter will detail the history, use and attainment of standards and their implications on the recreation experience in Urban America.

HISTORICAL BASIS OF CONTEMPORARY STANDARDS

Despite arguments to the contrary, the origin of standards was *not* accidental. This section will trace how they have emerged "as the codified aspirations of an interest group in response to situations in which resources are to be distributed."[1] The object is to discredit the common excuse for dismissing rigorous analysis of standards and show how their origin and development have been accepted by professionals over time without challenge.

EARLY REFERENCES

The standards now in use can be traced back to 1890 and the beginnings of public recreation as part of the social reform movement. Henry Curtis, who made some of this nation's earliest recre-

---

[1] Gans, "Recreation Planning for Leisure Behavior," p. 448.

ation surveys, wrote, "we don't know very well what adequate facilities for play are, but we know that they must be within walking distance of the children if they are to be attended."[2] In 1906, Olmsted described requirements for types of neighborhood playgrounds and recommended sizes.[3] Also, during this year, the first meeting of the National Playground Association of America unanimously adopted this resolution:

> That while there is no inherent relation between space and children, and the exact amount of space required cannot be determined, it is our belief that the present London requirement of 30 sq. ft. of playground for each child of the school is the minimum with which the proper amount of light, air and space for play and gymnastics can be secured.[4]

By 1910, facility concepts, service radii and approximate sizes of neighborhood facilities were developed. A survey made by Hubbard in 1914 "showed that concepts of adequacy were considered, and that the bases of contemporary standards were already in existence."[5] The NRPA, in its recent publication on *Recreation Space Standards,* summarizes the period with this statement:

> Quite early in the century someone proposed that a municipality should provide ten acres of recreation space per thousand of the population. The actual origin of this standard is not known; however the National Recreation Association accepted and promoted it as a desirable standard.[6]

Shivers and Hjelte analyze this period and conclude that these standards or "ratio was never based upon any factual knowledge or validated scientific analysis. It was, and is, a historical estimate of expert *opinion,* which was developed . . . in another country in 1900." They suggest that "no validated standards exist for the acquisition and development of recreational spaces in urban centers and

[2] Henry Curtis, "Provision and Responsibility for Playgrounds," *The Annals,* February, 1910, p. 125.

[3] Frederick Law Olmsted, "The Normal Requirements of American Towns and Cities in Respect to Public Open Space," *Charities and the Commons,* July, 1906, pp. 411-417.

[4] National Recreation and Park Association, *Outdoor Recreation Space Standards* (Washington, D. C.: National Recreation and Park Association, 1967), p. 2.

[5] Henry Hubbard, "The Size and Distribution of Playgrounds and Similar Recreation Facilities in American Cities," *Proceedings of the 6th National Conference on City Planning* (Boston: 1914), pp. 265-304.

[6] NRPA, *Recreation Space Standards,* 1967, p. 5.

metropolitan regions. The only standards are those of inconsistent estimate and guess, and these vary with local conditions."[7]

DEVELOPMENT AND CODIFICATION

The development of standards closely paralleled the growth of the Recreation Movement during the 1920's. A Committee on Recreation Problems in City Planning recommended to the Recreation Congress of 1923 a set of standards for play space needed around elementary and secondary schools which formalized the idea of a neighborhood playground.

In 1928, Butler's book *Play Areas* suggested a series of standards. This book was published by the Playgrounds and Recreation Association (soon to be renamed NRA) giving the standards that agency's official sanction.[8] In 1929, Hamner refuted the NRA's recommended standards of 200 square feet per child and concluded that "every child needed 100 square feet, and that given adequate leadership, the playground could attract one-fourth of the children of the neighborhood at a given time."[9] He suggested a per capita standard of 25 square feet per child, age 5 to 15 years, living within a radius of ¼ mile. The NRA felt that these standards were too low and, in 1934, issued a series of standards that are essentially the ones in use today. These standards assumed:

(1) a low density single family, white, middle class neighborhood, centered around an elementary school of 600 children, (2) baseball as a given activity on a site no smaller than 5 acres, (3) an average of 250 square feet per child and (4) maximum use of the facility by all children at the same time.[10]

These assumptions were soon translated into a standard which applied to the total population of a given neighborhood and became codified as the standard of 1 acre of neighborhood playground per 1,000 persons. This marked a departure from the above approach based on the number of children and a beginning of the gross assumption of acreage per 1,000 persons so common today.

---

[7] Jay S. Shivers and George Hjelte, *Planning Recreational Places* (Cranbury, N. J.: Fairleigh Dickinson University Press 1971), p. 210.

[8] Playground and Recreation Association, *Play Areas* (New York: Barnes, 1928), p. 74.

[9] Lee Hamner et al., *Regional Survey of New York and Its Environs*, Public Recreation, Vol. V (New York: Committee on the Regional Plan, 1928), pp. 118-121.

[10] George D. Butler, Ed., *Playgrounds* (New York: A. S. Barnes and Company, 1936), pp. 9-19.

TOWARD NATIONAL ACCEPTANCE

While NRA was careful to indicate that its standards were "guides," for lack of any alternatives these standards were soon widely applied without revision by their own personnel and were nationally accepted by many communities in the late 1930's. This had a compounding effect which increased the authority of the original standards and encouraged still more communities to accept them without revision or question. In 1943, the concept of the neighborhood playground as a family area began to assume an importance which had an impact on the existing standards based primarily on children. In 1948, Butler suggested:

> The playground . . . now also affords limited opportunities for informal recreation for young people and adults . . . where the people of a neighborhood can find recreation . . . with their families, neighbors and friends. The enlarged conception of the playground's function has made necessary a revision in the previous standards relating to children's playgrounds.[11]

This resulted in a decision to change the acreage standard from 1 acre of neighborhood playground per 1,000 to 1 acre per 800 people. At the same time, the NRA formulated a series of new standards for most types of municipal recreation facilities to support the growing emphasis on community planning and recreation systems.

In 1960, the NRA appointed a National Committee on Recreation Standards and requested them to "survey communities for plans which exemplified an application of adequate standards to a local situation."[12] This marked the beginnings of a search for adequacy in the Recreation Movement. The results of this survey were published in 1962 in *Standards for Recreation Areas* and are summarized in Appendix D, Table 1. The standards were defended and slightly revised, but *not* rationalized, in the NRPA's publication *Outdoor Recreation Space Standards 1967.*[13]

National acceptance of the NRPA standards as guidelines culminated in the Bureau of Outdoor Recreation's recent publication, *Outdoor Recreation Space Standards*[14] and *Guidebook for State Out-*

---

[11] George D. Butler, *Standards for Municipal Recreation Areas* (New York: National Recreation Association, 1962), p. 12.

[12] NRPA, *Recreation Space Standards, 1967,* p. 4.

[13] NRPA, *Outdoor Recreation Space Standards,* 1967.

[14] U. S., Department of the Interior, Bureau of Outdoor Recreation, *Outdoor Recreation Space Standards* (Washington, D. C.: Government Printing Office, 1967). Hereafter cited as BOR, *Space Standards.*

door Recreation Planning.[15] Both of these publications: (1) imply no other approach to recreation planning than the use of recommended standards, and (2) make no scientific rationalizations of these standards in terms of economic feasibility, recreation behavior, geography or any other variable.

In January of 1969, the NRPA convened a National Forum in Kansas City on park and recreation standards. Over 150 experts reached a consensus "that the Association should continue to determine standards."[16] This Forum produced a report, *National Park, Recreation and Open Space Standards* which recommends standards that "have resulted from years of observation, experience and consultation by top professionals in the park and recreation and allied fields."[17] The preface states:

> ". . . This report brings into focus recommended minimum standards that are current with the times; it provides targets or minimum goals and comes to grip with political realities. It also gives attention to the needs and desires of people and the recommended standards that are usable below the neighborhood level. . . . We would urge park and recreation and planning departments to adopt these minimum standards as a guide to further enhance their operations.[18]

REFLECTIONS ON THE PAST

When viewed in perspective it becomes easier to rationalize the origin, evolution and codification of recreation standards. Several points considered separately may not be impressive, but in combination they begin to reveal the reasons for much of the current thinking about standards and outdoor recreation.

Outdoor Romanticism

Most standards were developed at a time when neither city planning nor public recreation was vitally concerned with the problem of implementation. As reform movements, both were so certain of their cause that only moral persuasion was felt necessary for

---

[15] U. S., Department of the Interior, Bureau of Outdoor Recreation, *Guidebook for State Outdoor Recreation Planning* (Washington, D. C.: Government Printing Office, 1964).

[16] Robert D. Buechner (Ed.), *National Park, Recreation and Open Space Standards* (Washington, D. C.: National Recreation and Park Association, 1971), p. 7. This reference will hereafter be cited as Buechner, *National Park, Recreation and Open Space Standards.*

[17] *Ibid.,* p. 6.

[18] *Ibid.,* pp. 4-5.

implementation and this was reflected in the well-meant, but sometimes naive, optimism characteristic of the early 1900's.

Most publications have conspicuously warned against the unqualified use of standards, but most warnings have been disregarded in favor of largely emotional responses to the allocation of recreation resources. Small cities without adequate planning staffs have adopted NRPA standards without qualification, while larger cities have made only minor modifications. Even when some standards were found to be almost impossible to apply in high-density areas, most cities have persisted in maintaining them despite countless warnings from authorities:

> Standards, it should be kept in mind, can never be applied completely or without modification, because a typical or ideal situation is never found in a city. They need to be adjusted in the light of conditions, needs and resources of each locality. Standards are designed to indicate a norm or a point of departure; as such they afford a basis for the intelligent development of local plans.[19]

The historical justification for clinging to standards established over a half-century ago is understandable only in the light of the fervor of reform movements. However, this justification becomes questionable in light of current needs and methodologies. If there is any single past rationalization which is most vulnerable to criticism, it is this one; the standard which was established and codified as a measure of adequacy has never been qualified, tested or evaluated in human terms.

Methodological Deficiencies

The relatively primitive state of contemporary recreation-planning methodology and research is one indication of the lack of authoritative testing and evaluation of early standards. Whatever research has been done in this area has been based on questionable data which have made each study less dependable than the preceding one and subjected the area to further distortion. If any past rationalization can be justified, it is this one. Lack of standards of adequacy or social indicators has, in fact, been a persistent methodological deficiency of the Social Sciences. Shivers and Hjelte state:

> "The single greatest deficiency among those who plan for recreational facilities and places is a lack of knowledge concerning neces-

---

[19] George D. Butler, "Standards for Municipal Recreation Areas," *Recreation*, July, 1948, p. 161.

sary space for the provision of recreational activities of all types within the urban center. . . . There is no information, other than conjecture and pure estimation. . . . Some suggestions have been made as to the numbers of facilities to be supplied, but there has been no scientific validation of these ratios.[20]

Decision-Making Process

The decision-making process is perhaps the most visible area for attempting to rationalize the past use and acceptance of recreation standards. There are several possible reasons why standards, developed as guides, have been accepted in many instances as rules.

First, most standards are clear and simple. To the busy decision-maker or planner, they represent an expedient way to attain an objective usually established by the supplier of recreation. They require no study or research and can be applied as an instant recommendation or solution to problems.

Second, standards are established by a national organization specializing in recreation and are thus legitimized as "expert." Should anyone challenge them, most planners defend them simply by appealing to their authoritativeness. Also, their national origin gives standards a reference point outside the community and abstracts them from partisan politics or the claims of interest groups.

Third, standards are symbols of community pride and status. They stand for an ideal few can or will oppose, at least prior to the actual allocation of resources. In many instances they become ends rather than means, tools or guidelines. Communities are often evaluated by NRPA and others for how *much* rather than how *good* their facilities are, despite a wide range of demographic variables.

Finally, standards are useful in the typical community's decision-making process. Although conceived as planning tools, their most frequent use is often that of bargaining points by suppliers who compete with other municipal agencies for the community's resources. Because of their simplicity and authority, standards are often used to determine what a community should have. The demands implicit in these standards are scaled so high that decision-makers who accept the standards in principle can more easily be persuaded to shift additional resources to recreation, if only to reduce what appears to be glaring inadequacies.

Combined, each of the above factors plays a significant role in the historical evolution and acceptance of standards. There is

---

[20] Shivers and Hjelte, *Planning Recreational Places,* pp. 221-222.

no question that some of these factors can be rationalized in perspective as well-meant, but ill-conceived. There is, however, serious question as to whether or not standards can continue to be rationalized on this basis.

TYPES OF STANDARDS

Because the different orientations, planning units and activity relationships are a source of confusion, any consideration of standards faces a problem of classification. Since this book is primarily concerned with resource allocation for a neighborhood park or playground in the inner city, it will focus on those standards which relate to this area. However, the principles should relate to other areas and sets of activities.

The literature indicates no national effort to classify standards by type, function, orientation or scale. Several authors have attempted partial classifications, but no single source has developed anything comprehensive. There are five major orientations of standards and, within each, a number of variations. These variations or types are summarized in Table 11. The possible combinations and proportionate weights of each type of standard in any given situation could have a bearing on the relative effectiveness of all standards used to plan, develop or manage an area or park system.

For example, if standards are viewed as measures of the inputs of land, labor or capital in a given situation, a minimum standard for the allocation of land could be optimized with maximum standards for development, program or management to produce a higher quantity and quality recreation experience for the user than if the reverse, or some other combination, were attempted. The mix of standards is a research problem identified here and discussed later as one of the conditions which make it difficult to be precise in the consideration of recreation standards. This problem would be well adapted to simulation techniques because of the large number of possible variables.

Space Standards

The term "recreation space standard" is relatively new. Few sources make reference to it prior to the BOR and NRPA publications on space standards released in 1967. Since that time, the term has been widely accepted and is used in this book to mean those types of standards listed in the recreation use, development and

TABLE 11

A Classification of Selected Types of Recreation Standards*

General Orientation	Specific Type	Measurement Units	Illustrative Examples
Recreation use	Population ratio Recreation demand Percent of area	Area/population Area/user group Area/planning unit	1 acre neighborhood park/1000 pop. 1 acre playground/600 children 10% of planning unit area
Recreation development	Facility to site Facility placement Facility to activity Facility size	Units/acre Distance bet. units Units/user group Area/facility	16 picnic tables/acre Picnic tables 50 ft. apart 1 softball diamond/10,000 pop. 3-5 acres neighborhood playground
Carrying capacity	User to resource User to time	Users/site Users/time/site	400 people/mile of trail/hr. 50 people/mile of trail/hr.
Recreation program	Activity to population Leadership requirements	Activity/population Leaders/activity	1 arboretum/10,000 pop. 2 leaders/100 children
Recreation management	Supervision to users Maintenance to site	Staff/population Degree/area	1 supervisor/1000 users 1 laborer/10 acres playground

* Abstracted and adapted from a number of sources listed in the Bibliography.

carrying capacity orientations listed in Table 11. Because this book is concerned with user, rather than resource-oriented areas, the carrying capacity orientation will not be considered.

DEFINITIONS

The NRPA defines the recreation space standard as "a measure of land required to accomplish a specific objective." This standard is projected as "a measure which changes as the thinking of the people and conditions change . . . and an educated opinion as to how much land is needed to enable people to engage in wholesome outdoor recreation activities."[21] A more recent NRPA definition states: "Standards are relative rather than absolute requirements, and should serve as *guidelines* or *criteria* to aid in the planning and decision making process."[22] The BOR believes that recreation space standards "represent relative rather than absolute space requirements" and qualifies its compendium of standards with this statement:

> It is important to understand the conditions under which these relative requirements were developed. Standards developed in response to a specific set of resource, land-use, and cultural conditions in one area may not be relevant to another area with a different set of circumstances.[23]

Gans refers to "standards as rules or guides which permit the planner to determine the kind of facilities to be provided, their number, size and location within either the neighborhood or city."[24] His study identifies and criticizes this definition "as the quantified statements of an ideal recreation system as envisaged by the suppliers."[25]

Clawson refers to standards as "general guides and not as explicit directives." He concludes: "standards can never be rigid . . . and are meaningful only with respect to the types of areas." He also attaches an economic value to standards in his statement: "each community must determine what its citizens want, and what role

---

[21] NRPA, *Recreation Space Standards*, 1967, p. 17.
[22] Buechner, *National Park, Recreation and Open Space Standards*, p. 6.
[23] BOR, *Space Standards*, Foreword.
[24] Gans, "Recreation Planning for Leisure Behavior," p. 437.
[25] *Ibid.*, p. 511.

they assign to recreation. What can the community afford, and what is it willing to pay for?"[26]

Other authors are more absolute in their definition of standards. Meyer and Brightbill believe that "standards provide the framework for planning the recreation system and integrate the efforts of agencies to meet the needs of the people."[27] Doell looks upon standards as "guides to park management,"[28] but counters this by stating:

> In establishing [defining] standards which communities should be expected to attain, the job must necessarily devolve upon those who are especially versed in the study and the experience of the function in question, namely the professionals. . . . They, of all people, have the qualifications for establishing reasonably obtainable standards.[29]

Some authors define standards in a goal-oriented context. Young defines the standard as "a unit measurement which objectifies a value."[30] Gans refines this concept and defines standards "as the requirements in a total program to help achieve a desired goal."[31] Others equate and define standards as "measures of quality or adequacy . . . or basic tools required for planning a public recreation system.[32] One comprehensive definition states:

> Standards represent the goal the park and recreation department is striving to achieve and thus serve as a yardstick by which to measure progress and point out weaknesses. . . . Such standards serve as guidelines for improving inadequate programs. Standards represent relative rather than absolute space requirements . . . because they may not be relevant to another area with a different set of circumstances.[33]

---

[26] Clawson, *Economics of Outdoor Recreation*, p. 147.

[27] Meyer and Brightbill, *Community Recreation*, p. 454.

[28] Charles E. Doell, *Park and Recreation Administration* (Minneapolis: Burgess Publishing Company, 1963), p. 14.

[29] *Ibid.*, p. 257.

[30] Robert C. Young, "Establishment of Goals and Definition of Objectives," in Driver, *Elements of Outdoor Recreation Planning*, p. 264.

[31] Gans, "Recreation Planning for Leisure Behavior," p. 555.

[32] California Committee on Planning for Recreation, Park Areas and Facilities, *Guide for Planning Recreation Parks in California* (Sacramento: California Recreation Commission, 1956), p. 22.

[33] National Association of Counties, *Community Action Guides for Outdoor Recreation: Planning* (Washington, D. C.: National Association of Counties, 1968), n.p.

If there is any consensus on a definition of standards, it infers that they be used as *guidelines* rather than absolutes and be applied with sensitive discretion. The ideal or average combination of resources and values seldom exists and each situation or community represents a *different* set of variables. There also seems to be general agreement that if standards are used properly they can be one point of departure for estimating and evaluating the: (1) amount of land and facilities required to serve a population and sub-groups within the population, (2) number of people a given recreation area, facility or system can be expected to serve adequately, and (3) adequacy of an area, facility or system to accommodate the potential users in its service area.

It is interesting to note the omission of concepts or terms such as user preference, leisure objectives, recreation experience, optimum, form and function, time horizons, economic feasibility, and political efficacy in most definitions of standards. Perhaps these concepts are implicit, but there is evidence to indicate that they are not. Some of this evidence is discussed below and will be illustrated in Chapters VI and VII.

CONCEPTS

These four areas are important to a conceptual understanding of standards: (1) defense mechanisms, (2) degree gradients, (3) time and scale dimensions, and (4) feasibility. All are closely interrelated, but will be treated separately for greater clarity.

Defense Mechanisms

Despite the qualification of "flexibility" in most standards, existing concepts and practice seem to contradict this through a series of defense mechanisms commonly labeled requirements, restraints, custom or authority. Although most references to standards strongly imply the "guideline syndrome" in both concept and practice, there have been almost no constructive attempts to challenge or change existing standards.

To date, most of the conceptual effort has been directed toward rationalizing arbitrary standards. Rationalization often takes the form of emotional argument, status comparisons, professional pedanticism, and legal or administrative constraints. Conceptually, the standard meant to be a "guideline" is seldom considered as one. Most of the intellectual or technical effort associated with it is generally of a defensive nature which attempts to adapt it to a given situation no matter how irrelevant or inappropriate it may be. Gans makes this point in his dissertation which focuses primarily on the differences between user and supplier goals and the impact of this on leisure planning. He directs his criticism:

> . . . more at the planner who adopts supplier goals and standards unquestioningly than at the recreation movement which like other missionary movements is entitled to reshape the world in its own image . . . and recreation officials as municipal functionaries or professionals if and when they claim to speak for the entire community.[34]

The above statement is seldom questioned except in some enlightened plans which state:

> Standards for urban-design oriented open space have even less in the way of precedents than have many other sorts of standards. . . . quantified design standards indicating optimum acreages and distribution of urban open space do not exist. . . . applying quantitative standards to a problem that is essentially aesthetic is a superficial approach.[35]

Some of the plans examined for this type of thinking were apologetic, evasive and sometimes misleading. The following statement is typical of the apologetic stance:

> The subject of standards for recreational facilities is complicated, affected by many variables and most difficult to define in absolute terms. . . . It seems clear that standards will remain incomplete until better information than is now available is at hand and the goal and objectives of outdoor recreation can be more clearly identified.[36]

But even with this dismissal of the problem, the above plan develops a series of standards "to permit a desirable level of recreational experience" and then rationalizes them with this statement:

> Standards for recreational activities generally take the form of minimum requirements and tend to be regarded as basic necessities to serve the public. This presents the danger of the standard becoming an absolute requirement which it is not. They are more in the nature

---

[34] Gans, "Recreation Planning for Leisure Behavior," p. 510.

[35] Department of Commerce and Economic Development, *Washington Statewide Outdoor Recreation and Open Space Plan* (Spokane: Department of Commerce and Economic Development, January, 1967), p. 59.

[36] Illinois, 1967 *Addenda, State Outdoor Recreation Plan* (Springfield: Illinois Department of Business and Economic Development, June, 1967), pp. 9-10.

of guidelines or criteria to be followed under average conditions, designed to satisfy accepted levels of opportunities for recreation.[37]

Because of the lack of any apparent alternative, the conceptual distortions resulting from this defense mechanism tend to create more confusion and frustration. Styles illustrates this idea:

> While there is some reaction against them, space and facility standards are commonly used in local and state recreation plans. Despite the pitfalls involved, the stereotyped approaches and so forth . . . I fail to see how we can avoid the use of standards, particularly space standards.[38]

Degree Gradients

The gradient between minimum, maximum, desirable or optimum standards is a concept often discussed in the literature, but has had relatively little research. Clawson approaches this from an economist's point of view but reaches no conclusions. Instead he asks:

> How much park and recreation area is enough to meet the needs of the people? What is a reasonable goal? . . . standards of real adequacy can help answer such questions, if they are taken as general guides and not as explicit directives.[39]

Other leading authorities such as Chapin conceptualize standards as "a set of yardsticks established for measuring the excellence of quality in elements of the community's makeup." They reflect a legal concept of standards as minimums necessary for the public interest, but qualify this as a preference for "desirable standards . . . which are somewhere between the minimum and optimum situation."[40]

The confusion in this area is more than just semantic. It represents a genuine lack of rigorous thought by all concerned and especially those agencies and organizations most responsible for establishing or at least publishing compendiums of standards. For example, the NRPA states: "on the basis of present conditions, the standard of 10 acres per 1,000 of the population within an urban

---

[37] *Ibid.,* p. 9.

[38] Frederick G. Styles, "Variables Which Must Be Considered in Outdoor Recreation Planning," in Driver, *Elements of Outdoor Recreation Planning,* p. 57.

[39] Clawson, *Economics of Outdoor Recreation,* pp. 146-147.

[40] Chapin, *Urban Land Use Planning,* p. 376.

area can be accepted *as a minimum.*"[41] Yet in the same publication it contradicts this with: "parks should always be as large as possible."[42]

A review of over 200 state and local outdoor recreation plans and the literature reveals almost no discussion of the concept of adequacy or distinction between minimum, desirable and optimum standards. In general, these plans project an image of *desirable*, quality or optimum recreation opportunities, but, for the most part, utilize *minimum* standards to achieve these objectives.

Often the values of beauty or pleasantness are equated with the minimum space standard which lends further confusion, if not a thread of surrealism, to most plans. This is commonly illustrated in the NRPA statement:

> A recreation space standard is an educated opinion as to how much land is needed to make individual sites beautiful features which contribute in large measure toward making the community environment a permanently attractive place in which to live.[43]

There is no greater point of conceptual misunderstanding about standards than the area of gradient. It is paradoxical for this nation to seek such goals as "Quality of Life" or a "Great Society," but to measure them with the *minimum* values implicit in a *desirable* gradient. This is a contraction which can hardly lead toward these goals.

Time and Scale Dimensions

In concept, the closest most plans come to an acknowledgment of the dimensions of time and space in their use of standards are the designation of appropriate minimum standards for areas by type and location. The dimension of time is almost nonexistent in most plans, except for references to an "ultimate, not present population."[44]

The ambiguity of relating a plan to an "ultimate population" assumes either infinite wisdom or that the city is a relatively static entity. Both assumptions do little for the cause of standards because

---

41 NRPA, *Recreation Space Standards*, 1967, p. 24.

42 *Ibid.*, p. 26.

43 NRPA, *Recreation Space Standards*, 1967, p. 18.

44 *Ibid.*, p. 20. Also see Buechner, *National Park, Recreation and Open Space Standards*, p. 11.

they present the paradox of attempting to quantify something which is difficult to state in absolutes. For example, the ultimate population of even an inner city neighborhood is now subject to radical change in a period measured in years. How then can an "ultimate standard" be even considered in concept? Certainly its effectiveness in practice is marginal.

The dimension of scale is conceptually as ambiguous as time. At anything but the pedestrian scale the traditional concepts of community, district, city and region begin to have a marginal relationship to existing recreation standards unless they are rephrased in time/distance and circulation patterns to include types of movement by age or user groups.

Most plans present an intuitive scale or system of recreational opportunities and indicate recommended sizes and acreages per 1,000 population, but do not realistically consider items such as community social organization, demographic variables between and among potential user groups or private recreational opportunities. Sessoms identifies this conceptual deficiency:

> Space time, energy, human relations—these are the dominant concern of urban twentieth century America. . . .
>
> . . . .
>
> Recreation facilities are simply the physical manifestations of social needs. They are to provide an avenue for the fulfillment of expression of social and recreation needs through leisure experience. . . .
>
> . . . .
>
> The arbitrary drawing of a circle with a specific radius, and the enumerating of so many facilities and acres per 1,000 population . . . is as antiquated a planning concept as is the gridiron street pattern. . . .
>
> . . . .
>
> We need to put aside the traditional planning concepts based on distance traveled from home and the number of acres per 1,000 persons, and to plan according to function and need.[45]

Feasibility

The concepts of political efficacy, economic feasibility and urban form or function are lacking in most considerations of standards. Yet, it is precisely the standard which is either the cause or effect of the recommendations in most recreation plans. Thus, most plans

---

[45] H. Douglas Sessoms, "New Bases for Recreation Planning," *Journal of the American Institute of Planners*, May, 1965, pp. 26-31.

have a built-in dimension of conceptual contradiction in the area of feasibility.

This problem is not uncommon for many types of governmental services. However, the development of more sensitive approaches to economic and social feasibility in Planning-Program-Budgeting Systems has created a serious need to rationalize the recreation standard conceptually and relate it to other measures of public service.

The literature indicates no rationalization or technique to date other than the traditional benefit-cost ratios commonly used to justify many recreation projects. However, it does identify the need to rationalize standards from a political, economic and social standpoint. Clawson best illustrates this theme:

> In general, determination of desirable area of various kinds of open space in the past has depended primarily upon rather subjective considerations. . . . There is a tendency to think of public open space as a positive good . . . but in the long run, it seems questionable public policy to advocate acquisition or reservation of open space unless it meets a real purpose. [46]

Other authorities are seemingly indifferent in their concept of feasibility. The NRPA states:

> If all urban areas provide 10 acres of open space per 1,000 of the ultimate population . . . the probabilities are that the open space needs for recreation will be adequately met in the year 2000. A standard of 15 acres per 1,000 of the population in extraurban areas is feasible.[47]

Doell emphatically states:

> Standards are not merely idealized pictures arbitrarily arrived at by the professionals who have no regard for the ability to pay. . . . Nevertheless, experience, observation, and a logical reasoning from cause to effect have constrained them to express standards which can be expected to be attained, or substantially attained, by any self-respecting city.[48]

The most recent and authoritative study on feasibility concludes: "No two communities or sets of living conditions are exactly alike. There is little similarity between the park and recreation needs in

---

[46] Clawson, "A Positive Approach to Open Space Preservation," pp. 124-129.
[47] NRPA, Recreation Space Standards, 1967, p. 24.
[48] Doell, Park and Recreation Administration, p. 259.

our affluent suburbs, rural America, or the teeming poverty areas of the inner city."[49] On the same page the previous statement is contradicted with: "These policies are nothing more than good common sense and apply to almost *any* community."[50] With reference to feasibility this study recommends:

> To be effective in any situation standards should satisfy certain criteria: They must reflect the needs of the people in the *specific* area being served. They must be reasonably or substantially *attainable;* or adequate *alternatives* devised. They must be *acceptable* and *usable* to the practitioner and policy maker. They must be based on sound *principles,* and the *best available information.* They must stand the test of time.[51]

No conclusions can be drawn from the wide range of differing concepts in this area except to acknowledge at least two divergent concepts. One that makes little attempt to conceptualize the feasibility of standards, and simply rationalizes this with a humble apology or by dismissing the topic because of a lack of data. The second concept assumes a self-righteous stance which avoids feasibility by equating it with expertise or experience.

The results of both tactics have been to cloud the conceptual basis of standards with an aura of controversy in precisely the area where consensus is most needed. This not only compounds the conceptual shortcomings of the three previous areas, but it also discourages needed research in these areas.

CURRENT USE OF SPACE STANDARDS

Illustration of Existing Standards

STATE AND LOCAL PLANS

The collage of space standards now in use at all levels of government is best illustrated by a review of published plans. A systematic sample would be desirable, but because there is no national index of all recreation plans, a selected sample is considered valid. A representative collection of over 100 local, county

---

[49] Buechner, *National Park, Recreation and Open Space Standards,* p. 8.
[50] *Ibid.* (Emphasis added.)
[51] *Ibid.* (Emphasis added.)

and state outdoor recreation plans plus several summaries by the NRPA and other sources provide the basis for this discussion. Although this book is primarily concerned with the inner city, it is meaningful to illustrate all types of plans because the relationships are similar. In order to make comparison more systematic, the selected plans in Table 12 are classified by government level and geographic distribution.

TABLE 12

Illustration of Space Standards by Government Level and Region

Level	Region	Location	Space Standards[a] (Acres)
Municipal	North	Ann Arbor, Michigan	10
	South	Dallas, Texas	10
	East	Pawtucket, Rhode Island	6
	West	Tacoma, Washington	10
County	North	Detroit metro. region	15
	South	Baltimore County, Md.	15
	East	Erie County, Pa.	10
	West	Santa Clara County, Calif.	15
State	North	State of Connecticut	50
	South	State of Virginia	45
	East	State of Pennsylvania	45
	West	State of Nebraska	40 (1980)

[a] Minimum gross standards/1000 population. Does not include any other level of government. No time horizons evident unless stated.

Although this is not a stratified sample, it begins to point toward a pattern of national usage and acceptance of standards with only minor exceptions. Were it possible to consider all plans in a similar manner, most would follow the same pattern. Approximately 60 to 80 percent of the plans probably reflect the *same* standards, even though each planning area has a wide range of demographic, recreation resource, fiscal and climatic variables. Stated another way, there is probably less than a 20 percent standard deviation between space standards at each level of government.

SELECTED OTHER SOURCES

Beyond these plans an abstract of the literature is summarized in Table 13. Appendix F lists the most current NRPA recommended standards. A similarity between space standards, especially at the

TABLE 13

A Summary of Recommended Space Standards for Neighborhood Playgrounds

Reference Source	Acres/ Pop.	Maximum Service Radius (Mile)	Minimum Size (Acres)	Max. Pop. Served	Year Published
BOR[a]	1/800	½	4	8,000	1964
NRPA[b]	1/800	½	2.75	8,000	1967
Meyer and Brightbill[c]	1/800	½	3-5	5,000	1964
Butler[d]	1/800	½	3	7,000	1959
Nez[e]	1.5/1000	½	4	variable	1961
Chapin[f]	1/800	½	5	variable	1965
Doell[g]	1/1000	½	6	8,000	1963
FSA[h]	1/800	½	2.75	5,000	1955
APHA[i]	1/800	½	2.75	5,000	1948
Average	1/800	½	3	6,000	1960

[a] BOR, Guidebook for State Outdoor Recreation Planning, p. 47.
[b] NRPA, Outdoor Recreation Space Standards and other publications.
[c] Meyer and Brightbill, Community Recreation, pp. 402-404.
[d] Butler, Introduction to Community Recreation, p. 31.
[e] G. Nez, Urban Land, May 1961, p. 4
[f] Chapin, Urban Land Use Planning, p. 449.
[g] Doell, Park and Recreation Administration, p. 16.
[h] Federal Security Agency, Planning for Recreation in Small Towns and Cities, 1955.
[i] American Public Health Association, Planning the Neighborhood, 1948.

urban scale and with respect to the general range of urban types of facilities, e.g., playground, playfield, city park, should be noted. Although only the playground is illustrated in Table 13, it is indicative of the similarity in standards for most types of urban facilities.

This similarity is not as noticeable as the acreage totals indicated in Table 12 because the slight variances tend to balance each other. However, Table 13 and a review of most available sources indicate an unusual *similarity* between standards where the variables might *not* warrant such similarity.

It is invalid to draw any firm conclusions from only this sample, but there is enough evidence to support these observations: (1) the standards recommended by the NRPA are widely accepted and used throughout the country, (2) very few cities have deviated from these standards or attempted to innovate an alternative approach to recreation resource allocation, (3) there seems to be no relationship between demographic or geographic variables in the use of standards, and (4) most plans regard the standard as a goal or objective and make superficial goal statements which do not relate to stated policies, objectives and often the standards themselves.

Nationwide Attainment of Standards

"A completely unattainable standard is of little value."[52] The question of how the nation measures up to the standards it has set is obscured by divergent opinions. Those who feel that the standard has definite value and recommend its use are defensive and go to considerable effort to rationalize the attainment of these standards wherever possible. Conversely, those who believe that "it is not possible to formulate standards or norms for recreation space applicable to every community"[53] are skeptical and go to great lengths to show why standards are not attainable or have not been attained to any effective degree. This section will illustrate these arguments, present available data to substantiate each by level of government, and draw some tentative conclusions.

INNER AND CENTRAL CITY

To date, no single source has separated the degree of standard attainment between the central and inner city. What data are avail-

---

[52] NRPA, *Recreation Space Standards, 1967*, p. 11.

[53] International City Managers' Association, *Local Planning Administration*, p. 165.

able must be assumed to represent the central city and include the inner city. By field observation of several American inner cities* it is conservative to assume a 25 percent attainment of most standards. This means that the acreage per 1,000 population listed in the following tables and Table 3 in Appendix D should be reduced by at least 75 percent for a figure representative of the inner city.

Table 14 summarizes the results of a study of 321 cities in 1940 for their attainment of the existing space standard of 10 acres per 1,000 population or 1 acre per 100 population. Note how the following interpretations of the data differ according to the source. The NRPA states:

> About one fourth of those reporting had acquired more than one acre of parks for each 100 population. It is true that some of the largest park properties owned by a number of cities are outside the city limits, but for the most part they are fairly accessible.[54]

However, an analysis of this same study by the International City Managers' Association found:

> A comparison of the acreage now available for recreation pur-

TABLE 14

Average Ratio of Population to Park Acreage in 1,282 Cities, by Population Groups, and in 321 Selected Cities, also by Population Groups[a]

Population Group (1930 Census)	No. of Cities	Average No. Persons/ Acres of Park	25% Best Cities	
			No. of Cities	Av. No. per./ Acres of Park
1,000,000 and over	5	330	1	234
500,000 to 1,000,000	8	214	2	80
250,000 to 500,000	20	145	5	67
100,000 to 250,000	48	207	12	48
50,000 to 100,000	83	203	21	54
25,000 to 50,000	145	231	36	46
10,000 to 25,000	312	243	78	44
5,000 to 10,000	358	445	90	45
2,500 to 5,000	303	242	76	48
Total	1,282	300	321	47

[a] Exluding cities with no parks.

Source: United States Department of the Interior, National Park Service, *Municipal and County Parks in the United States*, 1940, p. 2. Cited in *Local Planning Administration*, Second Edition, 1948, p. 167.

---

* Detroit, Chicago, New York City, Philadelphia, Cleveland, Newark.
[54] NRPA, *Recreation Space Standards*, 1967, p. 12.

poses in the cities with the recommendation of one acre per 100 persons discloses that cities in each of the population groups as a whole fail to meet the standard . . . [especially] cities with a population of one million or more.[55]

The analysis also reported:

The situation may not be as favorable as it appears . . . because 62 per cent of the acreage in recreation areas of all types in the reporting cities is found in large parks . . . only 16 per cent consists of neighborhood recreation areas; and only 13 per cent of active recreation areas. The adequacy of a recreation system depends on the location and types of areas as well as on the total acreage.[56]

In 1955, a study of 189 cities showed that:

49 cities, or 27 per cent, have achieved the standard of one acre per 100 population. . . . Between 1940 and 1950 park acreage per capita decreased in 108 cities and increased in only 79. A still smaller number made a relative gain between 1950 and 1955.[57]

In 1961, the *Park and Recreation Yearbook* surveyed 50 of the largest cities in the country for their attainment of space standards and, based on the information obtained from 46 cities reporting, compiled the statistics listed in Table 2 of Appendix D. An abstract of the findings of this survey is given below.

1. The average acreage in 1960 was 7.0 acres of gross recreation area per 1,000 population. This comprised 7.8 percent of the total land area within the city limits. The total population gain in the 1950's was 6.7 percent and the average gross density of population was 7,118 per square mile.

2. Eleven (24 percent) of the cities had 10 or more acres per 1,000 of the 1960 population. Considering these eleven cities as a unit, there were 19.4 acres of recreation area per 1,000; 12 percent of the city area was in recreation area, there was a 28.7 percent increase of population between 1950 and 1960, and the population denstiy was 3,952 per square mile in 1960.

3. Twenty-two (46 percent) of the cities gained 10 percent or more in population during this period. Considering these as a unit,

[55] International City Managers' Association, *Local Planning Administration*, pp. 167-168.

[56] *Ibid.*

[57] International City Managers' Association, *Municipal Recreation Administration* (Chicago: The Association, 1960), pp. 67-68.

their population gain was 35.9 percent; average of recreation area was 10.8 acres per 1,000 population of the 1960 population, the population density was 3,724 per square mile, and only 6.3 percent of the city area was devoted to recreation space. Seven cities had more than the 10 acres of recreation land per 1,000 of the 1960 population, but with four minor exceptions, these were southern or western cities.

4. Seventeen (37 percent) of the cities lost population ranging from 0.3 to 13 percent between 1950 and 1960. Considering these cities as a unit, their population density was 14,638 per square mile, 11.6 percent of the city was in recreation area and there were only 5.1 acres of such space per 1,000 population.

These findings represent a distorted view of the attainment of standards, especially with reference to most of the cities listed. More careful analysis reveals that: (1) the average acreage per 1,000 for cities over 1 million is only 4.6 acres, city areas are only 9.7 percent and the population density is 14,736 persons per square mile, (2) the averages for cities in the 500 to 1,000,000 classification are only slightly better, (3) of the ten cities which exceed the NRPA recommendations of 10 acres per 1,000 population, five are in the far West and have park systems which include large holdings on the edge of or outside the city limits, (4) those areas with the last amount of recreational acreage per population lost the largest amount of population in the last decade and were, with the exception of New York City, among those with riots during the summers of 1967 and 1968.

The point here is not to belabor the apparent differences in interpretation of these data between the NRPA and the author, but to identify some statistical distortions which might have a bearing on the inner city. Tables 3 and 4 of Appendix D support these observations and supply a historical perspective. Tables 9 through 11 of Appendix D supply a current perspective and indicate no appreciable change in the attainment ratios.

What becomes clear from only a quantitative point of view is: (1) there is at least a 100 percent difference between standards and reality for the central city and (2) in many cases an estimated 400 percent difference for the inner city. Were it possible to include a number of other variables in this comparison, e.g., environmental conditions, density, mobility, demand and need, it does not seem unrealistic to project an estimated 1000 percent difference between current standards and reality for the inner city. Clawson states:

There is often a serious disparity in the availability of park and recreation areas within cities. The densely populated parts of the city

— often decadent with outright slums — frequently have the most inadequate areas. Children and adults from these areas often must play in the street, seek indoor recreation activities — for which facilities are often equally inadequate — or just plain do without.[58]

Clawson elaborates on this idea by stating: "in a great many American cities, park and playground acreage is more unevenly distributed than is personal income." He believes that:

The lowest income parts of the city have an even smaller share of recreation area than they have of personal income, while the higher income sections have relatively generous park and recreation areas. The poorest people, who most need easily accessible parks and playgrounds, often have them the least.[59]

Clawson concludes:

This situation is made still worse by the racial pattern of urban living. The low-income central city areas so deficient in recreation space are likely to be Negro; the suburban and outer city ring, generously supplied with recreation, are likely to be white. One of the great *myths* of the outdoor recreation field is that free public parks are a boon to poor people; actually, it is the *poor* who frequently lack them.[60]

TABLE 15
Recommended Acreage Standards for State and Local Government[a]

Level of Government[b]	Location[c]	Type of Area	Acres per 1,000 pop.[d]
Municipal	Central city[c]	Neighborhood parks	2.5
Municipal	Central city	District parks	2.5
Municipal	Central city	Large urban parks	5.0
County	Hour's travel	Large regional parks	15.0
State	Variable	State parks	65.0
		Total	90.0

[a] NRPA, *Outdoor Recreation Space Standards,* 1967, p. 20.
[b] Interpolated from text and above standards.
[c] Interpreted from "near-at-hand areas" cited in text.
[d] Acres per 1,000 ultimate population.

[58] Marion Clawson, *Land and Water for Recreation* (Chicago: Rand McNally and Company, 1963), p. 21.
[59] Clawson, *Economics of Outdoor Recreation,* p. 151.
[60] *Ibid.* (Emphasis added.)

SUBURBS AND EXURBS

Traditionally the suburbs and exurbs have been serviced by parks commonly provided by the county level of government. In 1961, the NRPA surveyed 51 of the largest county park systems and

TABLE 16

Guides to Per Capita Needs for Outdoor Recreation Areas by Type of Area

Type of Recreational Area	Acres per 1,000
In-city recreation: total	
(National recreation Association)	10.00
Playgrounds (4-7 acres, each)	1.25
Playfields (12-20 acres, each)	1.25
Minor parks (at least 2 acres, each)	2.50
Major parks (100 acres, each)	5.00
County and metropolitan regional parks and beaches	
National Park Service	
Intensive-use areas	5
Parks and natural areas	15
Denver Inter-County Regional Plan[a]	15
Detroit Regional Recreational Lands Plan[b]	15
Richmond Open-Space Study[c]	15
New York Tri-State Study[d]	12 plus
State parks (National Park Service)	
General recreation areas	15
Natural areas	30

[a] For regional recreation areas of 500 acres or more located within one hour's drive of major centers of urban population. Inter-County Regional Planning Commission, *Recreation in the Denver Region* (Denver, Colorado: The Commission, July, 1958).

[b] For regional parks within 30 minutes' drive from centers of population. Detroit Metropolitan Area Regional Planning Commission, *Regional Recreational Lands Plan* (Detroit, Michigan: The Commission, June, 1960).

[c] 7.5 acres for regional parks of 500 to 1,000 acres each within 20 miles from home and 7.5 acres for large regional reservations of 1,000 to 5,000 acres each within 40 miles from home. Richmond Regional Planning and Eeconomic Development Commission, *Open Spaces in the Richmond Region* (Richmond, Virginia: The Commission, January, 1960), p. 7.

[d] 12 acres of county parks per 1,000 persons, or at least 5 percent of the county area to allow for population growth beyond that projected for 1985. Regional Plan Association, *The Race for Open Space* (New York: The Association), pp. 143-45.

Source: U. S. Department of the Interior, Bureau of Outdoor Recreation, *Guidebook for State Outdoor Recreation Planning* (Washington, D. C.: Government Printing Office, 1964), p. 47.

found that: (1) only 20 counties had more than 10 acres per 1,000 of the 1960 population and (2) the average for all 51 counties was only 8.7 acres per 1,000 or approximately one half of its commonly accepted standard of 15 acres per 1,000, as indicated in Table 15. Table 16 gives some common standards for county parks.

Tables 5 and 6 in Appendix D list the results of the NRPA survey and present a representative sample of existing standards for regional or county parks. A comparison of these tables for only county parks indicates a similar level of attainment. Although the situation is not a favorable one in regard to national attainment of these standards, there are many who feel that this is not as critical as the shortage in the central cities. Clawson equates the suburbs with high-income levels and states:

> People from the very highest income levels may not use public park and recreation areas extensively . . . but this seems to be true . . . in part, they can substitute their own home or private club areas.[61]

STATE AND FEDERAL LEVEL

Very little data and almost no standards are available for the state and federal level largely because the traditional emphasis has been on resource-oriented areas for which there are no standards. However, some states have begun to equate their recreational opportunities with the space standards recommended by the NRPA and BOR.

In 1965, the NRPA surveyed all states and found that five had more than 65 acres per 1,000 of the 1960 population. Considering the 48 coterminus states as a unit, there are 32.4 acres of state park per 1,000 of the 1960 population and 268.1 acres of state forest and other lands for a total of 300.5 acres of state-owned open space per 1,000 of the 1960 population. The areas comprise 2.8 percent of the total land area of the 48 states. These statistics are shown in Table 7 of Appendix D. Estimates based on 1970 census data show no substantial increase in these ratios.

Again, the average attainment is approximately one half of the recommended standards; this coincides with a similar deficiency found at the local and county levels of government. There is reason to believe that this may be even greater at the state level because much of the area included in the total and averages is inaccessible or undeveloped for recreational use. A conservative estimate for

---

[61] Clawson, *Land and Water for Recreation*, p. 20.

attainment of state standards would place them at approximately 25 percent of the desired level.

Reasons for Nonattainment

Several possible reasons are commonly given for the nonattainment of space standards. At face value, most appear to be valid, but on closer examination some of these rationales are open to question. This section summarizes the traditional rationales for nonattainment and offers a concise criticism of these with reference to the inner city.

CONFLICTING GOALS AND OBJECTIVES

This is the most nebulous rationale. Gans devotes his landmark study to exploring the conflicting goals between the user, supplier and community decision-makers and concludes:

> There is a need to reshape the method of planning in the direction of an applied social science . . . which can integrate values of many . . . in a goal oriented approach to recreation planning for leisure behavior.[62]

Gans studies the expressed and latent goal differences between many groups, but focuses on the community decision-makers, supplier and user for his detailed analysis. An overview of his findings is listed in Table 10. These differences will be discussed and applied in Chapters VI and VII.

LACK OF RESOURCES

The proverbial rationale for not attaining a given standard is the lack of human, fiscal or natural resources. To some extent this can be justified, but there are some who believe that existing standards may not be *realistic* in relationship to these resources and should be revised or eliminated from the planning process. Clawson is one of the more forthright critics of this rationale. He believes:

> Cities of all types and sizes have difficulty providing adequate park and recreation area for their residents. Part of this difficulty is financial, but only part; parks and recreation must compete with many other essential services for the limited tax revenues available. But there is also the problem of suitable open area available for public

---

[62] Gans, "Recreation Planning for Leisure Behavior," pp. 735-739.

purchase and use. In the older and densely settled parts of the larger cities, it would be simply impossible to meet these standards, regardless of cost. For instance to meet this standard for the population of Manhattan would exceed the area of the island itself.[63]

Clawson argues his point with an example:

> In 1955, there were over 20,000 city parks in the United States with about ¾ million acres of land. . . . If even the minimal standard of ten acres had been applied to all cities, then 2 million acres of city parks would be required to meet this standard . . . with the population in prospect, by 2000 as much as 5 million acres of city parks would be required. It is most improbable that any such area can be provided.[64]

The lack of human resources generally refers to either a shortage or ineffective use of professionally trained staff and leadership to build, maintain and provide programs at recreation areas. To a large extent this appears to be true if professional personnel are viewed as the only source of staff for the effective operation of a recreation system. But there are some who question the Recreation Movement's emphasis on trained personnel as a means of self-perpetuation and suggest more voluntary leadership as an alternative.[65]

ENCROACHMENT OF EXISTING AREAS

> Throughout our nation today public parks are being chopped down, carved up, invaded or totally scraped away by the relentless blades of the bulldozers. The pace of this destruction is incredibly rapid. . . . There are many forces at work . . . a major one is the interstate highway program, which alone will consume some two million park acres.[66]

One valid and often invisible rationale for the nonattainment of standards is encroachment, defined as "the unjustified diversion, loss of, modification of, reduction in size or condition of any public park and recreation land, or water area or facility."[67] A national

---

[63] Clawson, *Land and Water for Recreation,* p. 20.

[64] *Ibid.*

[65] Goodale, "The Fallacy of Our Programs."

[66] Alfred Balk, "Progress and Parks," *National Civic Review,* October, 1960. Cited in *Current,* March, 1961, p. 57.

[67] Donald F. Sinn, "Encroachment Survey Findings," *Parks and Recreation,* November, 1960, p. 505. This author notes that the term "encroachment" does not apply to planned and acceptable changes in park land which are advantageous to the park and recreation system.

survey to determine the nature and extent of encroachment on park land concludes:

> Encroachment is increasing at an alarming rate and shows no sign of diminishing. . . . It shows losses of land and facilities valued conservatively at $9 million. . . . The chief offenders are: highways, private enterprises, schools, other public and quasi-public uses. . . . The major factors are: apparent unavoidability, assumed lower cost of park land compared to other land, failure of the park agency to plan and develop their land, political expediency and ineffectiveness of the recreation-park department.[68]

The recreation space standard when properly rationalized to a given situation could be used as a constructive force to defend many park areas threatened with encroachment. The area of encroachment lacks an adequate data base, but there is some evidence to identify it as a cause for the nonattainment of standards.

TIME AND SCALE DISCREPANCIES

This justification has already been discussed in several other contexts, but is identified here as a major reason for the nonattainment of standards. The statistical confusion it presents becomes an obstacle to understanding and implementation of plans or programs. Most standards do not have explicit considerations of time and scale while those few that do are too absolute for effective use in a rapidly changing Urban America. Moreover, this inflexibility often contributes to the loss of pending opportunities and discourages innovation.

SUMMARY OF COMMON REASONS

This summary is an overview of all previous discussion on standards and the basis of an alternative planning approach to be described in Chapter VI. It is aimed at the way the standard is typically used in the planning process and includes these 15 points which are *general* indictments, subject to *exception:*

1. Standards are not based on explicit goals being achieved through tested means. They are based on informally developed approximations or arbitrary judgments intended as guides, but expressed as authoritative requirements by planners, suppliers and community decision-makers.

---

[68] *Ibid.*, pp. 505-507.

2. Standards are quantified statements of an ideal recreation system or experience as viewed by the suppliers.

3. Although standards are stated as means to attain social goals, there is no evidence that this is true. More often than not, the standards become the goals of the supplier rather than the user groups or community which they serve.

4. The planner who applies standards indiscriminately takes each facility as an end in itself. The good area, facility or system is defined in terms of its adequacy with existing standards, regardless of whether these facilities contribute to the achievement of other ends which the community may hold to be important.

5. Because of the facility orientation of most standards, there is little concern for user behavior. The plans which evolve from this bias are based on the goals of individuals or interest groups primarily concerned with public recreation facilities.

6. The goals of these interest groups are expressed in quantitative terms which make them subject to acceptance, rejection or revision, but not to analysis that permits the consideration of alernative goals. They usually narrow planning to only what is given in the standards.

7. Standards are not appropriate to the development of priority decisions between different kinds of recreation facilities or between other municipal functions.

8. The NRPA standards, and those based on them, are essentially the goals of an organization devoted to advancing the cause of public recreation. Since they are costly to implement, these standards have a built-in or self-fulfilling priority determination with respect to the allocation of public resources.

9. The allocation of resources potentially available for other social needs is automatically reduced when recreation standards, which may be unattainable, are applied without discretion.

10. Standards presume judgment about the recreation experience, residential environment and public goals or objectives which have no empirical basis.

11. Because most standards are national in origin, they make no allowance for differences between communities. Thus, poorer communities aspire to the same goals as richer ones, despite the likelihood that they cannot afford to implement these goals, the possibility that their residents may have different goals, and the probability that existing conditions may require a different set of priorities for allocating resources. Here, standards can be an impediment rather than an aid in helping to solve community problems.

12. Standards do not make it possible to consider differences between areas of the community and the varying demands, behavioral patterns or cultural characteristics of users or residents in these respective areas.

13. Standards can and often do inhibit the function of the planner. Since all decision points are predetermined, there is no opportunity for innovation, imagination, demonstration, research or the application of new insights.

14. Because the plans resulting from most standards provide only facilities desired by the supplier, other techniques such as program must be designed to make them attractive to potential users. Program is justified, but should not be used to substitute for major shortcomings due to inappropriate standards.

15. Standards are only a quantitative statement of an ideal system or facility. They do not provide tools for implementation or generally motivate public involvement in the planning process.

IMPLICATIONS OF CURRENT STANDARDS

The implications of continuing to use inappropriate space standards constitute a critical area in recreation planning. The literature indicates almost no research on this topic with the exception of writings by Gans who dwells primarily on the goal implications. To measure the future quantitative and qualitative national consequences of standards is beyond the objectives of this book. However, it is an area for speculation with reference to the inner city and the immediate future.

Economic Growth

COST OF IMPLEMENTING STANDARDS

The national cost of implementing a standard of 10 acres per 1,000 population in the inner city is estimated at $37.5 billion.*

---

* Gans indicates the cost of acquisition and development for an acre of playground in built-up residential areas in 1955 with net densities of 180 or more persons per net acre to be $220,000 per acre. ("Recreation Planning for Leisure Behavior," pp. 457-467.) At 1970 prices these figures for land and development are conservatively estimated at $250,000 per acre for either a park or playground. Thus $250,000 × 150,000 acres = $37.5 billion.

This is a conservative estimate of what it would cost to acquire and redevelop 150,000 acres* of inner city land into effective neighborhood recreation areas. It does not include the additional cost of staff, program, leadership and maintenance for these areas nor does it include the social cost of relocating displaced persons. These items might place the possible cost of implementing existing standards in the vicinity of $50 billion or approximately 100 times the $500 million now being spent on the Model Cities Program.

BENEFITS OF IMPLEMENTING STANDARDS

If it were possible, a national investment of $50 billion to provide outdoor recreation opportunities in the inner city might have a considerable social benefit in terms of recreation and some economic impact on adjacent property values. This assumes that people would use these facilities and that the nation or inner city had no other priorities such as health, safety, education, jobs, environmental pollution and a host of other public services which generally outrank recreation on any priority scale of human needs.

Even if recreation were deemed to be a national priority, it would be imperative to explore the many leisure alternatives to this type of investment in land, facilities and program. Assuming the beginnings of an accepted program for birth control and family size of four individuals, a $50 billion investment could be viewed as a $10,000 investment per family. This sum might be used to provide any number of leisure experiences other than traditional parks or playgrounds to include: individual backyards, public commons, educational television, family vacations, cultural museums, ethnic theaters and private development of urban leisure opportunities. All of these possibilities might provide leisure experiences equal to, or better than, those generally provided by most inner city parks.

---

* Land area is based on an estimated 1970 inner city population of 20 million people (see Chapter III). At a standard of 10 acres per 1,000 population this would imply that 200,000 acres are needed. The amount of existing park land in all American cities over 10,000 population in 1970 is estimated at 1 million acres. An estimated 5 percent of this land is in the inner city of 25 SMSA's with populations of over 1 million in 1970 (see Table 8, Appendix D). Thus, 5 percent $\times$ 1 million acres = 50,000 acres. This area subtracted from the projected immediate need indicates a "deficiency" of 150,000 acres.

Social Change

URBAN VIOLENCE

The prospect of continuing alienation and civil disorder in the inner city seems apparent until constructive programs are implemented to relieve some of the inner city's critical problems. One cause of this alienation has been identified as a lack of recreational opportunities. This can be related to a relatively indiscriminate use of recreation standards in the inner city. The question is one of both quantity and quality. There is some rationale to justify the lack of quantity, but very little to justify the application of upper- and middle-class standards to activities or facilities for lower-class users. This implies that what little area is available, or could be made available, would probably not be effective because it would not meet the needs of most inner city populations.

The continued insensitive use of space standards in a planning process already resented by some inner city residents who have too few opportunities for constructive participation could have a severe impact on the public image of recreation, a negative effect on any value recreation might be able to contribute to individual users, and might be one of the contributing factors to urban violence.

ENVIRONMENTAL CHANGE

One implication of the continued use of existing standards in the inner city is more of the same type of public leisure opportunities. Here there is a serious question of how something which has not proven effective in the past can now have a positive effect on the corrosive physical and social environment of the inner city. There is no evidence to indicate that the problems of the inner city are primarily environmental, nor is there any reason to assume that 10 acres per 1,000 population is any better or worse than 5 or 15 acres.

Research is needed to determine what, if any, standard is relevant to the inner city. The continued use of an absolute standard might have a restraining influence on needed innovation in the use of space for environmental change. Perhaps *less* but more functional open space would be *more* effective than simply *more* open space; the same might apply for the leisure experience which would utilize these spaces.

CHANGING NEIGHBORHOODS

Nothing characterizes the inner city more than change. The continued use of relatively static standards with no dynamic time or space horizons can do little to accommodate change. Studies indicate that some areas in the central city now experience a change in racial patterns which can be measured in blocks per month.[69] Within the inner city, change is even more frequent when shifting economic opportunities, urban renewal, natural aging and a host of other variables cause one population to replace another.

Any standard which has not been receptive to the changing neighborhood is working against its intended purpose. The playground designed for white middle-class residents of the inner city in 1900 may no longer be relevant to the 1970 population. Moreover, a standard adopted to accommodate these populations today may not be relevant to the population five years or even one year hence. This is not an easy problem to solve, but it must be acknowledged for its social implications.

The Political Process

The thrust of politics in the inner city is toward more self-determination. This implies a greater degree of citizen participation in the planning process and more citizen review and selection of standards which should reflect citizen's goals and objectives. The continued practice of labeling standards "guidelines," but seldom varying them to meet the values of the population group for which they were intended, is capricious and undemocratic. It reflects an authoritarian approach to planning which may be a violation of constitutional rights to representation, equality and opportunity. The continued use of arbitrary standards may have significant political implications in these areas.

ADVOCACY PLANNING

Trends in the inner city point to disillusionment with traditional city planning and project a move toward some form of advocacy planning. The lack of effective recreational opportunities coupled with the continued practice of utilizing standards will probably alien-

---

[69] Downs, "The Future of American Ghettos," p. 2.

ate neighborhood groups and prompt them to adopt an advocate-planning approach for the provision of recreation facilities.

PUBLIC SUPPORT OF RECREATION

The continued use of insensitive recreation standards may become a contributing factor to a growing lack of political support for outdoor recreation. If people do not feel that they are involved in a constructive manner in the planning process by review and selection of their own standards, there is good reason to believe that they will not be motivated to support plans and funds necessary to implement these plans. Hence, the standard, in an unconscious way, may be undermining the very support the Recreation Movement needs, if it is to serve the public effectively.

FEDERAL AID FOR URBAN AREAS

Outwardly there would seem to be little relationship between the use of the recreation standard and federal aid, but it is possible to speculate on the effect that this can have on the equitable allocation of resources. For example, if the *same* standard is used to justify need for a suburban and inner city area, there is a built-in bias in resource allocation. The suburban area, which needs relatively less, obtains more aid, while the inner city, which needs substantially more, obtains proportionately less. One might argue that the suburb contributes more, hence, it should receive more and vice versa for the inner city. But, this argument becomes specious in terms of the expressed national goal of seeking a "quality of life" for *everyone*.

Outdoor Recreation Experience

In the final analysis, the continued use of space standards can have a negative effect on the total recreation experience, especially in the three areas discussed in the following paragraphs.

USER SATISFACTION

Although there has been no national study to indicate any trend in user satisfaction, observations of recreation use and the growing private leisure market indicate that many who use public recreation areas have very little choice or are dissatisfied with the general quality of the experience. A number of writers have referred to the growing congestion, inadequate range of facilities and generally

unimaginative or inappropriate character of many urban public recreation areas. The indiscriminate use of standards can be traced as
one of the possible causes and effects of this problem.

USER PREFERENCE

Another implication of standards is evident in the area of user
preference. There is reason to believe that the best and most effective use of limited urban open space is not for golf courses or
baseball diamonds, yet these continue as conspicuous consumers of
available land. The values and standards of the Recreation Movement may have assumed public preference for these facilities over
others such as creative playgrounds, nature interpretation, community gardens or any number of other activities. The ultimate
implication of this possible distortion of user preference may be
the decline of public recreation to a point where only those who
have no alternative will depend on it for a leisure experience. This
would imply either a reorientation of the Recreation Movement
toward urban populations who have no alternatives, or the beginning of a new movement which would supersede the traditional
approach to recreation as a public service in this country.

DEMAND DISTRIBUTION

The continued arbitrary use of recreation standards can have dis-
ruptive effects on the distribution of demand to available supply and
further strain an already overused system to the breaking point. The
disproportionate allocation of recreation resources in regard to demographic and geographic variables can so diminish the degree of user
satisfaction that it will ultimately compound both the problems of
nonuse and overuse of areas.

The implication of continuing to over-allocate in some areas and
under-allocate in others can distort demand analyses, especially
where standards are used to allocate more on the basis of participation rates. This usually results in those with more obtaining more,
while those with less receive nothing based on any system of priorities. This dilemma is not easily solved, but must be acknowledged
as one of the pitfalls in the current and continued use of standards.

Basic and Applied Research

Beyond the above implications is a need to initiate and pursue
meaningful research on the past, present and future effectiveness

of traditional standards and any possible alternatives. Almost every reference to standards makes an apology for a lack of substantiation and a plea for additional research. However, the record reveals little or no follow-through. The continued use of existing standards could have serious implications on needed research in these areas.

LACK OF EXPERIMENTAL ALTERNATIVES

Research is one approach to problem-solving. Experimentation requires a range of alternatives to test, analyze and evaluate. The lack of *alternative* standards currently being recommended by organizations that should be most interested in innovation, e.g., NRPA, BOR, leaves the researcher with relatively few alternatives to study. More important, it narrows the range of choice for applying research to action programs, e.g., the decision-maker, supplier and user.

The NRPA believes that its standards are "reasonable" or "feasible" because it apparently knows of no alternative that would offer more choice and some rationale for that choice. This is a serious dilemma for the recreation field which is trying to acquire many of the sophisticated traits of the Behavioral Sciences. One way for the field to overcome this shortcoming is to initiate research, even at the risk of exposing itself to criticism. Shivers and Hjelte conclude:

> Some way must be found to determine precise recreational space needs . . . within the urban center. The research instrument for such an undertaking has probably not been designed, nor is it likely to be, unless contemporary city planners and their recreation counterparts, . . . make a radical change in the thinking and direction to which they are now committed.[70]

NEED FOR SOCIAL INDICATORS

The need for social indicators is one vital component in any effort to move society from its preoccupation with "how much" to the nobler horizon of "how good." The social indicator is one means of beginning to deal with the "quality of life" in quantitative as well as qualitative terms. It is a new way to view man, his institutions and the relationship between both and the environment. "Clearly, the implications of the development of social indicators are revolu-

---

[70] Shivers and Hjelte, *Planning Recreational Places,* p. 223.

tionary"[71] and in keeping with Kenneth Boulding's conclusion "that we need a widening of agendas."[72]

The recreation standard might be useful as a social indicator for some aspects of the recreational experience. However, its arbitrary nature and insensitive use make it a marginal and distorted measure of opportunity. There is a possibility of developing and testing more appropriate and sensitive standards which might begin to serve as social indicators.

POSSIBLE NEW STRATEGIES

Despite the criticism directed at the current use of recreation standards in the planning process, these same standards may be a key to several new frontiers in a field which is tradition-oriented and inner-directed. For all of their shortcomings, standards may offer the perceptive researcher or professional a challenging and rewarding opportunity for study and action because they represent one of the few quantitative measures in recreation which can be related to the past, present and future.

The recreation standard can be made more responsive, especially to the needs of the inner city. There is an array of new tools, methodologies and techniques which can now be used to develop and test a new type of recreation standard. The task will not be easy, but it is possible and within the realm of existing professional expertise and technology. What is needed most is financial support and the courage to undertake speculative research.

What may now seem to be an illogical and irrelevant tool in the planning process may become, in time, the catalyst of needed change. If the standard can do this, it has at least justified its existence and moved Urban America toward a better understanding of its recreation problems and potentials.

---

[71] Raymond A. Bauer, Ed., *Social Indicators* (Cambridge: MIT Press, 1966), postscript.

[72] Kenneth E. Boulding, "The Ethics of Rational Decision," *Management Science*, XII (February, 1966), p. 161.

II

Techniques
and
Application

VI

Urban Outdoor Recreation Planning

In this chapter two approaches to urban outdoor recreation planning at the neighborhood scale are described and evaluated. These approaches are based on the information and ideas discussed in previous chapters. Substantiation is minimized in favor of a concise description, analysis and evaluation of how the standard is employed in the planning process. A neighborhood playground is used as an illustration; however, most of these concepts and techniques are common to the provision of many other types of indoor and outdoor recreation facilities in cities and suburbs.

The objective is to develop an alternative to the traditional approach which can correct some of the shortcomings of this approach and be more adaptable to the inner city neighborhood, the times and the future. The alternative or "innovative" approach* is still experimental. It has not been tested or evaluated in a real situation over time. One cannot assume that it can or will be successful in all cases, but it is worth trying even if the shortcomings of the existing approach were the only incentives.

---

* Innovative approach is hereinafter used to represent an alternative to the traditional approach in concept, technique, practice, values and meaning.

TRADITIONAL APPROACH

Concepts and Planning Techniques

There has been a gradual evolution in the traditional approach to outdoor recreation planning. Using the *ORRRC Report* as a chronological turning point in the development and application of commonly accepted concepts and techniques, two major periods can be defined. The main concepts and techniques of each period are outlined here.

PRE-ORRRC REPORT

This period dates back to the beginnings of the Recreation Movement and is the basis of most of the techniques in use today. Basically, it is characterized by an arbitrary, intuitive and relatively absolute approach to planning which does little to acknowledge or be responsive to community goals and objectives, user preference, citizen participation in the planning process, or change. This approach is codified in most existing textbooks on recreation or planning. It is so ingrained in the Recreation Movement that few challenges are recorded prior to 1962 when the *ORRRC Report* identified some shortcomings to this country's traditional approach to outdoor recreation planning.*

Most of the planning associated with the approach is generated by statements such as "just as schools are necessary for public education . . . so recreation areas and facilities are required in order to house recreation programs and services."[1] From this assumption, a classification of areas projecting a range of facilities oriented toward specific age groups, activities or geographic areas is made. The usual hierarchy ranges from the neighborhood tot-lot to a regional recreation area. Most classification tends to separate areas by form and function and isolate rather than integrate them with the environment. It also separates age groups, user groups and activities by design, program and scheduling. After classification, each type of area is subjected to a series of standards, locational concepts and facility requirements.[2] Although every reference reviewed cautions:

---

* These shortcomings are discussed in Chapter II.

[1] Meyer and Brightbill, *Community Recreation*, p. 25.

[2] See Doell, *Park and Recreation Administration*, p. 16, for illustrative example.

Standards are of value only insofar as they are pliable and can be carefully weighed against the needs, interests, resources and peculiar characteristics of the individual community, and even then only up to the point where they are within reach of the community.[3]

Most references and plans adopt these standards on a citywide basis with the following type of rationale:

Certain areas, such as the neighborhood playground and playfield are required in or near every residential neighborhood, and standards as to their size and development have been worked out and widely accepted.[4]

Once the amount of area needed and the location are determined, a detailed site plan is prepared to indicate placement of equipment or layout of areas for various activities. These plans are generally based on principles such as:

(1) to get the maximum use from the land available, (2) to produce an attractive playground viewed from within and without, (3) to simplify the problems of supervision and leadership, (4) to prevent accidents by careful segregation of activities, (5) to keep operating cost low and (6) to keep original construction cost low.[5]

The planning objectives listed by Butler are usually included. These are:

Effective use of the entire site, provision of essential areas and facilities, multiple use, adequate space for the facilities, ease of supervision or operation, utilization of natural features, safety, economy in construction, convenience of people using area and appearance.[6]

Based on these principles and objectives, the neighborhood playground is divided into separate areas by "these essential functions: apparatus play, team games, and sports, activities such as art and crafts and informal individual types of activity."[7] These areas are defined by function in spacial terms as shown in Table 18. Within each of these major subdivisions, each activity, its number of users and spacial requirements are indicated as illustrated in Tables 17 and 19.

---

[3] *Ibid.*, p. 454.
[4] George D. Butler, *Recreation Areas* (New York: A. S. Barnes and Company, 1947), p. 1.
[5] Gilbert Clegg, "Playground Planning and Layout," *Recreation*, June, 1935, cited by Butler, *Recreation Areas*, p. 99.
[6] Butler, *Recreation Areas*, pp. 6-7.
[7] *Ibid.*, p.98.

TABLE 17
Space Standards for Indoor and Outdoor Recreational Activities

Types	Location[a]	Area Required	Acreage Parity (Acres)
Aerial darts	O	30 ft. x 50 ft. (court)	1.50
Archery	O	50 yds. x 150 yds.	0.10
Archery	I	20 yds. x 30 yds.	—
Art	I	20 ft. x 20 ft. (room)	—
Badminton	O	20 ft. x 45 ft. (court)	—
Baseball	O	350 ft. x 400 ft. (diamond)	1.90
Basketball	I/O	50 ft. x 90 ft. (court)	0.10
Bowling	O	130 ft. x 140 ft. (green)	0.30
Cricket	O	150 yds. x 150 yds. (pitch)	3.00
Crafts	I	25 ft. x 40 ft. (room)	—
Croquet	O	30 ft. x 60 ft. (field)	—
Curling	I/O	25 ft. x 165 ft. (rink)	0.10
Drama	I/O	20 ft. x 36 ft. (stage)	—
Equitation	I	50 ft. x 100 ft. (arena)	0.10
Fencing	I	25 ft. x 30 ft. (room)	—
Field events	I	60 yds. x 130 yds. (field house)	1.70
Field events	O	220 ft. x 520 ft. (stadium)	2.30
Field hockey	O	200 ft. x 300 ft. (field)	1.50
Fly casting	I/O	60 ft. x 100 ft. (skish)	0.10
Football	O	160 ft. x 360 ft. (field)	1.60
Golf	I	Practice driving range (cage)	—
Golf	O	18 hole standard links (course)	180.00
Golf	O	9 hole course	60.00
Golf	O	Pitch/putt course	10.00
Gymnastics	I	50 ft. x 60 ft. (arena)	—
Handball	I/O	30 ft. x 40 ft. (court)	—
Hockey rink	I	60 ft. x 165 ft. (rink)	0.15
Horseshoe pitching	I/O	10 ft. x 50 ft. (court)	—
Lacrosse	O	225 ft. x 360 ft. (field)	1.80
Paddleball	I/O	20 ft. x 40 ft. (court)	—
Paddle tennis	I	30 ft. x 60 ft. (court)	—
Pistol range	I/O	150 ft. x 150 ft. (range)	0.50
Polo	O	500 ft. x 600 ft. (field)	6.90
Rifle range	I	50 ft. x 100 ft. (range)	0.10
Roller skating	I	50 ft. x 120 ft. (rink)	0.14

TABLE 17—Continued

Types	Location[a]	Area Required	Acreage Parity (Acres)
Rugby	O	300 ft. x 330 ft. (field)	2.30
Skeet shooting	O	150 ft. x 150 ft. (range)	0.50
Shuffleboard	I/O	6 ft. x 52 ft. (court)	—
Skiing	O	Any appropriate hill	—
Soccer	O	225 ft. x 360 ft. (field)	1.80
Softball	O	275 ft. x 275 ft. (diamond)	1.80
Swimming	I/O	50 ft. x 165 ft. (olympic course)	0.15
Swimming	I/O	42 ft. x 75 ft. (short course)	—
Stadium	O	450 ft. x 600 ft. (stadium)	6.00
Tennis	O	60 ft. x 110 ft. (court)	0.11
Trap shooting	O	200 ft. x 300 ft. (range)	1.10
Volleyball	I/O	30 ft. x 60 ft. (court)	—

[a] I means indoors, O means outdoors.

From Jay S. Shivers and George Hjelte, *Planning Recreational Places* (Cranbury, N. J.: Fairleigh Dickinson University Press, 1971), p. 130.

TABLE 18
Space Requirements for a Neighborhood Playground

Name of Division	Suggested Space (Square Feet)	
Preschool-age children	5,000	10,000
Apparatus area	4,000	8,000
Wading pool area	5,000	10,000
Free play and game area	10,000	25,000
Multiple-use paved area	20,000	30,000
Field games area	120,000	180,000
Quiet activities area	6,000	10,000
Older adults area	3,000	5,000
Shelter house	4,000	8,000
Landscape area	10,000	20,000
Total square feet	187,000	306,000
Total acres	4.29[a]	7.0[b]

[a] Suggested for a neighborhood of 3,000 people.
[b] Suggested for a neighborhood of between 5,000 and 6,000 people.

From George D. Butler, *Recreation Areas* (New York: A. S. Barnes and Company, 1947), p. 11.

TABLE 19
Space Requirements for Children's Play Area

Recreational Activity	Use Dimensions (Feet)	Space Required (Square Feet)	No. of Players
Archery	50 x 135	6,750	2+
Baseball	50 x 235	62,500	18
Basketball	50 x 75	3,500	10
Field hockey	150 x 250	37,500	22
Hopscotch	10 x 20	200	2–4
Horseshoes	12 x 40	480	2–4
Marbles	18 x 18	324	2–6
Paddle tennis	25 x 60	1,500	2
Soccer	125 x 240	30,000	22
Softball	175 x 175	30,625	18
Speedball	150 x 260	39,000	22
Dodge ball	60 x 60	3,600	20
Touch football	140 x 280	39,200	22
Volleyball	40 x 70	2,800	16

From George D. Butler, *Recreation Areas* (New York: A. S. Barnes and Company, 1947), p. 97.

Suggested types of apparatus are recommended "as the minimum standards for the *average* playground" with the usual caution: "it is recognized that it often becomes necessary to adapt the standard to meet local conditions and special needs" and the usual disclaimer: "the apparatus listed, however, is believed to include the various types having the *greatest* value."[8] Table 20 illustrates this technique. Appendix E, Tables 1 through 4 represent the latest recommended standards and Table 5 describes some current and authoritative "principles" and "standards" of recreation planning.

With reference to innovation or alternatives, statements of the following type are common in many references:

> Communities equipping playgrounds may well be guided by the committee's suggestions [Table 20] and install primarily the kinds of apparatus that have *proved* their worth. . . . The *newer* and less standard types therefore merit *careful* investigation.[9]

Implicit in this common technique is a self-righteous approach to planning which usually exhibits a conspicuous lack of citizen

8 *Ibid.*, p. 20. (Emphasis added.)

9 *Ibid.* (Emphasis added.)

TABLE 20
Minimum Standards for the Average Playground

Age Group	Apparatus Standard
Children of preschool age (under 6 years)	Chair swings (6) Sand box (1) Small slide (1) Simple climbing device (1)
Children of elementary school age (6-12 years)	Frame swings (6) Slide (1) Horizontal ladder (1) Giant stride (1) Balance beam (1) Horizontal bar (1)
Optional — if available funds, space and attendance justify	Traveling rings (1) Seesaws (4) Low climbing device (1)

From George D. Butler, *Recreation Areas* (New York: A. S. Barnes and Company, 1947), p. 20.

involvement, knowledge of user behavior, community goals or objectives and a narrow view of who is to do the planning. Statements such as "it is recommended that the plan be prepared by a competent landscape architect, if possible, in order to assure a good design as well as an effective use of the area"[10] or "as finally adopted the plan should be acceptable to the recreation authorities who are responsible for the operation of the area"[11] reflect a supplier instead of user orientation to planning.

With reference to the inner city, this approach not only dismisses the variables of the inner city as contrasted with other areas, but compounds the already arbitrary use of standards for the inner city by suggesting that citywide standards *avoid* these variables.

> Most of the largest cities over 100,000 population have slums, but the problem of creating recreational areas in slum districts must be regarded as peculiar to such districts. . . . In endeavoring to arrive at standards for general application to urban communities, it would be well to consider conditions which are not extraordinary or peculiar to areas of extreme congestion.[12]

[10] *Ibid.*, p. 5.
[11] *Ibid.*, p. 6.
[12] George Hjelte and Jay S. Shivers, *Public Administration of Park and Recreational Services* (New York: MacMillan Company, 1963), p. 129.

There is little question that this period was characterized by an intuitive, if not arbitrary, set of concepts and techniques which had no apparent rationale other than constant qualification as guidelines or minimums, but soon became adopted as desirables. Areas such as leisure behavior, community goals, alternatives, social or physical change of neighborhoods, user satisfaction, activity preferences, design innovation and benefit-cost analysis were generally not visible in this era. Also there is no evidence of anyone, except Gans, seriously questioning the "state of the art" during this period.

POST-ORRRC REPORT

This period is characterized by a reliance on most of the concepts and techniques of the previous period with several additions. Outdoor recreation was recognized as a component of leisure and codified in bureaucratic jargon by such terms as "demand," "participation rates" and "visitor days." The idea of visualizing recreation as an "experience" instead of an activity became accepted. A new way of classifying areas which integrated instead of separating their form and function came into use.[13] Existing areas began to be viewed as components of a "system." The concept of government responsibilities for different types of recreation became evident. A clear distinction was made between a "user" and "resource" oriented type of area and this was related to administrative responsibility*

The research effort necessary to prepare the ORRRC Report was the source of a number of questions directed at the use of standards in the planning process. There was also some frank criticism of the traditional approach to resource allocation and some recommendations for making the process more responsive to human needs.

These developments changed the "state of the art" from one quantitative technique to another. Arbitrary standards, e.g., 10 acres per 1,000 population, were replaced with sophisticated demand estimates based on population, income, mobility and leisure time. User surveys became popular to determine activity preferences which were translated into "demand" with an array of intricate calculations or elegant models. The results were projected in amounts of time, space and users.

---

[13] BOR Classification System. See Guidebook for State Outdoor Recreation Planning, 1964.

* These concepts are discussed in depth in Chapters II, III and V. See Glossary for definitions of these terms.

Traditional standards were applied to relate existing or projected demand to the supply of opportunities in the public sector to determine future needs which, in some cases, were projected to the year 2020! The product of this effort was an impressive display of statistics which supported or became the self-fulfilling objectives of suppliers, but had a questionable relationship to the user and reality.

On the surface, these planning concepts and techniques seemed deceptively simple, sensitive and appropriate to the nation's growing capability and fascination with computers. To some degree, they were justified because of the large amounts of data and number of variables associated with outdoor recreation. But some people began to seriously question the relevance and effectiveness of this quantitative approach to planning.

In 1968 a National Short Course on Elements of Outdoor Recreation Planning devoted a good share of its effort to questioning the legacy of the *ORRRC Report* and the relevance of its recommendations to the present and future. Many of the papers presented reflected skepticism concerning this report's narrow and quantitative approach to recreation planning and raised serious doubts about the consequences of continued reliance on distorted data instead of needed innovation. Wise states:

> Haven't we too often confused needs with past behavior and trends — and, in turn, confused trends with policy. Haven't we, in fact, sought to turn our backs on innovation and creativeness, in the name of a bunch of punch cards and so-called research efforts that in all reality lead one nowhere but to an extra fifty pages of gobbledygook which is supposed to prop up the conclusions that we either had before or had to dream up after we found that the research led to no logical conclusion at all . . . and all in the name of a federal grant.[14]

Davis amplifies this theme:

> It has been customary to base the causes of the so-called "Recreation Explosion" on four changes in our society [population, leisure, income, mobility]. Once these four changes have been identified, the recreation planners then usually start collecting masses of data which, in fact, appear to prove the validity of [these changes].[15]

---

[14] Harold F. Wise, "The State of the Art of Comprehensive Planning" (paper Recreation Short Course, 1968) pp. 2-3. Edited paper published in Driver, *Elements of Outdoor Recreation Planning*, pp. 225-234.

[15] Hugh C. Davis, "Technological Change and Recreation Planning," in Driver, *Elements of Outdoor Recreation Planning*, p. 113.

He describes the current planning process:

> Fascinating new computer programs were produced by equally fascinated computer programmers. . . . The amount of data that can be and is being processed in this fashion is truly staggering . . . the per unit cost of this information is extremely low. . . . Under the circumstances the urge to ask the machine more questions is almost irresistible. . . . However, the time to ask the questions is *before* the whole process gets under way.[16]

With reference to the inner city, Davis states:

> There seems to be a national myth that if something is "public" it is available to all. Only in the most theoretical sense is this true. for in reality, thousands of public recreation areas are well beyond the reach of the *poor*, the uneducated, the old and the infirm. Yet countless recreation plans ignore this fact and perpetuate the myth.[17]

He criticizes the traditional approach to urban recreation planning:

> For the past half century most outdoor recreation planning has focused on serving educated, white, young middle-class Americans. . . . Their values have been accommodated. It is difficult to call this comprehensive planning.[18]

Davis also describes "how the ORRRC Commission was directed by Congress to exclude consideration of *urban* recreation and . . . make recommendations for the provision of recreation for all people." He explains how "the [middle-class] myth was perpetuated by this contradiction" and how "major expenditures under the Land and Water Conservation Fund seem to follow this same naive belief." He asks these provocative questions:

> If outdoor recreation is for *all* the people should we not place greater effort on planning recreation for people *in* our cities? Should not recreation today be considered more an urban problem than a rural and natural resource problem? Should not the Bureau of Outdoor Recreation be moved to the Department of Housing and Urban Development? Should not our universities be training city planners in recreation as well as traffic circulation? . . . I suggest that the real recreation problems are where the *people* are.[19]

---

16 *Ibid.* (Emphasis added.)
17 Hugh C. Davis, "A Comprehensive Recreation Plan for the City" (paper presented at the annual meeting of the American Nature Study Society, New York, December 28, 1967), p. 1. (Emphasis added.)
18 *Ibid.*, p. 2.
19 *Ibid.*, p. 3. (Emphasis added.)

There is a growing awareness of shortcomings in the traditional approach to urban recreation planning. This awareness has developed despite the recent adoption of more sophisticated techniques which have lifted the traditional approach above the base level of "standards planning" to a seemingly *less* sensitive approach based on illogical assumptions, irrelevant data, a generation of ingrained recreation plans based on these assumptions and a government agency (BOR) dedicated to supporting all of this. Many of the possible advantages of the period ushered in by the *ORRRC Report* and the current trend toward more sophisticated methodologies in all areas of planning may not be effective to help solve present and future problems without drastic revision or the adoption of an *alternative* approach to planning.

Commonly Accepted Rationales

The more commonly accepted rationales used to defend the traditional approach to urban outdoor recreation planning are intriguing to study because they have no basis in fact. Some rationales seem to defy common logic and reason, yet they persist despite some of the questions raised in the foregoing paragraphs and others which will be raised here. For convenience, these rationales are classified into five related areas.

GUIDELINE SYNDROME

No rationale of the traditional approach is more conspicuous than the use of standards as "guidelines" or "minimums." However, widespread professional practice and the literature point out how and why most *minimum* standards used as guidelines soon become *desirable* goals and measures of adequacy. There is little question about these relationships, but there is question about why the semantics of "minimum" and "guideline" are so often used when something else is intended. One explanation and criticism of this condition is expressed by Wise:

> Maybe, we planners need some serious lessons in the fine art of semantics and logic. Today there is in planning a crying need for directness, for simplicity, for honesty, for confidence in one's self and in what one does, and for the need of exposing sham, particularly intellectual sham.[20]

---

[20] Wise, "State of the Art of Comprehensive Planning," p. 225.

Conversely, there is some political wisdom in holding to standards as guidelines because this allows what appears to be maximum flexibility and minimum opposition if and when priorities must be changed. In a pluralistic society governed by a partisan system which often changes, the guideline syndrome is valid. However, this does not imply that the guidelines for each community or neighborhood be the *same*, which is so often the case.

UNIFORMITY AND EQUALITY

This commonly accepted rationale is grounded in the "myth of uniformity and equality of opportunity."* The uniform recreation standard is often noted as one way of insuring *everyone* an *equal* distribution of public goods and services. However, it usually becomes a guise for distorting the allocation of resources in both a political and practical sense. This guise often results in those with more receiving more of the same, while those with less receive nowhere near what they realistically need. Davis states:

> The place to start [in planning] is to recognize and fully accept the implications of the fact that the city holds a wide spectrum of social, economic, racial and intellectual backgrounds. The recreation program [plan] should reflect this diversity and be equally broad.[21]

Sessoms focuses the inequity of the traditional approach on the poor:

> The relationship of urban poverty and urban blindness-to-poverty is too often overlooked in recreation planning, for those who provide recreation often assume everyone is like them. Recreation areas are planned primarily for the mobile middle-class which comprise 65 percent of this population, but what about the other 35 percent, especially the 40 million [20 percent] who are referred to by Harrington as the "economically deprived."[22]

Sessoms supports Davis and makes a plea against the continued rationalization of equality:

> They [the poor], too, have recreation desires and require special understanding when planning for their facilities and opportunities.

---

* See Chapter III for a discussion of "the myth of equality."
[21] Davis, "A Comprehensive Recreation Plan for the City," p. 5.
[22] Sessoms, "New Bases for Recreation Planning," p. 30. Reference is to Harrington, *The Other America*.

Their needs also serve as a reminder of the *inflexibility* and *questionable use* of current facility standards which do not take into consideration the role and impact of such variables as economic, residence, age, race, and educational attainment.[23]

Beyond the lack of social and economic awareness evident in any rationale for uniform standards are the physical dimensions of change, diversity, density, environment and the real estate market which contribute to a dynamic inequality in the physical and social nature of most cities. To rationalize standards for the purpose of uniformity and *not* acknowledge these variables is illogical. Moreover, it compounds the irrelevance of the traditional planning approach to the inner city where the physical environment is both a cause and effect of social decay.

ADMINISTRATIVE EXPEDIENCY

Although most standard texts on planning or recreation indicate that detailed surveys should be made prior to the application of standards to determine needs, this stage in the traditional approach to recreation planning is often treated superficially or omitted for expediency and a lack of resources or survey techniques. Political intuition and the supplier's values often prevail over analytical techniques. The administrator or planner usually seeks the most expedient concept and technique to help rationalize his recommendations, which are generally based on standards developed by someone else for a different situation.

The short-term effect of this rationalization is usually negligible. In the name of "progress" and the urge to accomplish something, few question the concepts or methodology used to determine needs. There is no record in the literature of anyone (except Gans and Sessoms) realistically questioning either his own or other's standards. This implies that most standards are either adequate or no professional is willing to evaluate them.

Criticism of this rationale should be viewed in the larger context of metropolitan government where administrative expediency is a common reason for many similar decisions. Although outdoor recreation is part of a much larger and more complex decision-making process, already strained by pressing needs and a lack of resources, this does not excuse the continued use of this rationale. On the contrary, it should be all the more reason for *not* using it.

---

[23] *Ibid.* (Emphasis added.)

PUBLIC ACCEPTANCE

There is developing evidence to indicate that what is often expressed as "public acceptance" is usually acceptance by the suppliers of outdoor recreation and the organizations which represent them. Gans proves this by indicating a wide difference between user and supplier goals. The rationale of precedent is often based on an abstract comparison with other communities and the nation. Many communities use this device to justify their budget requests for land, facilities and program. "The very unattainability of the standards provides them with the useful function of persuading municipal decision makers of the need to increase allocations towards a far distant goal of adequacy."[24]

With regard to precedent, Sessoms believes that "recreation planning innovations are at a premium."[25] Gans supports this with his conclusion that the field of recreation is inner directed and supplier oriented. Standards created over 50 years ago are still in common use today. Statements such as "the needs and role of the metropolitan area are basically the same today as 100 years ago"[26] still appear in the recreation literature. These are visible evidence of either a relative lack of innovation or reliance on precedent.

There is little question that one rationale for not attempting alternative approaches to recreation planning is professional reluctance or indifference to innovation and this may have ominous implications. For example, Sebastian DeGrazia told recreation planners that "it is too bad you people are part of a dying profession." He explains this as the profession's "lack of historical insight and willingness to innovate."[27]

LACK OF ALTERNATIVES

This rationale is often used to unconsciously summarize the preceding rationales. It is offered with humility and generally followed with a challenge or commitment to seek alternatives by additional research. It is well-meant and valid where available resources

---

[24] Gans, "Recreation Planning for Leisure Behavior," p. 415.

[25] Sessoms, "New Bases for Recreation Planning," p. 30.

[26] William L Landahl, "Park Standards, Open Space and Quality," *Trends in Parks and Recreation*, XV, No. 1 (January, 1968), p. 21.

[27] Sebastian DeGrazia, "Some Reflections on the History of Outdoor Recreation" (paper, Recreation Planning Short Course, 1968), p. 1. Edited paper in Driver, *Elements of Outdoor Recreation Planning*, pp. 89-97.

and techniques discourage experimentation. However, there have been adequate resources and techniques to attempt this type of research since the 1960 Census of Population and since 1962, when the Bureau of Outdoor Recreation was established.

To date no federal agency or national organization has realistically attempted to develop an alternative to the current use of arbitrary standards in the planning process. What appears worse is that both the NRPA and BOR continue to defend their traditional concepts and techniques and are not sponsoring a significant research effort to develop alternatives.* This infers that there is no possible alternative or perhaps that these institutions may be incapable of this effort, tradition-oriented or self-serving. I do not accept these possible inferences and will later illustrate how and why an alternative is both possible and desirable.

Relevance and Effectiveness

It is difficult to establish any positive relevance or attribute any effectiveness to the traditional approach to urban outdoor recreation planning, especially with reference to the inner city. If any reasons exist for a continuation of status quo other than the lack of an alternative, they are not apparent in the literature. In this section, some shortcomings of the traditional approach to planning will be discussed from a standpoint of their relevance and effectiveness to the present inner city. At best, the picture is a sober one.

Relevance and effectiveness are used as relative criteria to evaluate the traditional approach with reference to urban form and function, leisure behavior, governmental responsibility, community organization, the planning process and the residents of the inner city. The case against the traditional approach is finalized in five key areas.

USER PREFERENCE

There is little agreement in the literature about the effectiveness of user preference as a factor in predicting demand. In a positive vein, Reid states:

---

* Based on a review of research catalogs, personal correspondence and interviews with appropriate individuals. If a national research effort exists or is proposed, it is not visible.

Preference studies seek to identify human wants and desires. The optimal methodology remains to be perfected. Nevertheless, recreation researchers are convinced that in a free society . . . expressed preferences provide the best avenue for planning to adequately meet future needs.[28]

Twardzik is more negative:

Any attempt to wholly conceptualize, theorize, or implement the recreation desires of man and the needed facilities and places for recreation from a purely scientific base is not realistic nor logical. The process of relating man, his preferences, and satisfaction to recreation places requires too many of the sensitive qualities of a poet to fit exclusively into a science mold.[29]

The area of preference is clouded with value judgments and a lack of accepted methodology. Nevertheless, there is mounting evidence that if the outdoor recreation user is treated as a consumer, his preferences can be studied and predicted with market theory which basically expresses a relationship between what a consumer expects, wants and is willing to pay for a given commodity.[30] Outdoor recreation may have a unique set of measurement units, but the principles are the same.* It is possible to measure short-term user preferences if one is careful to structure his population sample. Reid elaborates on the common errors of samples in *Outdoor Recreation Preferences* and makes this overriding conclusion to the question "What do users prefer?":

Whatever the selected activity, recreationists prefer to be satisfied . . . that personal enjoyment above all else is the prime concern of the visitor . . . that the visiting group may be visiting the wrong area in terms of its desires is immaterial. If a group's desires are not

---

[28] Leslie M. Reid, "Utilizing User Preferences in Predicting Outdoor Recreation Demand" (paper presented at the National Recreation Research Conference, Pennsylvania State University, Nov. 7-10, 1965), p. 5.

[29] Louis F. Twardzik, "Expanding the User Approach to Recreation Area Planning" (paper presented at the Recreation Lands Conference, Detroit, Michigan, March 28, 1963), p. 3.

[30] See Clawson, *Economics of Outdoor Recreation*, pp. 41-141, ORRRC Report, Study No. 20 and 26, and Robert K. Davis, "Recreation Planning as an Economic Problem," *Natural Resources Journal* (October, 1963), pp. 239-249.

* Measurement units could include such items as: degrees of expectation, increments of psychological recollection, challenge, exhilaration, time instead of money budgets and educational stimulation.

met, there is a likelihood the group will be dissatisfied, regardless of how adequate the area is for its intended function.[31]

Reid also draws these conclusions: "An obvious relationship exists between user satisfaction and the ability of the visitor to fulfill his desires. User satisfaction increases as the ability of the visitor to fulfill his desires increases. . . . The objective of the user's visit is accomplishment of some anticipated action."[32]

Given these relationships, it is specious, to identify the relevance and effectiveness of the traditional approach to planning as a *representative* response to user preference. The practice of applying arbitrary standards to abstract populations does little to respond to expressed or latent preferences. If and where it does provide a response, it is coincidental, and a measure of expressed demand which is *not* preference. Most important, it provides no way of translating preference into a recreation experience in terms of time, space, activities, program, supervision, cost and a number of other critical variables.

Wise summarizes this point when he criticizes the current approach to recreation planning in which "demand" is generally arrived at by measuring participation and preference rates based on household interviews:

> In our experience such surveys don't begin to answer the real gut questions relating to: What kinds of new recreation or . . . where do you put it, or how big should something be, or . . . how should it relate to where people live. . . . We need to be innovative and creative. . . . An extrapolation of past behavior and past demonstrated desires simply isn't enough. . . . The need for a symphony orchestra, for example, in Western Kansas would be found to be zero based upon the needs justification techniques required by the Bureau of Outdoor Recreation simply because there has never been one there before.[33]

In a similar manner, many suburbanites might prefer tennis and inner city residents, horseshoes. This would be translated into needs

---

[31] Leslie M. Reid, *Outdoor Recreation Preferences: A Nationwide Study of User Preferences* (East Lansing, Michigan: an unpublished Ph.D. dissertation from the University of Michigan, June, 1963, p. 183). Note that use of the term "group" implies a family of adults and children in which only one adult member was interviewed.

[32] *Ibid.*

[33] Wise, "State of the Art of Comprehensive Planning," p. 223.

with arbitrary standards to compare supply with demand. The fallacy here is that each population has not had any opportunity to develop or express a preference for other activities because they are unavailable or unknown. Hence, not only are the standards irrelevant, but so is the preference sample that they are based on, especially if no time dimension is evident.

There are many examples of this paradox. The traditional approach to planning does little to respond to user preference in a manner which is both relevant and effective to present and especially future leisure behavior which should be the focus of recreation planning. This may be the cause of many problems in the areas of nonuse, vandalism, overuse and the diminishing quality of a public recreation experience in cities. We have too often looked back instead of ahead in attempting to determine user preference.

COMPREHENSIVE PLANNING

Where comprehensive planning exists the traditional approach to recreation planning and the use of space standards can have a critical role in this process. However, on close examination the relevance of existing standards to comprehensive planning is marginal. Davis summarizes the problem:

> Different elements in an urban population hold very different values concerning leisure. A comprehensive recreation plan for any city should strive to respect these diverse values. . . . Almost by definition a comprehensive recreation plan must involve the total range of facilities. . . . There is no substitute for imagination, empathy and effort.[34]

The guidelines for a model neighborhood in the Demonstration Cities Program state:

> Standards are flexible responses to local conditions and capabilities. They are to be applied in a way which will encourage maximum local initiative and *innovation*, . . . a comprehensive program might consist of . . . a recreation and cultural component concerned with providing a broad range of recreational opportunities both active and passive, public and private, designed to serve the particular interests, tastes, and abilities of area residents.[35]

---

[34] Davis, "A Comprehensive Recreation Plan for the City," p. 8.

[35] American Society of Planning Officials, "HUD's Guide to Model Neighborhoods in Demonstration Cities," *ASPO Newsletter*, XXXIII, No. 2 (February-March, 1967), p. 24. (Emphasis added.)

Although both statements imply a very discrete use of standards in the comprehensive planning process, the record indicates that this is not the case.* In almost any sense, the traditional approach to recreation planning can be considered comprehensive only for a relative minority of the population and irrelevant or ineffective for the majority. This raises the question of "comprehensive planning and social responsibility" detailed by Webber:

> Since we are a long way from achieving equal opportunity, our plans must account for wide variations in degrees of freedom and in capacities to consume. Poverty and the deprivations of racial minority groups persist as the most pressing social issues. . . . They call for an all-out reappraisal of programmatic priorities and for imaginative new programs.[36]

Webber criticizes planners for having accepted a responsibility for the physical environment and for using values, concepts and techniques that have had a negative effect on the individual's welfare. His plea is for the comprehensive planning process to "find those wealth producing approaches that will benefit all members of the society," and for a marriage of the social sciences with planning which should result "in imaginative social inventions that will increase the city's riches, while distributing them to all the city's people."[37]

This nation's continued reliance on the traditional approach to recreation planning can do little for the cause of comprehensive planning. If the city is to be recognized as more than a physical problem and planners seriously intend to assume a social responsibility "to expand freedom in a pluralistic society" they should begin to ask "What are our purposes? In what ways can we, who hold such large responsibilities for the physical city, so conduct our affairs to affect positively the lives of residents?"[38]

In this light, arbitrary standards which cannot be rationalized for certain segments of society should be reevaluated. More important is the need to explore alternative techniques which could result in a more comprehensive and responsive approach to recreation planning. Webber feels that "there is cause for much optimism."[39]

---

* Chapter V indicates a nationwide similarity of standards despite wide regional differences in leisure behavior and recreation resources.

[36] Melvin M. Webber, "Comprehensive Planning and Social Responsibility," in *Urban Planning* and *Social Policy*, p. 21.

[37] *Ibid.*, p. 22.

[38] *Ibid.*, p. 10.

[39] *Ibid.*, p. 15.

RESOURCE ALLOCATION

The relevance and effectiveness of the traditional approach to recreation planning for resource allocation are summarized by Knetsch:

> The myth persists that somehow we are able to multiply population figures by recreation activity participation rates of some form and call it demand; and then use such figures to justify doing just about anything we care to in the name of satisfying recreation needs. While such number manipulation occurs, it is economic and planning *nonsense* to treat resulting magnitudes seriously as guides for improving the provision of recreation opportunities.[40]

A detailed consideration of demand is beyond the scope of this book, but it is important to summarize some of the major conceptual difficulties pointed out by others and relate them to the use of standards. For example, Knetsch condemns the *ORRRC Report's* concept of demand:

> Recreation demand has often been used in . . . a fairly disastrously misleading way. This in large part stems from confusion of recreation demand terminology given wide currency by the ORRRC studies. Many have unfortunately and uncritically read into this early work, and subsequently propagated, erroneous concepts of demand.[41]

Knetsch cites ambiguity in two areas: (1) the price-quantity relationships which lie behind the concepts of demand and supply are ignored, and (2) the participation rates which are observed are quantities taken at prevailing opportunities. Hence, "demand" is *not* demand at all, but what economists commonly call "consumption." Moreover, participation is only a reflection of available opportunities. Knetsch cites this example:

> It should not surprise us, for example, that people in Colorado or Montreal ski in far greater numbers than people in Washington, D.C. This difference does not by itself indicate differences in demand for skiing. The figures are the result of the interaction between demand and supply factors.[42]

He continues: "this is more than a semantic quibble. It is an ambiguity which can increasingly cause mischief to well-intentioned planning efforts." He concludes:

---

[40] Jack L. Knetsch, "Assessing the Demands for Outdoor Recreation," in Driver, *Elements of Outdoor Recreation Planning*, p. 131. (Emphasis added.)
[41] *Ibid.*
[42] *Ibid.*, p. 132.

> What we have . . . is an extremely arbitrary determination of what outdoor recreation demands really exist, and their relative importance. Improper accounting of supply . . . leads to the assumption that people demand only increasing quantities of what they now have, and therefore can perpetuate present imbalances.[43]

With reference to participation rates as a technique of resource allocation, Knetsch observes their popularity because they:

> (1) appear right, (2) are straightforward and easily institutionalized, and (3) usually give large numbers which support supplier goals. [However, he believes] the reality seems to be that (1) they are wrong, (2) they give erroneous planning guides, and (3) it is a waste of effort that pre-empts the opportunity to undertake something useful.[44]

Knetsch concludes:

> What is needed is not a collection of miscellaneous facts, but an understanding of the relationships inherent in recreation behavior and the ability to forecast the effects of proposed alternative actions. A more efficient and equitable provision of recreation opportunities is dependent upon the recognition of the wide spectrum of outdoor recreation possibilities . . . and an assessment of the relative demands for different segments of this spectrum for these are tangible expressions of personal values that are most significant as guides to what people want.[45]

There can be little question in light of Knetsch's incisive analysis that decisions to allocate land or facilities based on the current approach to urban recreation planning are superficial, if not inadequate, and lead toward a *misallocation* of resources.

PROGRAM EVALUATION

Program evaluation is often linked to objectives where standards usually become both the objective and a quantitative measure of results. It is difficult to visualize how the traditional approach to planning can measure results with standards established by the supplier when there is such a radical difference between the objectives of most suppliers and users.*

---

[43] *Ibid.*

[44] *Ibid.*, p. 133.

[45] *Ibid.*, p. 134.

* See Table 10, Chapter III.

During a period when recreation is being asked to rationalize its objectives for public support and compete with other national priorities, it has no relevant or effective measures of utility in terms of social welfare. What measures do exist, e.g., 10 acres per 1,000 population, are meaningless in terms of leisure behavior, user satisfaction, program planning and budgeting concepts and existing national goals or objectives.

If the national search for social indicators[46] bypasses outdoor recreation because of its lack of meaningful measures, this might bias national priorities against outdoor recreation simply because outdoor recreation will not be able to compete for limited public funds in the statistical dialogue. The results could be very detrimental to a social service which does have a place on the scales of resource allocation.

ADVOCACY PLANNING

> Planning initiative on the part of individual groups and communities within urban areas has been made necessary for the increasing bureaucratization and technical basis of decisions in current urban society. . . . Advocacy planning takes many forms depending on its sponsor. . . . It fills a crucial need for managing latent conflict in the cities and for humanizing public opinion.[47]

The concept of advocacy planning is not new, but it has become one alternative in an attempt to make urban government and the political process more responsive to human needs. In many instances, advocacy planning has become a vehicle of "hope" for the long-neglected inner cities of Urban America. It has become a challenge and viable alternative to the traditional approach to planning. The traditional approach to recreation planning is particularly vulnerable to this challenge because of its value positions which do not necessarily represent those of inner city residents. Davidoff states: "Appropriate planning action cannot be prescribed from a position of value neutrality, for prescriptions are based on desired objectives.[48] Peattie expands this concept and applies it to community dynamics:

---

[46] U. S Department of Health, Education and Welfare, *Toward A Social Report* (Washington, D. C.: Government Printing Office, 1969).

[47] Lisa R. Peattie, "Reflections on Advocacy Planning," *Journal of the American Institute of Planners*, XXXIV, No. 2 (March, 1968), p. 80.

[48] Davidoff, "Advocacy and Pluralism in Planning," p. 331.

Advocate planners take the view that any plan is the embodiment of particular group interests, and therefore they see it as important that any group which has interests at stake in the planning process should have those interests articulated. In effect, they reject both the notion of a single "best" solution and the notion of a general welfare which such a solution might serve. Planning in this view becomes pluralistic and partisan — in a word, overtly *political*.[49]

Peattie continues: "advocacy planning here appears as a new kind of politics . . . it falls with a number of other current efforts to decentralize the work of government."[50] Davidoff relates this to poverty and the inner city:

Pluralism and advocacy are means for stimulating consideration of future conditions by all groups in society. But there is one social group which at present is particularly in need of assistance by planners. This group includes organizations representing *low-income* families. . . . It would be appropriate for planners concerned with such groups to find means to plan *with* them.[51]

In this perspective, the traditional approach to outdoor recreation planning cannot be responsive to the emerging emphasis on advocacy planning especially in the inner city, because it is too far removed from the problem in its values, concepts and methods. To hope for a radical change in the "Middle-class Protestant Ethic values implicit in the Recreation Movement"[52] is naive, if not presumptuous. Even if this change were possible, it would probably take at least ten years.*

There are many who believe that the inner city cannot and need not endure another decade of inaction.[53] The most recom-

---

49 Peattie, "Reflections on Advocacy Planning," p. 81. (Emphasis added.)

50 *Ibid.*, p. 81.

51 Davidoff, "Advocacy and Pluralism in Planning," p. 334. (Emphasis added.)

52 Barbara Sedlin, "Leisure Time Planning and Open Space Programming" (paper presented at the annual meeting of the Michigan Academy of Science and Arts, Cranbrook School, Bloomfield Hills, Michigan, March 19, 1961), p. 3.

* Because most universities with recreation programs are still using texts and concepts (see Chapter II, "Conventional Wisdom") which reinforce the middle-class Protestant Ethic values of most students in the programs. If immediate change in university programs were possible, it would still take approximately five years before graduates might be in responsible field positions to initiate or influence institutional change, and perhaps another five years to implement these changes.

53 Donald Canty, *A Single Society* (New York: Praeger Publishers, 1969), pp. 162-174.

mended course of action is integration with immediate enrichment of the ghetto to help alleviate some of its intolerable conditions. If this course is seriously pursued in the area of recreation, it will mean not only new concepts and techniques for leisure planning, but also an alternative approach to planning to help correct the shortcomings of the past and innovate needed changes for the future.

INNOVATIVE APPROACH

In this section an alternative to the traditional approach to urban outdoor recreation planning at the neighborhood level is described. The inner city is used to illustrate this approach, but the principles and method can be adapted to most cities or suburbs. The concept and techniques are presented in a format which can be easily understood and tried by others. Although this approach is still experimental, it is described in pragmatic terms based on an assumption that the reader is already aware of the problem and the need for an alternative approach to recreation planning.

Concept and Planning Techniques

The innovative approach is the opposite of most concepts and techniques now used in the traditional approach to outdoor recreation planning. Its emphasis is on experimentation, demonstration and citizen participation. It has no precedent and no proof that it will succeed or fail. It is offered as a challenging alternative to status quo in a field dominated by tradition. The concept is summarized in the following paragraphs.

Outdoor recreation planning at the neighborhood level is an incremental process for the determination of opportunities based on the expressed goals and objectives of residents. The allocation of public resources for outdoor recreation is a direct reflection of resident values. These values are expressed in the opportunities, space standards and priorities selected from alternatives by a representative body of the residents or their advocate.

The emphasis is on a short-range, goal-oriented, value-directed, representative and advocate planning effort which is adaptable, effective and relevant to the inner city neighborhood. The advocate emphasis is based on Davidoff's concept:

Planners should be able to engage in the political process as advocates of the interests both of government and of such other groups, organizations, or individuals concerned with proposing policies for the future development of the community.[54]

This concept reflects Davidoff's belief: "City planners represent and plead the plans of many interest groups. . . . Appropriate policy in a democracy is determined through a process of political debate. The right course of action is always a matter of choice, never of fact."[55] The essence of this concept is to make central planning more representative and responsive to the needs of special groups in society which are generally overlooked, bypassed or given inappropriate treatment.* Davidoff states:

Urban politics, in an era of increasing government activity in planning and welfare, must balance the demands for ever-increasing central bureaucratic control against the demands for increased concern for the unique requirement of local, specialized interests. The welfare of *all* and the welfare of minorities are *both* deserving of support.[56]

The innovative concept views government as the advocate of a neighborhood's interests. Residents are justified in employing planners or seeking volunteers to advocate their interests if government cannot or will not assume this responsibility to their satisfaction. In most cases, the volunteer option will be used because of institutional restraints and current lack of governmental resources to accomplish this effort.*

A given neighborhood may have "plural plans" prepared by several competing interests. "Lively political dispute aided by plural plans could do much to improve the level of rationality in the process of preparing a public plan." At this point Davidoff encourages full participation by citizens in plan making:

---

[54] Davidoff, "Advocacy and Pluralism in Planning," p. 332.

[55] *Ibid.*

* Special groups can include: the rich, poor and middle classes, racial or ethnic minorities, senior citizens, physically or mentally handicapped, preschool children, teens or others.

[56] *Ibid.* (Emphasis added.)

* This does not dismiss the difficulty of residents finding the resources and professional planners to represent their interests, but neither are impossible. There are some planners who will donate their services to an advocate cause, e.g., Planners for Equal Opportunity and other socially motivated professional organizations or individuals.

If the planning process is to encourage democratic urban government then it must operate so as to include rather than exclude citizens from participating in the process. "Inclusion" means not only
permitting the citizen to be heard. It also means that he be able to
become well informed about the underlying reasons for planning
proposals, and be able to respond to them.[57]

From a base of active citizen participation which has one or
several representative bodies to articulate goals and objectives, the
process is incremental for planning and implementation with a normal time horizon of no longer than *two* years from the beginning
to the end of one cycle.

The incremental dimension of this concept is based on a belief
that: (1) residents can and will organize to achieve short-term gains;
(2) in a ghetto of "hope,"* immediate enrichment can help to reinforce that hope; (3) in a ghetto of "despair," short-term enrichment
might help to stimulate some hope; (4) an entire neighborhood
population can change in this period; (5) if the residents do not
change in this period, their goals, objectives, values and recreational preferences might; (6) developing technologies and innovations elsewhere can radically change existing objectives, programs
and plans or priorities for both the neighborhood and the city; (7)
short-term tangible results might be instrumental in reducing urban
unrest; (8) no adults or especially children should have to wait longer
than this period for some incremental improvement in their living
environment; (9) government, with the help of the private sector, can
create and develop appropriate opportunities in this time period;
and (10) action is the best way to find out what will work in a given
situation.

Beyond the advocate aspect of this concept is a professional
imperative to view leisure in a light far different from the traditional
approach which clings to outdated, quantitative and static standards,
i.e., so many picnic benches for so many people. Instead of starting with conventional facilities for the formulation of goals and
objectives, recreation planning should begin with human needs[58]
and then see how these needs relate to potential recreational pat-

---

[57] Davidoff, "Advocacy and Pluralism in Planning," p. 332.

* See Chapter III for a description of ghettos of "hope" and "despair."

[58] See Driver and Tocher, "Toward a Behavioral Interpretation of Recreational
Engagements, with Implications for Planning," in Driver, *Elements of Outdoor
Recreation Planning,* pp. 9-31.

terns. "The activity allocation should be the end product of the planning process."[59]

In a rapidly changing world, Satterthwaite projects three possible functions for recreation as a human need: "(1) fulfilling or expressing, (2) testing, skill or challenge, and (3) forgetting or escape."[60] She places these in a recreation environment "where parks and open space are woven into the total fabric of social and economic programming. . . . An environment which blends amenities and recreation opportunities into the urban pattern of living." She outlines a number of imaginative possibilities and stresses that "the need for people to participate in and express themselves to the point where some impact of themselves can be seen or felt is something all too often forgotten by recreation planners." She states:

> Playground design perhaps best illustrates the need for recreation planning to take better account of these self expression desires. The traditional playground . . . except for the sand . . . provides no opportunities for a child to change or move things. . . . This points to a need for playground equipment to be designed so there is some sense of exploration, of discovery, or doing something on one's own.[61]

With respect to human values, Satterthwaite believes that "when planning ahead we must bear in mind the needs and demands of the mainstream of America." She qualifies this by identifying "the poor, the ghetto dwellers, the unemployed" as overlooked social groups outside the mainstream of an affluent society who "represent social priorities."[62] She feels that these people have critical social and economic needs, but:

> This does not mean that recreation should overlook the poor. All too often public agencies have just provided middle class opportunities and private charitable organizations have stepped in with elitist and patronizing attitudes. Public and private recreation plans and programs must try to reach these people with programs and activities geared to their *values* and needs.[63]

Satterthwaite makes a plea for more imaginative programming, accessibility and psychological awareness in planning recreational opportunities for the poor and gives this vivid example:

---

[59] Ann Satterthwaite, "Some Thoughts on Planning the Recreation Environment," in Driver, *Elements of Outdoor Recreation Planning*, p. 105.

[60] *Ibid.*, pp. 107-109.

[61] *Ibid.*, p. 108.

[62] *Ibid.*, p. 110.

[63] *Ibid.* (Emphasis added.)

It may be hard to understand how the crowded beach at Coney Island throbbing with transistor radio music can be more inviting than the glories of the Tetons, yet for someone who has not ventured beyond a block or two-block radius of his Bedford-Stuyvesant tenement those Tetons are alien and terrifying.[64]

The following sections describe and illustrate the innovative concept which will be applied in Chapter VII to a hypothetical situation. The focus of each section is to suggest one or more techniques for further development, testing and application to different situations. All techniques conform to the model in Figure 3 and the evolutionary aspect of this approach shown in Table 21. Note the change between supplier and resident standards and the emphasis on alternatives, citizen participation and revision in the innovative approach. This is in direct contrast to a general lack of these in the traditional approach.

---

[64] *Ibid.*

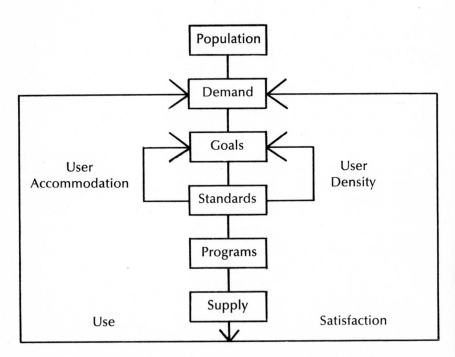

Fig. 3. Innovative approach to urban outdoor recreation planning.

TABLE 21

Development of Innovative Concept and Techniques

Approach	Time	Concepts/Techniques
Traditional	Past[a] Present[b]	Population + A Standard[c] → Allocation Pop. → Demand + A Standard[c] → Allocation
Innovative	Future	Pop. → Demand + Goals[d] + Alternative Standards[d] → Programs → Allocation → Review → Revision

[a] Pre-ORRRC Report (1900-1962).
[b] Post-ORRRC Report (1962-1968).
[c] Supplier Standard.
[d] Resident Goals and Standards.

SURVEY AND ANALYSIS TECHNIQUES

The innovative approach requires a data base or at least a survey of existing conditions prior to goal formulation by residents or the groups which represent them. It also requires a much more sensitive analysis of social and environmental problems, latent and expressed leisure preferences, existing and potential public and private leisure facilities, circulation patterns, weather and climate, community psychology, social disorders, public safety and the human and fiscal resources available to help implement any possible alternative.

Most of these areas are either omitted or only token efforts in the traditional approach. Some of this information is already available from existing social and welfare agencies. Additional data could be obtained through a number of conventional and unconventional survey techniques.

Webb details a number of unusual techniques, such as examination of physical evidence for wear or deposition to indicate use, investigation of archival records to determine the physical or mental trends and individual or group responses to set situations.[65] These techniques can apply to recreation studies and could be far more sensitive than the usual user survey which asks a selected population to sample their outdoor recreation preferences at home or interviews users at public recreation areas. Both methods give

[65] E. J. Webb, et al., *Unobtrusive Measures* (Chicago: Rand-McNally, 1966).

a distorted view of preference because they omit significant components of the population and types of leisure other than those normally supplied by the public sector. Some possible survey and analysis techniques which might be adaptable to the inner city or elsewhere and appropriate to the innovative approach include:

1. Surveys to determine what people are not using public parks and why.

2. Photographic time-sequence analysis of both public recreational areas and streets to record use, problems and potentials.

3. Surveys of children and teenagers to find out their specific desires, values and perceptions of things, activities and the environment.

4. Use of mobile play apparatus to observe how and where it is moved and why.

5. Requesting a sample of the population to maintain time budgets, diaries which use simple but novel techniques, e.g., marking hours for given activities on IBM cards or units of money deposited in a personal home bank which reflects time accounts.

6. Designing survey forms which utilize graphic symbols instead of complicated words and instructions.

7. Closing streets, opening rooftops, detouring pedestrian or vehicular traffic patterns to observe impacts on recreation use and nonuse.

8. Transporting a representative sample of the population to other neighborhoods or demonstration areas at periodic and continuous intervals to observe any marked change in preferences, values or participation.

9. Aerial photography to inventory vegetation, circulation and recreational use patterns of given areas or the entire planning unit.

10. Surveys of and by school children to identify recreational problems and potentials, preferences of nonusers, parental goals, objectives and values with regard to leisure, outdoor recreation and other community needs and wants.

GOAL AND OBJECTIVE FORMULATION

Based on the survey data and analysis by an advocate planner,* the neighborhood should have a series of problems and potentials on which to base their goals and objectives. Within the goal formulation framework outlined in Chapter IV, "outdoor recreation" would be a sub-objective under the objective "leisure" which might support a goal such as "the quality of life."

---

* Either their own planner, or one from the central planning agency whom they will accept, who can and will represent neighborhood goals and objectives.

The time horizon of objectives is no longer than *ten* years. It is divided into five planning-action cycles of no longer than *two* years each with a requirement of constant updating, review and revision on a *monthly* basis. Revision is the rule rather than the exception. Argument, controversy and issues are encouraged as a healthy sign of citizen or group dynamics and involvement. Decisions are made in any manner which is appropriate to the majority of the residents or their elected or appointed representatives and advocates.

If a neighborhood cannot or will not articulate its goals and objectives, the central planning agency formulates whatever goals they perceive as appropriate. The residents should be made aware of this strategy, with a condition that action programs for their area will have *lower* priority than other areas which have already articulated their goals. Enforcement of this strategy should be a positive motivation for even the most reticent neighborhood to seek its share of public benefits. These are not easy strategies to implement, but they are appropriate to the current trend toward more self-determination in the inner city and elsewhere.

SELECTION OF ALTERNATIVES

Once a neighborhood's goals and objectives are expressed, formulated and accepted by a *majority* of the residents, the problem becomes one of finding alternative means of reaching them. Three related devices are described here and will be applied in Chapter VII. They are: (1) Recreation Opportunity Index or Social Indicator, (2) Representative Space Standard, and (3) Recreation Resource Allocation Matrix.

Recreation Opportunity Index

This index quantifies alternative opportunity levels of a playground or neighborhood type of park based on: (1) the precent of the total possible users that the residents would like to have accommodated at any given peak hour of use and (2) the density at which the residents would like this use to be accommodated. Both can vary from approximately 1 to 100 (or 100 to 1,000) as shown in Table 22. Each can be used in combination with the other to produce 10,000 theoretical alternatives (100 x 100 = 10,000). In practice, the use and density scales would be more usable in sets of 10 each, which would imply 100 alternatives.

Each alternative implies a given spacial requirement and a corresponding set of activities which can be tailored to the available

TABLE 22
Recreation Opportunity Alternatives

Percent of users	Users/ Acre	Key	General Activity[a]	Specific Activity[a]
1	100	A	Passive[b]	Variable (see Table 23 for options)
20	200	B	Passive	
		C	Picnicking[c]	Same
40	400	D	Picnicking[d]	
		E	Area sports	Same
60	600	F	Field games	
		G	Court games	Same
80	800	H	Challenge areas	
100	1,000	I	Social interaction	Same
		J	Mass crowds[e]	

[a] Assumed for theoretical purposes. Requires field testing.
[b] Relative "solitude" in high-density urban area.
[c] Family groups.
[d] Organization groups.
[e] Spectator sports, rallies, festivals, public meetings.

space using the activity dimensions shown in Table 23. The general activity options are determined by the choice of a set of user accommodation and user density alternatives; the specific activity options are determined within each general option.

Theoretically, if it were possible to know the use intensity and preference variables for each individual in a given neighborhood, the above technique could begin with the individual and be employed in a manner which would be even more sensitive. In practice this would be quite difficult; however, it might lend itself to computer simulation.

A Recreation Opportunity Index can be constructed from Table 22 by assigning an index number to the sets of use and density alternatives and by assuming that: (1) the greater the percent of users which can be accommodated at a given time, the higher the value to the residents, and (2) generally, the lower the density of users, the greater the recreation experience in congested areas such as the inner city where open space is at a premium. This index is shown in Table 24.

TABLE 23
Selected Leisure Activity Space Needs and Possible Number of Users[a]

Leisure Activity[b]	Use Dimensions[c]	Space Required[d]	Peak Users[e]
Archery	50 x 300	15	50
Baseball	300 x 300	90	25
Basketball	60 x 100	60	15
Challenge apparatus	40 x 50	2	100
Football	150 x 300	45	20
Handball	25 x 40	1	8
Horseshoes (4)	40 x 50	2	16
Paddle tennis (5)	100 x 40	4	20
Family picnicking (5)	100 x 100	10	30
Group picnicking (1)	200 x 200	40	200
Shuffleboard (4)	40 x 50	2	16
Soccer	200 x 300	6	25
Softball	200 x 200	4	25
Table tennis (5)	10 x 20	1	25
Tennis (1)	50 x 100	5	8
Volleyball	50 x 60	3	20
Movies/television	200 x 100	20	1000
Combative sports (2)	50 x 50	5	50
Creative skills	100 x 100	1	100
Environment games	100 x 100	10	500

[a] Adapted from many sources to inner city conditions. Spacial requirements for most activities reduced by approximately 20 to 30 percent. Requires field testing to determine feasibility, safety factors, user satisfaction, etc.

[b] Selected for their adaptability to inner city conditions. Activity could take place indoors, in several areas or on several levels.

[c] Approximate dimensions in feet. Where more than one facility is listed, e.g., horseshoes (4), dimensions are for a battery of four horseshoe pits.

[d] Space required in thousands of square feet.

[e] Peak users implies the maximum number of players or users at a given activity to include spectators, umpires, alternates, etc. Hence, the number is higher than only players for many of the traditional sports. Watching is considered a leisure activity implicit in all others.

A Recreation Opportunity Index could provide one type of social indicator for outdoor recreation opportunity in densely populated residential areas with little or no recreational open space. It could also become the basis of a measure to compare different neighborhoods, revise objectives and serve as a means for a given neighborhood to determine its level of recreation opportunity by selecting

TABLE 24
Recreation Opportunity Index

Benefit Value[a]	Percent of Users	U/Index Number[b]	User Density	D/Index Number[b]	Social Indicator[b]
—	0	0	1,000	0	0
	10	1	900	1	1
	20	2	800	2	4
	30	3	700	3	9
	40	4	600	4	16
	50	5	500	5	25
	60	6	400	6	36
	70	7	300	7	49
	80	8	200	8	64
	90	9	100	9	81
+	100	10	0	10	100

[a] Note that although the index places a higher value on low density this is to accommodate normal recreation use which would not take place during the special events or times when high densities would preempt the entire space for a desired community purpose.

[b] U index number × D index number = Social Indicator (SI).

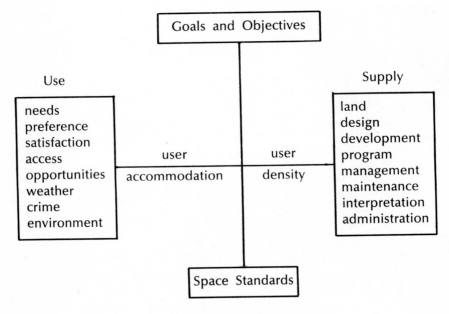

Fig. 4. Variables and relationships: innovative approach.

the indicator which it feels appropriate to its needs and resources. Figure 4 shows the important variables and relationships involved in developing this technique.

Representative Space Standard

It is possible to develop a space standard which reflects the percent of use accommodation and user density relationship already described. This standard is *representative* of the combination of activities, spacial requirements, objectives of a particular neighborhood, and is related directly to the given population of that neighborhood at a given time.

Use is calculated by counting every individual in a neighborhood as one user and assuming that no more than 20 percent of the total population would desire or be able to use public recreation areas at a given peak hour of use. This percentage could vary with each situation, but seems reasonable when based on estimated time budgets, age and sex ratios, employment patterns, and possible leisure behavior preferences of most inner city neighborhoods. Testing and field surveys would be necessary to determine this use estimate for each area.

Beginning with a use potential of 100 percent of the population, this is translated into the number of actual users at any given peak hour. The actual users become the percent of use which can be accommodated as determined by a selection from 100 alternatives or the more likely set of 10 alternatives illustrated in Table 22.

The density or users per acre is implied by the general or specific activity orientations selected by the residents. The total actual use divided by the density at which this use is to be accommodated for specific activities determines the potential need in acres. This potential need, divided by the total population, yields a space standard of acres needed per 1,000 population. If an existing supply of recreation land is available, it is subtracted from the acres needed. This technique and the use of a social indicator are expressed here:

1. 100 percent of total pop. (TP) = potential users (PU).
2. 20 percent of total pop. (TP) = users/peak hours (U).
3. Users/peak hour (U) = actual users (AU).
5. Activity orientations (AO) = persons/acre = density (D).
4. Goals and objectives (GO) = activity orientations (AO).
6. $\dfrac{U}{D}$ = potential need (PN).

7. Potential need (PN) minus supply (S) = actual need (AN).

8. $\dfrac{\text{AN}}{\dfrac{\text{TP}}{1,000}}$ = standard in acres needed/1,000 pop. (STD).

9. U index x D index (Table 24) = social indicator (SI).

10. Social indicator (SI) = recreation objectives.

Once the amount of area needed is determined, this does not have to be provided outdoors or provided on a single plane. There is no reason why many of these activities cannot be provided indoors, or above and below the ground if space is costly or unobtainable without displacing large numbers of residents. This concept encourages the design of recreation environments which can utilize existing areas, rooftops, streets, basements or abandoned buildings adaptable to multiple use. It also raises the possibility of providing high-rise recreation buildings instead of the traditional city park, decking over or tunneling under existing or proposed playgrounds and the acquisition of air rights over land uses such as parking lots, freeways, railroad rights-of-way and industrial developments.

In this perspective, the recreation environment can be vertical as well as horizontal. It can take place indoors and outdoors. In many instances, this flexibility can maintain or increase the range of opportunities where they are most needed, despite environmental conditions such as inclement weather, air pollution and temperatures that discourage the use of some facilities. There is no reason why playgrounds cannot be heated or air-conditioned "fieldhouses" and vice versa, or picnic and nature areas cannot be "greenhouses" and vice versa. These and other innovations are technologically possible and economically feasible based on increased use.

Recreation Resource Allocation Matrix

The major components of recreation resource allocation are: land, development, program, maintenance and administration. Each can be expressed in units which represent the combined resources of land, labor and capital to produce a desired result. There is a complementary and sometimes substitutable relationship between certain components which can be used as alternatives to create and manage recreational opportunities to meet desired objectives of social welfare, urban form or function.

For example, if land is one unit, it might be possible to double the output or effectiveness of this unit by doubling the input of program. Likewise, it might be possible to incrementally improve the use of an area by different inputs of design and development. If more maintenance and supervision are necessary for effective use, they might also be incrementally increased.

In terms of cost where residents are able to voluntarily provide their own resources for development, program and maintenance of recreation areas, this is an option which can be reflected in the matrix. This is especially important in the growing trend toward more "self-generated parks." Moreover, this system's approach to recreation resource allocation could be one way of simulating and evaluating each input on the matrix in terms of a desired objective. The matrix could also serve as a vehicle for benefit-cost analysis. Table 25 indicates what a hypothetical allocation of resources might be for a ten-year period, in five two-year increments, for a given neighborhood and one million dollars in public funds.

TABLE 25

Recreation Resource Allocation Matrix[a] (in Units of $1,000)

Two-Year Cycles	I		II		III		IV		V		Resource Totals
Each Year	1	2	3	4	5	6	7	8	9	10	
Land	200	..	..	..	25	25	25	25	25	25	350[b]
Development	..	50	25	25	20	20	20	20	20	20	220
Program	..	25	50	50	50	50	50	50	*	*	325
Maintenance	..	15	15	15	*	*	*	*	*	*	45
Administration	..	10	10	10	5	5	5	5	5	5	60
Totals	200	100	100	100	100	100	100	100	50	50	1,000

[a] Based on $1 million in public funds.
[b] One acre of land in high-density area.
* Voluntary resident effort.

INCREMENTAL IMPLEMENTATION

The array of alternatives allows maximum flexibility and response to change. The technique of incremental implementation complements this strategy by requiring the planning unit to review and revise its plans monthly and implement these plans in two-year cycles.

This approach should help to: (1) minimize a misallocation of resources, (2) coordinate local planning within the short-range time horizons of the political process, (3) maximize unforeseen opportunities, (4) minimize delays by prompting the bureaucratic process to act on realistic deadlines, and (5) produce tangible results for further resident motivation and participation in the planning process.

This approach adopts an action-oriented posture toward research and professional practice. It assumes that demonstration and action are the best examples of what will work and what will not in the inner city or elsewhere. It acknowledges the possibility of short-term failure for a probable long-term gain in human welfare. More important, this approach seeks to minimize the long-term risks of static programs or standards and to maximize benefits for a segment of the population long overdue in receiving its share of this nation's resources.

Some Possible Rationales

Beyond those already listed, two rationales are timely and worth mentioning. Both focus on experimentation, but each has different objectives, time horizons and methods. Each is discussed briefly here and detailed in Chapter VIII.

BASIC AND APPLIED RESEARCH

The field of outdoor recreation is acknowledged by many for its lack of basic and applied research on leisure behavior. Its relative lack of emphasis on the inner city has already been discussed in Chapters II and III. If the innovative approach has no other purpose, it could be a sensitive research vehicle to motivate professional interest in disproving it as a viable challenge to traditional concepts and techniques. Beyond this, the questions it could raise might draw some public attention to the imbalance of recreation resource allocation between inner city and suburb.

If the innovative approach is valid, it could become one avenue to many other areas of research in leisure behavior, citizen participation, benefit-cost analysis, goal-supplier differences and the application of developing technologies to recreation planning. Finally, what might have research value in recreation planning would probably have application in other areas of social welfare planning and prompt more professionals to study people instead of things.

DEMONSTRATION OPPORTUNITIES

Innovation and total attack are the key words in guidelines issued by HUD for its Demonstration Cities Program. Cities chosen for grants will have to include new, innovative programs . . . every element in the plan must have a direct impact on some of the basic problems of . . . lack of recreation.[66]

There has never been a more opportune time for needed research, innovation and action with respect to urban recreation planning. The Federal mandate for innovation in the Demonstration Cities Program is one rationalization for attempting the innovative approach. Federal guidelines emphasize that any program selected for a grant:

> Provide for widespread citizen participation. . . .
>
> . . . .
>
> Serve the poor and disadvantaged of the area. . . .
>
> . . . .
>
> Serve a broad range of recreational opportunities. . . .
>
> . . . .
>
> Develop realizable goals to be achieved at the end of 5 years.[67]

These are precisely the hallmarks of the innovative approach which need application, testing and evaluation. Thus, there would seem to be a possibility of receiving the type of funding necessary to implement needed demonstration programs.

Relevance and Effectiveness

By using the same definitions and approach to relevance and effectiveness described for the traditional approach, it is possible to evaluate the innovative approach on its own merits. Much of this evaluation has been implicit in all preceding discussion and specifically in the negative substantiation for the traditional approach. The following discussion covers only those points not already treated.

USER PREFERENCE

The essence of this approach is to encourage and provide diversity through innovations in development and program which directly reflect what users do or might like to do. It does not weigh past preferences, values or activities unless residents choose them and even here the innovative approach stresses choice by showing resi-

---

[66] American Society of Planning Officials, "Demonstration Cities," p. 23.
[67] *Ibid.*, pp. 23-28.

dents the alternatives available to them through the use of educational television, movies, field trips to other portions of the city and portable types of facilities brought into the neighborhood for trial by potential users.

COMPREHENSIVE PLANNING

If this concept is proven over time to be effective for one neighborhood, it could be applied to others. In practice the central planning agency could have an instant and continuous evaluation of its efforts and be able to better relate recreation to other priorities. Far from decreasing the effectiveness of centralized comprehensive planning, Davidoff feels that advocacy planning at the neighborhood level "would stimulate city [comprehensive] planning in a number of ways":

> It would serve as a means of better informing the public of the alternative choices open, alternatives strongly supported by their proponents. . . . Advocacy and plural planning would improve planning practice [by] forcing the public planning agency to compete with other planning groups to win political support. In the absence of opposition or alternative plans presented by interest groups the public agencies have little incentive to improve the quality of their work or the rate of production of their plans . . . . Plural planning would force those who have been critical of "establishment" plans to produce superior plans, rather than to carry out the very essential obligation of criticizing plans deemed improper.[68]

RESOURCE ALLOCATION

In terms of the residents of a given area, the innovative approach has a decided advantage over the traditional approach which has several built-in biases against the inner city. There is no question that the traditional approach is far more expedient for the decision-makers and the suppliers of outdoor recreation, but neither group exists for the sake of expediency. The functions of both are to represent and serve the goals and needs of their constituents and clients. If both fail because of their own ineptness this can be rationalized. However, if the suppliers cannot succeed because of an approach to planning which does not clearly express the goals and objectives of the people whom they represent, they cannot be expected to make rational decisions for the allocation of scarce resources.

---

[68] Davidoff, "Advocacy and Pluralism in Planning," pp. 332-333.

PROGRAM EVALUATION

The current emphasis on Program-Planning and Budgeting as a technique for evaluating programs in light of desired goals and objectives needs indicators to measure social benefits. To date, the field of outdoor recreation has developed few effective measures which can be considered social indicators. The traditional approach presents little more than distorted measures with existing space standards, demand estimates, participation rates and visitor days which do not relate to user goals, objectives or human needs in the sense described by Satterthwaite.[69] Conversely, the innovative approach can provide measures which clearly reflect the objectives and values of a neighborhood and can be used in program evaluation.

ADVOCACY PLANNING

This topic has already been discussed in detail and is the primary source of relevance and effectiveness for the inner city. It is both the cause and possible effect of an alternative to traditional urban recreation planning. In a period where *more* rather than less self-determination is a critical issue for residents of Urban America, there can be little doubt about the value of this approach to urban recreation planning.

COMPARISON OF APPROACHES

A comparison of the two approaches is possible with a modified Likert Scaling Technique because all items "measure the same thing" —relevance to the inner city.[70] Ten criteria are selected as most important and each is given the same weight because the ten are all closely related to each other. However, it would be possible to selectively weigh each item if more were known about each *after* the innovative approach has been *tested in several case studies.* The scale in Table 26 ranges from the most relevant to least relevant with reference to the typical inner city neighborhood.

---

[69] Satterthwaite, "Some Thoughts on Planning the Recreation Environment," pp. 105-112.

[70] A. N. Oppenheim, *Questionnaire Design and Attitude Measurement* (New York: Basic Books, Inc., 1966), p. 133.

TABLE 26

Comparison of Approaches for Relevance to the Inner City

Least Relevant[a]	Traditional Approach[b]	Innovative Approach[c]	Most Relevant[a]
Objective attainment			Objective attainment
Resource allocation			Resource allocation
User satisfaction			User satisfaction
Advocacy planning			Advocacy planning
Flexibility			Flexibility
Research applications			Research applications
Conflict resolution			Conflict resolution
Social indicator			Social indicator
Fiscal programming			Fiscal programming
Simulation potential			Simulation potential

−5   −4   −3   −2   −1   0   +1   +2   +3   +4   +5

[a] Relevance to residents and users and to provide an optimum level of recreation opportunity.
[b] Traditional approach: numerical total is 32, median score is 3, and average score is 3.2. All on *negative* scales.
[c] Innovative approach: numerical total is 45, median score is 5 and average score is 4.5. All on *positive* scales.

VII

The Innovative Approach

In this chapter the innovative approach is applied to a typical situation to illustrate some of its merits and shortcomings. Several ways of trying this approach are suggested and its relevance for the inner city is summarized. The innovative approach is described in general terms in order to emphasize important concepts and show how these techniques could be adapted to most urban and suburban areas. The inner city is used as an extreme example of specific recreational needs. An upper-class suburban area would represent the other extreme. The same concepts and techniques apply, only the variables would be different.

TYPICAL SITUATION

All data and conditions are hypothetical, but are based on inner city conditions described in Chapter III. Many of these conditions are representative of cities in the Northeastern Megalopolis described by Gottman,[1] including Boston, New York, Philadelphia, Newark, Baltimore and Washington, D. C. The conditions are also characteristic of the inner cities of Detroit, Chicago, Cleveland, St. Louis, Oakland (California) and other cities listed in Tables 9 through 13 in Appendix D.

---

[1] Jean Gottman, *Megalopolis* (Cambridge: The M.I.T. Press, 1961).

Although many aspects of urban living might be illustrated, only five are considered here. Each is described in only enough detail to illustrate an application of the innovative approach to the provision of public recreation areas or series of areas in a single neighborhood. The emphasis of this application is on allocation and location rather than design, management or maintenance.

Environmental Conditions

Six types of environmental conditions are important here. Although listed independently, they are closely related and influence each other in positive or negative ways.

PHYSICAL SETTING

The area occupies approximately 500 square blocks (approximately 5 square miles) and is within 2 miles of the central business district of a SMSA with a total population of two million persons. It has well-defined physical boundaries, no change in topography, no significant natural features and no access to water frontage. It has a distinct social, physical and economic character or image which identifies it as a Negro ghetto to both residents, visitors, and decision-makers.* Because of its physical boundaries and social character, it is treated as a single planning area and called "A Community" which, in turn, is composed of "Neighborhoods."

POPULATION DENSITY

The area's total population is 500,000, distributed at a uniform net density of 1,000 persons, or 200 families of 5 persons each, per square block. An average of 200 persons per net acre or of 40 dwelling units per net acre is implied. Each square block has an average total gross area of 5 acres. In relation to the urban area, amount of available open space and amenities, this is high-density housing which consists of tenements, row houses and low-rise apartments. It does not meet most of the desirable and minimum density standards listed by authoritative sources.[2]

---

* These characteristics are described in detail in Chapter III. Such areas as Harlem or Bedford-Stuyvesant in New York City, Hough in Cleveland and Elmwood in Detroit serve as examples.

[2] Chapin, *Urban Land Use Planning*, pp. 430-431.

HOUSING

Most of the dwellings consist of structures built between 1890 and 1920. They are owned by absentee landlords and are poorly maintained and rapidly deteriorating. Building-code violations are common and are generally ignored by authorities. Rents are relatively high for the number of square feet per unit and person. For most units the utilities, off-street parking and children's play areas are inadequate. More than 50 percent of all units were classified as substandard in the 1970 Census of Housing; this figure may now be as high as 75 percent. Several urban renewal plans have been proposed for this area, but none has been implemented to date. Approximately 10 to 20 percent of the units are vacant because of their condition and there is an increasing number of abandoned buildings because of damage in the recent riots, tax foreclosures, insurance cancellations and lack of adequate utilities.

CIRCULATION

The area is traversed by a number of congested major and secondary streets lined with commercial uses. Local streets are also congested, subject to through traffic and extensive double parking. There is no off-street parking or vehicular circulation pattern separating local from through traffic or pedestrian thoroughfares. Sidewalks and alleys provide the only means for pedestrian circulation.

WEATHER, CLIMATE AND AIR POLLUTION

The region is characterized by four seasons: a short, cool spring; a hot, humid summer; a cool fall and a long, cold winter. Precipitation averages 50 inches per year. The average January temperature is 32 degrees Fahrenheit and snow covers the ground. The average July temperature range is 70 to 90 degrees and the humidity often matches this temperature range creating uncomfortable conditions. Approximately 6 out of every 10 days are sunny during the summer season. Extremes in weather are common, but short in duration. During the summer, irritating levels of air pollution can be expected 10 to 25 percent of the time. Most of the housing, stores and public buildings are not air-conditioned.

EXISTING PUBLIC RECREATION AREAS

The total amount of existing public outdoor recreation space is 50 acres or one tenth of 1 acre per 1,000 population. This is equally distributed in ten playgrounds of 5 acres each which are owned by the local school board and cooperatively managed by the parks and recreation department. These areas all have the same limited range of facilities, poor level of maintenance, marginal program and ineffective supervision, and were designed with existing standards for traditional types of equipment and activities.

Population Profile

Because the area is a Negro ghetto, its population is relatively homogeneous in terms of race, income levels, social mobility, educational levels and age and sex distributions.* At this point in time, problems outweigh potentials; this is a "ghetto of despair." There is little immediate hope that the occupants will be integrated into the mainstream of American society without drastic help. Even if such help were forthcoming, it might take a decade or two to have a significant impact on the quality of life for this population.

RACE AND CULTURAL BACKGROUND

The area is more than 90 percent Negro as reported in the 1970 Census. Most of the adult population have lived there at least 10 years after migrating from the rural South in search of employment opportunities. Most of the young adults are offspring of these migrants and are already beginning to raise a generation of children who recall nothing of their rural past and know only the ghetto as a way of life. This ghetto was formerly a white middle-class residential area which rapidly changed in racial composition after World War II. Although Negroes are a minority group in terms of the SMSA population composition, they are no longer a minority in terms of the population composition of the central city, now over 50 percent Negro, and the inner city, which is over 75 percent Negro.

INCOME AND EDUCATIONAL LEVELS

Most of the families are below "the poverty level of $3,335 established for a family of four" and are receiving some form of public assistance for food, shelter and necessities.[3] The average rate of unemployment for adults is 30 percent. Under-employment in menial, low-status jobs for "sweat man's pay" is common for most

---

* These characteristics are described in detail in Chapter III.
[3] *U. S. Riot Commission Report*, p. 462. 1973 level is $4,250.

adult wage earners.[4] The average annual high school dropout rate is 60 percent. Unemployment among teenagers and young adults ranges between 70 to 90 percent. Adults have a median of 8 years of school.

PERSONAL MOBILITY

Public transit to other portions of the city and within the planning area is unreliable and costly. Schedules are reduced during the times when most people have the most leisure. Public transit to regional parks is nonexistent. Personal mobility is limited to walking, bicycling, and, for a few, motorcycling. Only 20 percent of the families have automobiles, many of which are in poor mechanical condition for travel to regional parks.

AGE AND SEX DISTRIBUTIONS

The overall age distribution is weighted toward young and old people in five major groups: preschoolers (under 5), 15 percent; elementary school age children (6-14), 15 percent; young adults (15-24), 25 percent; adults (25-64), 25 percent; and senior citizens (65+), 20 percent. Sex ratios are evenly distributed for all groups except the adult group in which there are 10 percent more females than males.

Political Organization

Because of increased alienation from authority and widespread disappointment with local institutions and government, the traditional lack of effective citizen participation has changed to citizen involvement in a wide range of social, economic and political issues. The recent riots in this area and elsewhere have prompted residents and their leaders to organize in order to "(1) Present to the hostile white world a single voice of protest and rebellion, and (2) Allow no issue to take precedence over the basic issue of race, and, specifically racial oppression."[5]

The organization has a mandate from residents to improve the quality of life and environment by demanding the attention and resources of "the system" which includes the municipal government, labor unions, business and commerce, local universities, fraternal

---

[4] Kenneth B. Clark, *Dark Ghetto* (New York: Harper and Row, 1965), p. 35.
[5] *Ibid.*, p. 194.

groups, community service and social welfare organizations, and the Federal government.

NEIGHBORHOOD COUNCIL

Each of the 500 Block Clubs have equal representation on the Neighborhood Council. For planning purposes, the entire area is divided into 10 planning units of 50 blocks each or an area of approximately 200 or 300 acres, depending on such variables as streets and public facilities.

COMMUNITY COUNCIL

The churches, labor unions, organizations such as CORE, The Urban League, NAACP and teenage groups each have representation on the Community Council which is composed of representatives from these groups and the Neighborhood Council in a ratio consistent with the membership of each group. Membership allows each group at least one vote, but the Citizens Council automatically has 50 percent of the seats. This is to insure that no single group other than one which represents *all* the residents can control the Community Council. Each special interest has at least *one* or more votes, but cannot control the Community Council unless the majority of residents support it.

The Community Council might consist of 20 individuals, 10 who represent the 10 planning areas of the Neighborhood Council and up to 10 who represent other groups. If more than 10 other groups exist, the number of representatives for each planning unit could be increased to maintain the ratio of Citizens Council representatives to other groups. Hence, if 20 other groups exist, the Community Council would consist of 40 members.

All meetings are public, provide for citizen participation and are televised and tape-recorded for playback on the local radio and television stations at convenient times. Copies of all plans, minutes and proposed actions are posted at a designated area in each block and are available in the local school, library and police and fire stations. They are written to be easily understood by anyone with a fourth-grade reading level.

POLITICAL PARTIES

Fifty percent of the potential voters are registered and belong to a single party. They generally vote as a block on most issues and are cognizant of the growing power of their vote in the political process, regardless of their knowledge of the issues. In the national, state and local elections of 1960-1972 they have a consistent voting pattern.

Planning Situation

The city has attempted comprehensive planning in the ghetto area for the last 20 years, but has yet to complete an adequate plan and present it to the residents for their review, comment and suggestions. The only contact most residents have had with central planning has been through several abortive attempts at urban renewal which would replace the area with high-income housing. Residents have usually been requested to react to plans prepared by outsiders. They have never really had the opportunity to participate constructively in the planning process by offering anything other than opposition to the plans of others.

An accumulation of negative experiences has eroded any confidence that the citizens or their leaders may have had in centralized planning as a constructive means of solving their problems. Disillusionment with the traditional planning process, riots during the summers of 1966 through 1970 and the development of Negro militancy of "Black Power"[6] mark the beginnings of self-determination for this neighborhood.

CENTRAL PLANNING AGENCY

A standoff now exists between the central planning agency and the inner city. Because of the political pressure to help cope with the "ghetto problem," the planning agency would now like to do some sensitive planning for this area. The planning agency now lacks credibility with the residents and they do not want to cooperate in the planning process without a realistic opportunity for self-determination.

Despite its resistance to central planning, the Community Council does not have the technical and fiscal resources for the planning effort needed to enrich the area until integration becomes a realistic choice for residents who can and wish to leave the area.* The Council is reluctant to appeal to the central planning agency for help because of mutual distrust and antagonism. It also realizes that

---

6 "Black Power" in a positive, constructive sense of self-determination. See Stokely Carmichael and Charles V. Hamilton, Black Power (New York: Vintage Books, 1967). Also The Negro and the City (New York: Time-Life Books, 1968).

* The Integration Choice is described in Chapter III.

the immediate action needed for its continued political support from residents is beyond the resources and commitment of the central planning agency. It has no realistic alternative but an advocate planning effort.

ADVOCACY PLANNING EFFORT

To overcome its lack of resources, the Community Council appeals to several local professional organizations, the local university and interested citizens for technical help and receives a voluntary response from 15 professionals who will donate one man-day each week to an advocate planning effort. The professionals have organized themselves into an Advocate Planner Team called "ATP"* and have committed their professional efforts for at least one 2-year planning/action cycle. This team includes the services of a sociologist, a lawyer, a political scientist, a social worker, an economist, a landscape architect, an architect, a recreationist, an urban planner, a recreation planner, a psychologist, a community organization specialist, a civil engineer, an educator and a systems analyst.

To overcome its lack of financial resources, the Community Council appeals to several national foundations, local industry and citizens for funds and receives a total of 50 million dollars for planning and implementation of demonstration programs in the areas of employment, education, health, public safety and leisure consistent with its goals and objectives. In terms of its own priorities, the Council designates 5 million dollars for public recreation. This money is received and allocated for one two-year planning/action cycle with the condition that the local recreation agency match it. The local agency agrees to do this which means that the planning effort has 10 million dollars over a 2-year period to spend on public recreation. There is also the possibility of an extension of this level of funding over a 10-year period for a total of 50 million dollars, depending on the needs, priorities and performance of this area. All concerned consider this a demonstration program with high priority and are committed to its success.

Expressed Goals and Objectives

The recent riots and growing frustration of most residents coupled with a lack of governmental response to their repeated requests

---

* "Apt" is defined in Webster and standard dictionaries to mean unusually fitted or well qualified, ready, suited to its purpose, keenly intelligent and quick.

for action prompt them to establish and actively pursue two related goals: (1) Quality of Life, and (2) Quality of Environment. Their goals are supported by these overall objectives: (1) full employment or a guaranteed annual income, (2) adequate low-cost housing, (3) maximum educational opportunities, (4) adequate provisions for public health and safety, and (5) adequate leisure opportunities.

Under the overall objective of leisure opportunities, public recreation is a target objective which can take place in an indoor or outdoor setting. It can be achieved through *alternative* public policies, plans, programs, practices and standards. The following sections illustrate *one* set of alternative policies and practices which the Community Council has adopted to reach its goals and objectives. These alternatives were recommended by the Council's Advocate Planning Team and represent one of several alternatives considered by all residents and adopted by consensus.

The list is conceptual and illustrative of a wide range of alternatives possible within the community. It does not reflect any economic analysis. However, it is realistic in terms of available public and private resources and the potential for commitment to help this area, if the Nation does not accept the Integration Choice recommended by the *U. S. Riot Commission Report.*[7]

In order to abstract the listing, letters are substituted for specific projects, areas or actions. All items in the list could be consistent with a 10-year program, for many inner city neighborhoods, in planning/action cycles of 2 years each. All could be revised on a monthly or quarterly basis in a formal manner which involves direct citizen participation or decisions made by the citizens' elected representatives on the Neighborhood or Community Councils.

POLICIES

Land Acquisition

1. Preserve all existing recreational sites and public open space from encroachment by other uses.
2. Coordinate land acquisition with other recreation agencies, institutions and private recreation efforts.
3. Encourage and accept appropriate gifts of land.
4. Acquire land within convenient access of most users.
5. Utilize the most expedient methods available to acquire needed lands.

---

[7] *U. S Riot Commission Report,* pp. 406-407.

Facility Development

1. Provide an optimum range of recreation facilities to reflect the latent and expressed leisure preferences of residents which are consistent with their social values, problems and aspirations.
2. Develop all facilities to the highest standards consistent with safety, good design, user convenience and the maximum possible source of revenue.
3. Utilize the most imaginative, efficient and economical methods of developing recreation facilities.
4. Develop all facilities to achieve a maximum degree of flexibility and multiple use.
5. Coordinate the development of all facilities with other municipal service projects and programs.

Recreation Program

1. Encourage the optimum use of all existing and proposed recreation land and facilities.
2. Provide the widest possible range of programs which appeal to the needs, values and interests of all residents.
3. Encourage and solicit voluntary leadership to supplement the best available professional leadership.
4. Sponsor programs, consistent with seasonal and daily use patterns, which offer a maximum range of choice, satisfaction, challenge and meaning to the resident.
5. Coordinate all programs with other community recreation programs and the private sector to provide a maximum range of opportunity, user satisfaction and a meaningful recreation experience.

PRACTICES*

Land Acquisition

1. Use urban renewal to redevelop needed lands into appropriate recreation areas.
2. Purchase cemetery X for park land and school park sites A, B, and C as indicated in the comprehensive plan, prepared by APT and approved by the central planning agency.

---

* Note that ordinarily detailed practices would be developed only after a determination of needs, priorities and resources. For illustrative purposes they are listed here to complement the goals, objectives and policies and to indicate how each relates to the other.

3. Require any new residential construction to place 10 percent of the site in recreational open space or donate a like amount of land or money toward neighborhood recreation areas.
4. Purchase the air rights over railroad tracks Y, warehouse Z and parking lots D, E and F.
5. Close local streets X, Y and Z and redevelop them into recreational areas.

Facility Development

1. Enlist the aid of voluntary labor to build playgrounds A, B and C.
2. Grant company X permission to build and operate a concession and toilet building in each neighborhood park.
3. Deck over all existing playgrounds to increase their area, help to separate activities or age groups and provide heated and air-conditioned ground-level recreation facilities for year round use.
4. Acquire and redevelop an abandoned warehouse into a teenage night club and recreation area.
5. Build demonstration play areas in planning units Q, R and S which allow residents to evaluate potential play apparatus and manufacturers to display and test their new products at no cost to the city.

Recreation Program

1. Keep all recreation areas open until 2:00 a.m. on summer nights and weekends and illuminate all areas. Maintain an active program and supervision at these areas.
2. Enlist the aid of senior citizens and others to voluntarily serve as program leaders for preschoolers and young children.
3. Hold a different type of neighborhood festival or party each month in which each block has some responsibility and the residents provide their own entertainment, food, activities and decorations.
4. Cooperate with organizations A, B and C to sponsor activities Q, R and S at parks X, Y and Z on the second Tuesday of every month.
5. Contract with University C for students who need practical experience in recreation leadership, teaching and social work.

The emphasis in all policies and practices is on *resident* and *user* objectives instead of objectives held by the supplier or decision-maker. This is a direct contrast to the traditional approach. In this planning situation, the community advocates its own objectives as a starting point for compromise with the suppliers and decision-makers. Compromise may not be necessary if all have the same objectives, but this is seldom the case.

APPLICATION AND DEMONSTRATION

In this section an application of the innovative concept and techniques outlined in Chapter VI is illustrated. Concentration is on the determination of needs, action programs and citizen review aspects of the innovative approach. For simplicity, only *one* of the 10 neighborhoods in this community is used in the calculations. However, if desired, all 10 neighborhoods could be calculated at the same time by multiplying the results by 10, or each could be calculated separately and the results combined for the entire community of 500,000 people. This approach can be generalized to any neighborhood or population in the central city or suburbs and the results could be aggregated at the regional scale.

Determination of Needs

By any or *all* of the concepts and techniques listed in Chapter VI, the leisure preferences of a stratified, random sample[8] of the neighborhood residents are surveyed and prorated to the age distributions in Table 27.

The leisure objectives, values, problems and potentials of each group are analyzed and prorated to the general recreation opportunity alternatives indicated in Table 22. The range of general activities found to be most appropriate to this population tends to be in the active category and emphasizes the challenge and escape types of recreation as opposed to more passive and self-fulfilling activities.

---

[8] John Madge, *The Tools of Social Science* (Garden City, N. Y.: Anchor Books, 1965), p. 233.

TABLE 27
Neighborhood Age Distributions

Group	Age	Percent	Population
Preschool	under 5	15	7,500
Elementary	6–14	15	7,500
Young adults	15–24	25	12,500
Adults	25–64	25	12,500
Senior citizens	65+	20	10,000
Totals	17 average	100	50,000

TABLE 28
Potential and Actual Users by Age Group

Group	Age Range	Potential Users	Actual Users[a]
Preschool	under 5	7,500	1,500
Elementary	6–14	7,500	1,500
Young adults	15–24	12,500	2,500
Adults	25–64	12,500	2,500
Senior citizens	65+	10,000	2,000
Totals		50,000	10,000

[a] Estimated at 20 percent of the potential users. See Chapter VI for a rationalization of this percentage.

TABLE 29
Neighborhood Activity Space Needs and Possible Number of Peak Users[a]

Leisure Activity	Facility (Units[b])	Sq. Feet (1,000s)	Peak Users (Per Hr.)
Archery	10	150	500
Baseball	2	270	75
Basketball	9	54	105
Challenge apparatus	4	8	400
Combative sports	20	50	500
Creative skills	5	5	500
Environmental games	1	10	500
Group picnicking	5	20	1,000
Handball	8	8	64
Horseshoes	40	20	160
Movies/television	5	100	5,000
Shuffleboard	12	6	48
Softball	3	120	75
Table tennis	20	4	100
Teen club	1	30	900
Volleyball	6	18	120
Totals		873[c]	10,047

[a] Based on Table 23 Chapter VI.

[b] Units prorated to resident goals, values, and expressed or observed leisure preferences.

[c] Slightly over 20 acres (20.04 acres).

This range of general activities is translated into the specific activities listed in Table 23. These activities are related to the number of potential and actual users in each age group shown in Table 28 and translated into units, square feet and number of possible users per peak hour shown in Table 29.

The total area needed and number of potential peak-hour users are approximated at 20 acres and 10,000 users. At this stage, all concerned (resident, community leaders, the Community Council and Advocate Planning Team) reconsider the range of alternatives possible, as shown in Table 22, and the relationships between supply and use, goals and standards shown in Figure 4. They reach this consensus: (1) 100 percent of the actual number of users should be accommodated at peak-use periods, and (2) this use should be accommodated at an average density of 500 users per acre. These decisions are translated into a space standard and social indicator in the steps and calculations listed here.

Space Standard and Social Indicator Calculations

1. **100% of total population (TP) = potential users (PU):**
    50,000 = 50,000.

2. **20% of total population (TP) = users/peak hour (U):**
    20% x 50,000 = 10,000.

3. **Users/peak hour = actual users (AU):**
    10,000 = 10,000.

4. **Goals and objectives (GO) = activity orientations (AO):**
    GO = activities D through J (Table 22).

5. **Activity orientations (AO) = users/acre = density (D):**
    AO = 500 users/acre = D.

6. $\dfrac{U}{D}$ **= potential need (PN):**
    $$\dfrac{10,000}{500} = 20 \text{ acres.}$$

7. **Potential need (PN) − supply (S) = actual need (AN):**
    20 acres − 5 acres = 15 acres.

8. $\dfrac{\dfrac{AN}{TP}}{1,000}$ = standard in acres needed/1,000 population (STD):

$\dfrac{\dfrac{15}{50,000}}{1,000}$ = 0.3 acres/1,000 population.

9. U Index x D Index (Table 24) = social indicator (SI):

10 x 5 = 50.

10. Social indicator = recreation objectives (RO):

50 = recreation objectives.

The space standard is the *end* product of the needs determination process in the innovative approach. This is opposite to the traditional approach in which the space standard is usually the *beginning* of the process. The innovative space standard relates *directly* to the *expressed* goals, objectives, values, recreation preferences and desired opportunity levels of the residents and users. This is opposite to the traditional approach which does not generally reflect these variables in the planning process.

There is also a time horizon and distinct scale to the innovative space standard and social indicator which is related to the 2-year planning/action cycles of a 10-year program. Should the actual number of users change because of changes in activity preferences or use patterns after the completion of *one* 2-year cycle, these changes would automatically be reflected in the surveys and analyses for the next 2-year cycle. Hence, both the space standard and social indicator are likely to change every 2 years, or whenever the residents can rationalize a change which best meets *their* goals and priorities. This is opposite to the traditional approach which generally has *no* provisions for a rapid change in time horizons, scale or recreation preferences and does *not* normally reflect the expressed goals and objectives of potential users.

Action Program

Once the amount of area needed and activities desired are determined, a wide range of alternative *practices* for land acquisition, development and program can be used and organized into a *program*. The preceding list of practices is just one illustration of several ways in which these needs might be met. For example, if the neighborhood would rather not have homes taken to create recreation areas, they might insist on closing appropriate streets for recreation use. Likewise, if an abandoned warehouse becomes available for use as a teen club, a new club does not have to be built. At this point *opportunity, flexibility* and *choice* are used to determine which alternative practices are best.

The action program is related to available funds with the Recreation Resource Allocation Matrix shown in Table 25. This assumes that 50 million dollars are available over the 10-year period and each neighborhood can count on 5 million dollars to support its recreation needs over the next 10-year period.

The neighborhood divides its allocation into the priorities and items indicated in Table 30. The emphasis is on *action* and tangible *results* in *each* cycle with the major portion of funds being used in the first half of the 10-year action program. Also the *incremental commitment* of money to land and development allows for a change in priorities should it prove necessary after one cycle. This is to avoid a total misallocation of resources and give the residents and planners a continuous opportunity to reevaluate their ideas.

It is possible that these priorities and allocations might change as additional funds become available, preferences change and use increases or decreases. Sudden opportunities or new technologies could radically alter priorities. Also, as resident motivation builds

TABLE 30

Neighborhood Recreation Resource Allocation: A 10-Year Action Program (In Units of $1,000)

2-Year Cycles	I		II		III		IV		V		Resource Totals
Each Year	1	2	3	4	5	6	7	8	9	10	
Land	500		500		500		500				2,000[a]
Development		700		100		100		100			1,000[a]
Program	100	100	100	100	100	100	100	100	100	100	1,000
Maintenance		50	75	75	50	50	50	50	50	50	500
Admin.	50	50	50	50	50	50	50	50	50	50	500
Total	650	900	725	325	700	300	700	300	200	200	5,000

[a] Based on acquisition and development cost of $200,000/acre for 15 acres of land in this neighborhood.

with the sense of accomplishment through self-determination, there is the possibility of securing voluntary help especially for development, program and maintenance. This would allow a shift of funds from these areas to land acquisition or other programs. It also raises the possibility of one neighborhood helping another or making resource trade-offs which will best further the neighborhood's own objectives.

Review and Revision

The essence of the innovative approach is adaptation to *change* based on a continuous review and evaluation of the results by residents and planners. The 2-year planning/action cycles prompt constant review and response to change on at least a monthly or quarterly basis which coincides with each meeting of the Community Council. Some present and futuristic measures for review and evaluation might include any of these ideas:

1. A Mothers' Cooperative to periodically evaluate the functional use of each facility or activity.

2. Television monitors on selected areas or activities which can be viewed in the APT office, the Community Council headquarters or in the central planning agency.

3. Television surveys of various areas or activities which can be viewed at home and evaluated by dialing designated telephone numbers to indicate viewer response.

4. Electronic counters on selected pieces of equipment or areas to monitor use frequencies, intensities or noise levels.

5. Electronic suggestion boxes in all areas to allow users to tape record suggestions or press designated buttons to indicate their satisfaction or dissatisfaction.

6. Exchange of Advocate Planner Teams between neighborhoods to act as reviewers of each other's plans.

7. Holding the weekly meetings of the Neighborhood or Community Councils and Block Clubs in different recreation areas or facilities to familiarize these decision-making bodies with the areas and allow them a first-hand opportunity to evaluate the use of the areas or facilities.

8. Hold monthly criticism contests with substantial prizes for the best criticism and solution.

9. Request a formal annual review of all areas by the municipal recreation agency or the sponsors who have donated resources to this effort.

10. Post the results of all reviews in places where they could prompt public interest and discussion.

The APT acts as a central clearing house for all ongoing review and evaluation by residents, outside researchers and others. It prepares monthly evaluations and recommendations for review and action by the Community Council. The APT also coordinates needed research beyond its own capabilities by encouraging students from local universities to use this neighborhood for their studies.

All reviews and evaluations become public documents. They are posted in public places. All proposed plans and projects are on display in the "community planning van" which circulates to a different neighborhood each month. Any resident may phone a special number to record his or her comment, criticism or suggestion on any plan or project at any time. The recorded messages are played back during the monthly meetings of the Community Council and are available to all interested groups or individuals.

The reason for these elaborate procedures is to insure that each resident has ample opportunity to express himself through a variety of feedback loops. Fundamental to the innovative approach is the concept that people, planners and decision-makers are not infallible and need a continuing and constructive review of their efforts. These review procedures imply a conscious emphasis on self-evaluation as a parallel to self-determination.

TESTING AND EVALUATION

The assumptions, concepts and techniques of the innovative approach must be field-tested and adapted to each situation. There are many available and developing techniques which seem appropriate. All have been described by other authors in a wide range of publications on simulation, demonstration projects and community-action programs.

Simulation

The merits of simulation to represent a real or hypothetical model of a system, situation or process have made simulation a valuable technique for testing the feasibility or possible results of an idea, concept or approach.[9] Simulation allows one to test and evaluate his solution to a problem in an experimental situation which requires no commitment of resources or actual change in the item being

---

[9] Harold S. Guetzkow, *Simulation in the Social Sciences* (Englewood Cliffs, N. J.: Prentice-Hall, 1962).

studied. It could provide a number of imaginative ways to test and evaluate the relevance and effectiveness of the innovative approach to the inner city or elsewhere without a commitment of resources or risk of failure.

Because the innovative approach relies heavily on the roles of the resident, planner and administrator in the decision-making process, it lends itself to gaming simulation.[10] Its adaptability to systems analysis, linear programming and program-planning and budgeting techniques make simulation an ideal method for testing this approach and comparing it to the traditional approach. The innovative approach can also be used as a teaching and research device to explore many of the behavioral, political and economic aspects of urban recreation planning in a laboratory situation.

Demonstration Areas

A parallel or subsequent step beyond simulation is demonstration of the innovative approach under controlled conditions. Support could be obtained for this type of demonstration project under several programs which emphasize most of the features of the innovative approach.[11] There is also good precedent for private foundations to fund this type of research effort.

The estimated cost for research and implementation of one demonstration area similar to the example used in this study is 5 million dollars over a 10-year period. This would include the cost of land acquisition, development, program and research. This effort could be one component of the proposed system of "Urban Observatories."[12]

There are also many aspects of the innovative approach which are adaptable to planning for new communities. There is evidence to indicate the new community has many of the same characteristics of the inner city because of its relative homogeneity, isolation and motivation toward self-determination or citizen participation in the

---

[10] Richard L. Meier and Richard D. Duke, "Gaming Simulation for Urban Planning," *Journal of the American Institute of Planners* (January, 1966), pp. 3-16.

[11] See Nesbitt, Brown and Murphy, *Recreation and Leisure Service for the Disadvantaged,* pp. 559-569 for a list of current federal programs.

[12] Several papers by noted authorities detail the concept of "Urban Observatories" in the *Proceedings of the 1966 Graduate Colloquium,* Fels Institute of Local and State Government (Philadelphia, Pa., 1966), 54 pp.

planning process. Although it does not have the environmental, social and economic problems of the inner city, it may have a different set of problems, such as excess leisure, which lend themselves to the more sensitive aspects of the innovative approach.

There is also the dimension of innovation in new communities which would make them responsive to this approach. New communities planned with *traditional* recreation standards and suppliers' goals cannot reach their real potentials for providing meaningful leisure opportunities. There is much to recommend a demonstration of the innovative approach in a new community, if only to contrast its merits and shortcomings with a similar demonstration in the inner city.

Actual Situations

There is also an opportunity to test the innovative approach in a number of community-action programs, e.g., urban renewal, conservation and Model City Programs. This strategy is not without risk until such time as the innovative approach can be thoroughly tested and refined through simulation and demonstration. However, within limits, there is reason to believe that a community could attempt many aspects of the innovative approach with effective results. Various components of this approach might be tested in proposed urban renewal projects with relatively little extra effort or expense except for the humility of local administrators or urban planners in attempting an alternative to the traditional approach.

ANTICIPATED RESULTS

It is possible to speculate here on what might be some consequences of an application of the innovative approach in a real or simulated situation. There is as much reason to believe that this approach will fail in some cases as there is that it will succeed. It should be considered as a "calculated-risk decision" with these possible results.

Probable Risks

Six possible categories of risk seem evident: (1) misallocation of resources, (2) false expectations, (3) public apathy or misunderstanding, (4) bureaucratic obstacles and (5) political conflict. Each is discussed with respect to the inner city, the present and the immediate future.

MISALLOCATION OF RESOURCES

There is no question that the first or second 2-year planning/ action cycle of the innovative approach may misallocate resources because the values and preferences of residents have been misjudged, despite all the safeguards to minimize this possibility. At the neighborhood level, if there is no immediate response to misallocation of resources, the resulting delay can diminish resident motivation to participate in the planning process and compound the misallocation. At the community level this risk is even greater because of severe political and economic implications.

If the community organization is to retain the support of its constituents, it must not only show progress, but also must compete with other communities for limited public resources, which are often granted on the basis of past performance. This presents the risk that neighborhoods or communities which properly allocate their resources will obtain more, while those who make mistakes will obtain less, on the basis of past performance.

FALSE EXPECTATIONS

Many studies have identified one of the major sources of inner city problems as that of false expectations. The induced hope of improvement fades easily with the lack of quick response to pressing needs. Response need not be total, but it must be positive, visible and immediate to enlist the confidence and participation of ghetto residents. The innovative approach bases its success on incremental improvement in leisure opportunities which are relevant to expressed or latent tastes. If this approach raises the level of expectation and then fails to deliver what is promised, it may not have a second chance to prove itself.

PUBLIC APATHY

There is good reason to believe that a demonstration of the innovative approach would be viewed by residents as another ill-conceived panacea for their problems. In many cases, past experience with bureaucratic bungling and the patronizing attitude of many professionals have produced a general apathy for innovative programs directed at the inner city. Public apathy is a real risk that can only be overcome by better communication, patience and action.

BUREAUCRATIC OBSTACLES

Bureaucracy is an obstacle to innovation and the implementation of many public-action programs, especially in the inner city where there has been very little political leverage to expedite action. This, added to the dimensions of the innovative approach which challenge tradition and status quo, the personalities and professional niches of some, and the conscience of others, could create even more bureaucratic obstacles. It is a significant problem. Given the minimization of all other problems, this obstacle could thwart a fair demonstration of the innovative approach.

POLITICAL CONFLICT

The realities of the political process suggest that this approach could be mired in controversy, compromise and antagonism to a point where residents and their elected representatives or acknowledged leaders would not endorse it as a viable alternative to the traditional approach. Beyond conflict is the usual inability of the political process to rationalize its decisions in other than political terms which often neglect the long-term logic of planning and the public interest. The political-conflict risk can be compounded by the short-term emphasis of most political decisions and the rapid turnover of local politicians.

Potential Rewards

Six possible categories of potential reward seem evident: (1) research applications, (2) satisficing* user demand, (3) a more responsive planning process, (4) bureaucratic responsibility, (5) adaptability to rapid change, and (6) support for advocacy planning. Each is discussed with reference to the inner city, the present and the immediate future.

RESEARCH APPLICATIONS

One important reward in an application of the innovative approach is its wide range of research applications for scholars and government. The need for this type of study has already been documented in previous chapters. However, one area which has not been mentioned is that of using the innovative approach to evaluate the

---

* "Satisficing," a combination of satisfaction and suffice, is commonly used in contemporary social and economic contexts.

traditional approach. The results of such research could provide a measurable improvement in each approach and perhaps create a third approach integrating the best of both. The breadth of research skills required for an application of the innovative approach might prompt many reticent researchers to consider the study of leisure respectable. This could provide the needed research impetus and interdisciplinary approach in an academic area long deficient in both.

SATISFICING DEMAND

There is no simple solution to the dilemma of satisficing demand, nor is the innovative approach a sure remedy for the already over-burdened recreation resources of this nation. But it does provide *one* alternative that the traditional approach does not. By active participation in the planning process, individuals may begin to understand the dimensions of the problem and be motivated to constructive action. Given the approaching crisis in recreation use and the dilemma of increasing leisure, this hope is realistic. In addition, if people cannot have their demands accommodated, at least they can understand why, and, perhaps, reassign their priorities to help relieve the imbalances.

If the innovative approach is successful in satisficing local demands, it could also have a possible impact on the preservation of wilderness or resource-oriented areas.* One effective way to help keep the use levels of wilderness areas within ecological limits is to increase the attractiveness and utility of *local* recreation opportunities. There is also reason to believe many urban dwellers are fleeing the city each summer to avoid civil unrest and racial tension. The combination of these two causes can have disastrous results on resource-oriented areas not intended for mass use and will result in a diminishing recreation experience in these areas. There is a relationship between satisficing inner city recreation demands and wilderness preservation which could become critically important in the near future.

RESPONSIVE PLANNING PROCESS

One theme underlying civil disorder is a drive for more self-determination, equality and participation in the mainstream of Amer-

---

* This does not apply to most inner city residents who do not commonly use wilderness areas. It does apply to many central city and suburban populations.

ican life. This is often expressed in a growing resentment toward central planning and some of its insensitive techniques which alienate some individuals from the planning process. The traditional lack of responsiveness in the current approach to leisure planning for the inner city is a fact.

There is good reason to believe that, given the opportunity to become more involved in the planning process and decision-making, many people might begin to change their current disappointment with planning and government. There is also ample evidence to indicate that citizen involvement is the best way to improve the planning process and help make people more aware of complex problems which have no simple answers.[13] The innovative approach could provide one vehicle to give the planning process and government more credibility.

SUPPORT FOR ADVOCACY PLANNING

Advocacy planning, as a vehicle for citizen participation in the planning process, needs examples of success. If the innovative approach is ultimately to become an alternative to central planning, it needs the probable initial failures and results to refine its techniques. There is reason to expect both *success* and *failure* as the early results of a controlled application of this approach. Even failure should be considered as a reward because it will eliminate alternatives and prompt the development of other alternatives.

BUREAUCRATIC RESPONSIBILITY

A successful application of the innovative approach could have a significant impact on the bureaucratic responsibility of agencies charged with the planning and supply of recreation opportunities in the inner city and elsewhere. In terms of action, it could prompt the agencies to rationalize their own goals and actions and more carefully justify their proposed programs and past performance.

Advocacy planning might in time diminish the status of agencies which cannot or will not respond in a positive manner to the needs and demands of their clientele. This will be a strong inducement toward more bureaucratic responsibility. It should also increase the effectiveness of agencies by inputs of citizen action and outside professional help. This could bolster the strained resources of most

---

[13] Alan A. Altshuler, *The City Planning Process* (Ithaca, N. Y.: Cornell University Press, 1965), Parts II and III, *passim.*

agencies and allow them to concentrate better on long-range comprehensive programs at a city-wide scale. In effect, it would place problem-solving at the level of the problem.

ADAPTATION TO RAPID CHANGE

The basis of the innovative approach is change in leisure patterns and the urban environment. This approach can be both the cause and the effect of change. The merits of using it as an alternative to the traditional approach can only be measured over time. However, it is safe to assume that the innovative approach is more adaptable to rapid change than is the traditional approach which has built-in restraints to change.

DIMENSIONS OF RELEVANCE

Urgency in the face of realistic alternatives and challenges is an inescapable condition of Urban America. There is no doubt that this nation is at a crossroads in its acknowledgment and commitment to cope with the problems of the inner and central city. There is also no question about the consequences of approaching these problems with traditional and ineffective solutions. The dimensions of relevance have been explored by many over the past decade, yet relatively little has been accomplished.

Realistic Alternatives

At this point in time, two alternatives seem evident for recreation planning in Urban America. The first is a continuation of present policies, or status quo. This implies the usual platitudes, panic programs, token remedies, and well-meant efforts which might yield some incremental improvement in opportunity, but do relatively little to actually enrich the inner city especially or make it more tolerable.

At the same time, a continuation of current policies runs the risk of increasing the alienation of residents to dangerous levels. Individuals or their institutions, prompted by government inaction, might take measures which would effectively negate any constructive response from local governments and divide this country into two societies—one white and suburban, the other black and urban.

If status quo is an intenable alternative and enrichment of the inner city improbable, given the nation's current set of priorities, demonstration is one realistic option. This choice will involve humility, commitment and the willingness to acknowledge failure, all of which are difficult for many professionals or decision-makers. Despite these admitted obstacles, there is much to recommend a *trial* of the innovative approach. If it succeeds, there is some hope for incremental progress in the area of recreation planning. Progress here could lead to hope for other areas such as housing, health and education.

Luxury of Delay

To date, the Recreation Movement has overlooked many opportunities for innovation.* In a rapidly changing world the point may soon be reached where traditional suppliers of public recreation for the city may be replaced by other institutions; people will no longer rely on public agencies to supply their leisure needs.

This change could have severe impacts on the cost and quality of the recreation experience. If such basic facilities as the neighborhood playground cannot be effectively supplied by the public sector, there is evidence to project the loss of this opportunity or its provision by the private sector at a higher price and lower quality.[14] This is a remote possibility, but certainly one conceivable consequence of delay.

Conceptual Challenges

Conant said, "a scholar's [professional's] activities should have relevance to the immediate future of our civilization."[15] Cain expands this idea by associating professional courage and risk with the conceptual challenges of leisure planning. He states:

> We need to find the means and the mass courage to define and accept *humanistic* as well as technological goals. . . . There can be no real progress toward solution of our present problems without individuals who take the *risk* of discriminatory judgments. . . . Some-

---

* Such as adventure play areas, self-generated parks, day-care centers for children, environmental education or the use of gaming simulation in the planning and decision-making process.

[14] Clawson, *Economics of Outdoor Recreation*, Part IV, *passim.*

[15] James B. Conant, commencement address at Michigan State University, June, 1967, published in *Michigan State University Publication*, Vol. 62, No. 5, November, 1967, p. 18.

how we must translate our knowledge and technology into effective social action. . . .

. . . .

> If we find ourselves unable to meet the challenges of technological change, it will be because we have failed to generate the discriminating thinkers who *challenge* the herd psychology and modify it enough to preserve the group structure by shifting, perhaps only slightly, the centers of *traditional* belief.[16]

The intellectual barriers to innovation form a most difficult obstacle. Boulding's call for "broader agendas" describes these intellectual barriers as "agarophobia . . . fear of open spaces, especially open spaces in the mind."[17] Michael relates this conceptual challenge to the professional and the city:

> In the next few years, the contrast between the poverty-stricken portion of our population and that enjoying a high standard of living will present a blatant challenge to our egalitarian ethos. The distinction made between those who cannot or will not and those who can and do . . . will gradually emphasize that this is becoming an elite society with the prizes going to those best endowed and best trained.[18]

The essence of Michael's statement is professional relevance. Those willing to accept the conceptual challenge of innovation will be rewarded; those unwilling to risk their professional reputations may not share in the rewards. Michael's plea is for more courage and commitment to improve the quality of life and environment in Urban America. A new approach to urban recreation planning is one place to begin.

---

[16] Stanley A. Cain, "Concluding Remarks," in Driver, *Elements of Outdoor Recreation Planning*, p. 311, emphasis added.

[17] Kenneth Boulding, *The Meaning of the Twentieth Century* (New York: Harper and Row, 1964).

[18] Michael, *The Next Generation*, p. 170.

VIII

Summary

This chapter summarizes what has been discussed or omitted in this book and why, describes the major implications of the problem and solutions to it, and makes some recommendations for future study and action. The emphasis is on what needs to be done, responsibility and timing.

The objective of this book has been to develop a concept and technique for outdoor recreation planning in the inner city that could also be used elsewhere. This has been done by a critical analysis of the traditional approach to recreation planning and use of space standards. The shortcomings of the traditional approach have been identified and an alternative called "the innovative approach" has been developed to compare the differences between the two approaches. The innovative approach has been applied to a typical situation to illustrate its possible results, and several means of testing it have been suggested.

There are several conceptual and methodological areas which could be the focus of future study and action. All will require extensive field studies. Both the time and costly nature of the required studies will require a national commitment to recreation research of the scope and scale described in *A Program for Outdoor Recreation Research.*[1]

---

[1] National Academy of Sciences, *A Program for Outdoor Recreation Research.*

255

NEEDED RESEARCH

One conclusion of this book has been the need for more research and professional knowledge in the area of outdoor recreation. Five problem areas are most critical: (1) user behavior, (2) supplier and community goals, (3) goal-program relationships, (4) costs and benefits, and (5) implementation.

USER BEHAVIOR

There are relatively little data in the literature on who uses what facilities, where, when, why and with what effects. Quantitative data on the characteristics of users beyond the usual age, sex and income level are almost nonexistent. Little is known about urban leisure behavior and relatively few studies have been made of recreation for the urban poor, especially the Negro. No studies have been made to contrast these populations with current trends and past behavior. There are also relatively little data on user groups; the need for program and leadership; frequencies of use by activity, challenge levels, satisfaction levels; reasons for nonuse; and conflicts in the use of a given facility or system of opportunities.

The use of recreation as a vehicle for social interaction, advocacy, conflict resolution, escape and self-testing has received very little attention to date. This void contributes to the knowledge gaps on use patterns, participation rates, user preference, and what role the public and private sectors should play in supplying opportunities.

SUPPLIER AND COMMUNITY GOALS

Generalizable information on the goals of the suppliers and consumers of recreation opportunities is a serious obstacle to research in many other areas because it leaves the researcher with only hypothetical measures of achievement. It also creates difficulties in attempting to justify the actions or inactions of each user group or planning unit. This is particularly true for the approach to urban recreation planning described in this book, which is difficult to apply if either the practiced or latent goals are not expressed.

Isolation of the explicit goals of different groups would open several other research areas such as policy formulation, benefit-cost analysis and time budgets. It also would be an inducement for the application of systems analysis techniques to leisure behavior. These techniques could be used to identify and help solve many other problems now generally avoided by professionals for lack of information on goals, objectives, policies and the criteria, standards or principles which they imply.

GOAL-PROGRAM RELATIONSHIPS

A major information gap exists in the historical analysis of goal-program consequences. There are very few authoritative case studies to relate the results of a given goal on programs or vice versa. Almost no quantitative or qualitative meaures of performance exist in the form of social indicators. What little data are available are largely intuitive and have never been tested and evaluated in a controlled situation with contemporary social research methods.

The lack of case studies is why this book had to use hypothetical goals and programs for evaluation. Were actual ones available, the task of description, analysis and evaluation would have been much simpler and more conclusive. This deficiency also restricts comparative research between recreation and other fields. The problem might be overcome if Federal agencies were to realistically require all local units of government to state their goals, objectives, policies and practices in order to receive Federal assistance. This could result in a national data bank of local recreation goals which researchers could analyze and develop into case studies. It could also result in the synthesis of national leisure goals and priorities.

COSTS AND BENEFITS

The lack of unit cost data for various aspects of public recreation is an obstacle to the development of necessary social indicators and sets of attainable objectives. Data on land cost, operating expenditures, depreciation and user fees are relatively scarce for most types of urban recreation facilities. Information on user benefits is almost nonexistent except in terms of attendance figures. A lack of participation rates as a function of price or the availability of other opportunities is one reason why it is difficult for researchers to derive actual demand estimates for recreation use or economists to price recreation as a social service.

IMPLEMENTATION

A general lack of historical information on the planning process, political strategies, critical path programming, program evaluation and innovation is evident in the field. What data exist are usually distorted by value judgments or arbitrary techniques which make them questionable for research and action programs.

The area of strategy is particularly lacking in documentation. Two kinds of research are needed to help correct this situation. First, the existing planning and decision-making process could be studied to provide insights into how decisions are reached and compromised in the process of implementation. Second, studies which deal with the "art" of compromise are needed to help indicate ways and means in which citizens, planners and decision-makers can maximize their ultimate goals, yet accomplish their immediate objectives in an expedient manner. Fundamental to all of these is the area of communication and understanding which has received very little definitive research as it relates to recreation issues.

RESEARCH PRIORITIES

If it were necessary to assign research priorities to the above areas, the highest would be a nationwide effort to study user behavior. Specifically, these studies should emphasize user goals, objectives and preferences; actual use patterns; user groups; the extent and frequency of use for given activities; and the area of nonuse, in approximately this order. Were it possible to obtain data in these research areas, all others would become far less difficult.

If this type of research were attempted, its approach and methods must be broadened to adopt the latest social research techniques. Because this may not be possible within the existing framework of most agencies in the recreation field, it might best be accomplished by universities, research foundations or private consultants. Hopefully, the pragmatic constraints of operational agencies and the innovative dimensions of the university could be blended in a joint effort supported by a national commitment to recreation research.

MAJOR IMPLICATIONS

The implications of this book on people living in Urban America, their recreation opportunities and the planning or recreation professionals responsible for providing these opportunities are provocative and can have serious consequences for all. Despite good intentions, the traditional approach to urban recreation planning has not been and will not be effective in today's cities without a drastic change in its level of responsiveness to user needs and self-determination.

While this may be a sobering conclusion, it is realistic in light of all available evidence. Perhaps others may be more optimistic than realistic about the future of the central city, central planning and public recreation, especially in the inner city, but their evidence has escaped this writer. Clark describes with candor:

> The dark ghetto's invisible walls have been erected by the white society, by those who have power, both to confine those who have no power and to perpetuate their powerlessness. The dark ghettos are social, political, educational and — above all — economic colonies. Their inhabitants are subject people, victims of the greed, cruelty, insensitivity, guilt, and fear of their masters.

He continues:

> The objective dimensions of the American urban ghettos are over-crowded and deteriorated housing, high infant mortality, crime and disease. The subjective dimensions are resentment, hostility, despair, apathy, self-depreciation, and its ironic companion, compensatory grandiose behavior.

He concludes:

> The ghetto is ferment, paradox, conflict, and dilemma. Yet within its pervasive pathology exists a surprising human resilience. The ghetto is hope, it is despair. . . . It is aspiration for change, and it is apathy. It is vibrancy; it is stagnation. It is courage, and it is defeat-ism. It is cooperation and concern, and it is suspicion, competitive-ness, and rejection. It is the surge toward assimilation, and it is alienation and withdrawal within the protective wall of the ghetto.[2]

In this context the innovative approach to recreation planning can have these major implications for institutional change, the recreation experience, citizen participation in the planning process and the future of Urban America.

INSTITUTIONAL CHANGE

"The times cry for change and the disaffected demand it. Yet our institutions are sluggish, resistant, painfully slow to respond. They were designed for another kind of nation, an earlier societal self-image."[3] This feeling is characteristic of many institutions in Urban America. However, recreation seems to be one area very responsive to change because it does not produce the controversy

---

[2] Clark, *Dark Ghetto*, p. 11.

[3] Donald Canty, *A Single Society*, p. 175.

and polarized attitudes seen in areas such as housing, education and employment.

The traditional approach to recreation planning in most cities is irrelevant and ineffective. Responsible public agencies should either modify their current concepts and techniques to make them more responsive to user needs or seek an alternative approach which can respond to these needs. If these agencies cannot or will not innovate change, change will innovate new institutions to plan, provide and administer recreation opportunities.

THE RECREATION EXPERIENCE

Many of the traditional activities, facilities and "conventional wisdoms" about the recreation experience do not apply in the central and inner city because of a vast difference between user and supplier goals, objectives and values. Supplier goals often encourage nonuse and do not provide the measure of social service possible in the area of leisure. In general, the arbitrary space standards and planning techniques which have been used elsewhere do not apply to inner city conditions and populations. In many cases they are socially, economically and politically infeasible.

CITIZEN PARTICIPATION

The traditional approach to recreation planning does not encourage direct citizen participation in the planning process. Its concepts, techniques and standards have been essentially established by an elite and supported by a professional organization which has not scientifically tested or evaluated them in terms of their relevance to any populations other than white, middle-class Americans. The result of this insensitive approach to coping with a human need is resident dissatisfaction and alienation expressed in vandalism, nonuse of public facilities and riots to protest grievances which include the lack of adequate recreation opportunities.

One implication of this alienation is a more militant stance of residents to demand a planning process which is more responsive to their goals and objectives. If professionals cannot or will not respond in a constructive manner, either through action or an acceptable rationalization for inaction, one probable alternative is a trend toward more self-determination in the form of advocacy planning. This could have serious consequences on the scope, scale and nature of urban recreation systems.

THE FUTURE OF URBAN AMERICA

Leisure, outdoor recreation and open space are vital components of the quality of life and environment possible in the city. They do not rank with other needs such as employment, housing, health, and education, but they do have a role in enriching the life and environment of cities and suburbs. This role is especially critical in the inner city until such time as integration becomes a reality or a commitment to separate, but *equal* societies in America is visible.

Recreation planning has a place and a purpose which have been largely overlooked. It should provide residents with optimum recreation opportunities reflecting their goals, values and needs. In this sense, responsive recreation planning is one way to make life more tolerable in cities and sustain the hope for a better Urban America.

CONCLUSIONS

In this book an attempt has been made to reshape the current approach to urban recreation planning in the direction of an applied social science. The plea for planning and recreation professionals to adopt the techniques of the behavioral scientist calls for institutional change beginning with professional education and continuing through the political process.

Institutional change and innovation have seldom been easy, but they can be a rational avenue to problem-solving in cities. Tradition is difficult to forsake, especially in times of economic or political uncertainty and social crisis. The risk of failure lends an unrealistic pallor to new ideas and there is a strong tendency to look back instead of ahead.

The methods and techniques of social science and the innovative approach to recreation planning outlined here are far from perfect, but they can provide an alternative for understanding or creating change which is the essence of Urban America. All too often in our preoccupation with time, space and things, *people*, the justification for cities, social science, leisure and planning, are forgotten. Hopefully, this book has remembered them.

Appendices

APPENDIX A

TABLE 1

Estimated Outdoor Recreation Use in 1960, 1980 and 2000*
(Millions of Visits)

Type of Recreation	1960	1980	2000
National parks	72	175	485
National forests	93	1,700	24,000
State parks	259	1,200	5,200
Corps reservoirs	109	2,000	32,000
TVA reservoirs	53	360	2,300
City and county parks	213	290	470
Totals	799	5,725	64,455

* Adapted from Marion Clawson, *Economics of Outdoor Recreation* (Baltimore: Johns Hopkins Press, 1966), p. 119. By simple trend extension procedure, 1953-1960 trend.

263

TABLE 2

Participation in 16 Major Summertime Outdoor Recreation Activities*
(Millions of Occasions)

Recreation Activity	Rank	1965[a]	1980[a]	2000[a]
Walking for pleasure	1	1,030	1,539	2,581
Swimming	2	970	1,671	2,982
Driving for pleasure	3	940	1,423	2,146
Playing outdoor games or sports	4	929	1,594	2,940
Bicycling	5	467	617	860
Sightseeing	6	457	705	1,169
Picnicking	7	451	668	1,022
Fishing	8	322	422	574
Attending outdoor sports events	9	246	352	535
Boating[b]	10	220	387	694
Nature walks	11	117	173	274
Camping	12	97	173	328
Horseback riding	13	77	111	179
Water skiing	14	56	124	259
Hiking	15	50	89	159
Attending outdoor concerts, plays	16	47	80	144
	Total	6,476	10,128	16,846

[a] 1965 Bureau of Outdoor Recreation Survey and Projections.

[b] Other than canoeing or sailing.

* From U. S. Department of the Interior, Bureau of Outdoor Recreation, *Outdoor Recreation Trends* (Washington, D. C., Government Printing Office, 1967), p. 20.

TABLE 3

Participation in 16 Major Summertime Outdoor Recreation Activities*
(Millions of Occasions)

Recreation Activity[a]	Rank	1965	1980	2000
Walking for pleasure	3	566	922	1,569
Swimming	2	672	1,310	2,307
Driving for pleasure	1	872	1,508	2,215
Playing outdoor games or sports	4	474	915	1,666
Bicycling	8	228	314	452
Sightseeing	5	287	499	825
Picnicking	6	279	446	700
Fishing	7	260	364	521
Attending outdoor sports events	9	172	272	416
Boating[b]	10	159	316	557
Nature walks	11	98	167	263
Camping	12	60	127	235
Horseback riding	13	55	88	143
Water skiing	14	39	94	189
Hiking	15	34	72	125
Attending outdoor concerts, plays	16	27	49	92
Total		4,282	7,463	12,275

[a] Outdoor Recreation Resources Commission, National Recreation Survey, 1960.

[b] Other than canoeing or sailing.

* From U. S. Department of the Interior, Bureau of Outdoor Recreation, *Outdoor Recreation Trends* (Washington, D. C., Government Printing Office, 1967), p. 21.

TABLE 4

**Outdoor Recreation Activity in U.S. Metropolitan Areas
1960, 1976 and 2000***

Outdoor Activity[a]	1960	1976	2000
Driving for pleasure	298	502	952
Walking for pleasure	277	442	892
Swimming	260	498	1,107
Playing outdoor games or sports	187	356	810
Sightseeing	118	201	408
Picnicking	106	172	325
Bicycling	71	104	188
Attending outdoor sports events	59	95	180
Fishing	58	89	159
Boating other than sailing or canoeing	56	110	248
Nature walks	37	63	124
Camping	17	36	88
Hunting	14	21	36
Hiking	14	28	62
Water skiing	12	30	79
Horseback riding	11	18	39
Attending outdoor concerts, drama	11	20	45
All activities	1,606	2,785	5,742

[a] Millions of occasions for selected recreational activities, actual and projected, by persons 12 year of age and over, residing in large metropolitan areas. Number of separate days on which persons engaged in activity during June–August, except hunting, for which September–November was used. Areas with population of 1,000,000 and over.

* From *Outdoor Recreation for America* (A report to the President and Congress by the Outdoor Recreation Resources Review Commission, Washington, January, 1962) cited in *Open Space in Northeastern Illinois* (Chicago: Northeastern Metropolitan Area Planning Commission, 1962), p. 38.

TABLE 5

Rank Order of Top Six Activities Reported by Localities 1960 and 1965*

Ranka	Youthb		Adult	
	1960	1965	1960	1965
1	Baseball	Baseball	Picnicking	Softball
2	Swimming	Basketball	Softball	Swimming
3	Softball	Swimming	Swimming	Tennis
4	Picnicking	Tennis	Tennis	Basketball
5	Tennis	Volleyball	Baseball	Volleyball
6	Basketball	Picnicking	Basketball	Picnicking

a Ranked according to number of localities reporting this activity.

b 18 years of age or over [sic], should read under.

*From National Recreation and Park Association, *Recreation and Park Year-book 1966* (Washington, D. C.: National Recreation and Park Association, 1966), p. 53.

APPENDIX B

TABLE 1

Acreage of Nonurban Public Designated Recreation Areas, by Region and Level of Government, 48 Contiguous States, 1960*

Region	Acreage (1,000)				Percentage of Regional Total Acreage		
	Federal	State	Local	Total	Federal	State	Local
New England	1,058	643	115	1,816	58	36	6
Middle Atlantic	541	6,707	41	7,289	7	92	1
East North Central	5,564	5,854	2,395	13,813	40	42	18
West North Central	9,821	4,634	22	14,477	68	32	(a)
South Atlantic	9,491	1,794	8	11,293	84	16	(a)
East South Central	3,800	954	8	4,762	80	20	(a)
West South Central	6,058	1,008	79	7,145	85	14	1
Mountain	106,555	2,959	89	109,603	97	3	(a)
Pacific	51,188	4,334	113	55,635	92	8	(a)
Total, 48 States	194,076	28,887	2,870	225,833	86	13	1

a Less than 0.5 percent.

* From ORRRC Study Report 1, Tables 11 and 12, pp. 16-17. This table includes only areas of 41 acres or more, hence it includes only 20 percent of the areas but about 97 percent of the total acreage. Cited in Clawson, Economics of Outdoor Recreation, p. 200.

TABLE 2

Municipal and County Parks: Number and Acreage by Regions,
Total and per Million of Urban Population*

Region	Urban Population (1,000)	Parks Total		Parks Per Million Urban Population	
		Number	Acres	Number	Acres
New England	8,033	2,152	52,389	268	6,522
Middle Atlantic	27,810	4,235	127,246	152	4,576
East North Central	26,439	5,205	282,108	197	10,670
West North Central	9,047	1,884	70,591	208	7,803
South Atlantic	14,853	3,752	101,382	253	6,826
East South Central	5,834	917	31,906	157	5,469
West South Central	11,479	1,740	62,572	152	5,451
Mountain	4,600	1,021	119,937	222	26,073
Pacific	17,190	3,459	167,330	201	9,734
Total, U.S.	125,285	24,365	1,015,461	195	8,105

* From National Recreation and Park Association, *Recreation and Park Yearbook, 1961* (Washington, D. C.: National Recreation Association, 1961). Cited in Clawson, *Economics of Outdoor Recreation,* p. 198.

TABLE 3
Recreation and Park Statistics for 1965[*]

	Cities	Counties	Totals[a] City & County
Park and recreation areas			
Total number	26,360	4,149	30,509
Total areas	805,336	691,042	1,496,378
Number acquired, 1961-1965	3,525	1,100	4,625
Acres acquired, 1961-1965	114,700	220,676	335,376
School recreation areas			
Number	14,413	2,126	16,539
Acres	96,965	19,741	116,706
Playgrounds under leadership			
Total number[b]	22,304	1,994	24,298
Year-round	6,076	350	6,426
Summer only	16,142	1,558	17,700
Baseball diamonds—90 ft.	8,230	1,105	9,335
Bathing beaches	883	378	1,261
Golf courses			
9-hole	305	50	355
18-hole	545	105	650
Softball diamonds	15,441	2,026	17,467
Swimming pools			
Indoor	447	21	468
Outdoor shallow	1,596	66	1,662
Outdoor deep	2,418	197	2,615
Tennis courts	18,631	1,295	19,926
Recreation buildings			
Large	1,945	156	2,101
Other	3,774	611	4,385
Indoor recreation centers			
School	12,905	1,389	14,294
Other	1,542	205	1,747
All paid personnel			
Full-time, year-round	54,646	10,567	65,213
Seasonal and part-time	158,508	19,449	177,957
Volunteers			
Total leaders	373,353	47,239	420,592
Total other	60,814	13,001	73,815

[a] Reported by 3,142 agencies: 2,784 city and 358 county authorities.

[b] These totals do not reconcile.

[*] From National Recreation and Park Association, *Recreation and Park Yearbook 1966* (Washington, D. C.: NRPA, 1967), p. 59.

TABLE 4
Local Recreation Trends 1940-1965*

Expenditures

Since 1940, the amount of money spent by park and recreation agencies has increased from 31 million dollars annually to more than 905 million dollars. Since 1940, operating expenses soared from less than 26 million dollars to more than 611 million dollars, while spending for capital improvements climbed from some 5 million dollars to nearly 300 million dollars.

Management

From 1960 to 1965, the number of combined park and recreation agencies jumped from less than 500 to more than 1,300, with a corresponding decline in the number of separate recreation departments, and school districts reporting park and recreation services. Until surpassed in 1965, separate recreation authorities were reported in greater numbers than other managing authorities since 1940.

Professional Personnel

Since 1940, the number of employed park and recreation professionals has risen nearly fivefold from approximately 24,000 to nearly 120,000, increasing at a steady rate of about 3,500 every year. From 1960 to 1965, the number of professionals employed full-time has more than doubled from 9,216 to 19,208 persons, while the growth rate for the number of professionals employed part-time has leveled off slightly.

Outdoor Playgrounds under Leadership

Since 1940, the number of playgrounds under leadership has increased almost 2½ times from 9,921 to 24,298. In 1965, there were nearly three times as many summer-only playgrounds as year-round playgrounds under leadership—17,700 to 6,426.

Major Sports Facilities

From 1940 to 1955, major recreation facilities maintained a rather steady increase, but from 1955 to 1965 the growth rate jumped sharply. Since 1955, the number of tennis courts increased from 13,188 to 19,926, softball diamonds from 11,834 to 17,467, and regulation (90 feet) baseball diamonds from 5,452 to 9,335.

Selected Facilities

Since 1955, golf courses and outdoor swimming pools — both requiring major capital investments — have more than doubled, with the highest rate of increase in the period 1960-1965. Since 1955, the number of public bathing beaches has increased from 830 to 1,261.

---

* From National Recreation and Park Association, *Recreation and Park Yearbook 1966* (Washington, D. C.: NRPA, 1967), p. 41.

TABLE 4—Continued

Other Findings

In 1950 — the first year figures were available — city and county agencies reported 17,142 park and recreation areas with 644,067 acres; in 1965, the number of park and recreation areas had increased to 30,509, and the acreage more than doubled to 1,496,378 acres. From 1940 to 1965, the number of recreation buildings more than tripled from 1,750 to 6,486; while during the same period, indoor recreation centers jumped fourfold from 3,986 to 16,041.

TABLE 5

Comparison of Selected Activities 1960 and 1965*
(Percentage of Local Public Agencies That Reported Particular Activity)

	1960		1965	
Activity	Youth[a]	Adults	Youth[a]	Adults
Games and sports				
Archery	28.3	17.1	45.6	31.5
Athletic tests	32.9	5.4	43.8	9.6
Badminton	37.0	21.3	36.8	25.4
Baseball	69.9	41.5	84.2	42.9
Basketball	54.7	37.7	79.8	62.2
Bowling — indoor	14.0	6.7	30.7	21.0
Football — regulation	16.1	2.9	36.8	7.8
Football — touch	26.9	6.5	53.5	19.2
Golf	20.6	20.7	42.1	39.4
Handball	7.9	6.6	14.0	11.4
Horeshoes	45.3	36.7	52.6	39.4
Paddle tennis	26.2	9.5	29.8	12.2
Shuffleboard	30.9	22.1	35.0	28.0
Soccer	13.8	4.4	18.4	7.8
Softball	61.1	52.3	73.6	69.2
Supervised roller skating	13.9	4.9	15.7	7.8
Table tennis	42.4	24.0	53.5	36.8
Tennis	56.6	48.4	74.5	64.0
Track and field	33.2	5.5	54.3	16.6
Tumbling and gymnastics	20.6	4.7	39.4	7.0
Volleyball	44.0	28.8	62.2	52.6
Outdoor activities				
Supervised bicycling	9.6	0.7	21.9	6.1
Camping — day[b]	16.5	2.7	37.7	14.9

TABLE 5—Continued

Activity	1960		1965	
	Youth[a]	Adults	Youth[a]	Adults
Outdoor activities—continued				
Camping — family[c]	4.0	4.4	7.1	7.1
Camping — overnight	9.4	4.9	42.9	21.9
Gardening	2.1	3.6	5.2	7.0
Hiking — organized	12.1	2.1	22.8	9.6
Horseback riding	3.8	3.9	15.7	12.2
Nature activities	21.6	6.1	30.7	15.7
Picnicking	58.8	58.7	57.0	49.1
Shooting	7.3	7.3	17.5	15.7
Trips and tours	21.2	10.4	41.2	27.1
Water sports				
Boating	12.3	13.9	29.8	33.3
Fishing	16.7	9.7	42.1	33.3
Swimming	61.3	50.3	77.1	65.7
Synchronized swimming	14.7	7.1	29.8	7.8
Water carnivals	16.4	7.8	22.8	10.5
Water skiing	3.7	3.6	15.7	14.0
Winter sports				
Coasting	11.9	17.6	22.8	14.0
Ice hockey	8.6	4.2	15.7	7.8
Skating	33.6	30.8	47.3	37.7
Skiing	8.6	7.1	18.4	16.6
Tobogganing	5.6	4.2	17.5	15.7
Winter carnivals	3.6	2.1	5.2	5.2
Crafts				
Clay modeling	34.0	7.1	41.2	10.5
Ceramics	22.3	13.3	35.9	24.5
Leathercraft	33.8	9.6	39.4	13.1
Metalcraft	22.3	7.7	44.7	17.5
Needle craft	19.7	8.1	30.7	15.7
Papercraft	38.7	6.0	51.7	9.6
Plastics	18.5	4.6	25.4	12.2
Weaving	28.4	6.9	35.9	17.5
Woodwork	23.9	7.8	31.5	12.2
Fine arts				
Drawing	25.1	8.4	37.7	25.4
Painting	24.0	11.8	38.5	28.0
Other graphic arts	5.4	3.3	14.9	14.0
Sculpture	4.7	2.8	12.2	13.1

TABLE 5—Continued

Activity	1960 Youth[a]	1960 Adults	1965 Youth[a]	1965 Adults
Performing arts				
Ballet	10.5	1.8	21.0	5.2
Band concerts	21.9	23.1	29.8	30.7
Choral activities	9.2	8.0	22.8	22.8
Community theater	7.5	7.4	16.6	19.2
Creative dramatics	12.3	2.3	21.9	6.1
Festivals	12.3	5.8	13.1	9.6
Folk dancing	18.5	10.5	20.1	22.8
Informal instrument groups	7.6	3.9	21.9	10.5
Modern creative dancing	10.6	3.7	20.1	6.1
Music shows	9.7	6.2	21.0	13.1
Orchestral concerts	6.3	6.2	15.7	14.9
Pageants	8.7	2.3	13.1	7.8
Puppets and Marionettes	11.9	1.0	16.6	2.6
Rhythms	14.4	2.5	13.1	2.6
Social dancing	37.0	21.7	32.4	29.8
Square dancing	27.0	24.7	31.5	35.0
Story telling	33.5	1.6	40.3	6.1
Special services				
Equipment loan or rental	22.5	26.0	6.1	7.8
For ill and handicapped	12.2	6.9	24.5	6.1
For preschool children	14.5	. .	19.2	. .
For older adults	. .	22.9	. .	28.0
For service personnel	3.1	6.2	5.2	11.4
Miscellaneous				
Art and hobby shows	24.2	14.2	38.5	27.1
Community celebrations	22.3	20.2	36.8	35.9
Flower shows	5.0	9.3	14.0	16.6
Forums and discussion groups	3.2	5.7	5.2	17.5
Model artcraft	10.8	4.9	14.9	6.1
Motion pictures	20.5	12.3	28.0	12.2
Photography	4.6	5.8	7.0	16.6
Radio and TV shows	6.7	4.6	16.6	6.1
Supervised parties	30.9	15.8	45.6	20.1

[a] 18 years of age or over [sic] should read under.
[b] This activity listed for adults may be specifically related to senior-citizen day-camping or use of adults as volunteers in youth day-camp programs.
[c] Since a family camping program involves both young and adults, the differential between adults and youth in 1960 is probably due to error on the part of survey respondents.
* From National Recreation and Park Association, *Recreation and Park Yearbook 1966* (Washington, D. C.: NRPA, 1967), pp. 53-55.

TABLE 6
Recreation and Park Personnel and Volunteers*

Type of Personnel	Number Reported By		
	Cities	Counties	Total
Full-time year-round	54,646	10,567	65,213
Seasonal and part-time	158,508	19,449	177,957
Total paid personnel	213,154	30,016	243,170
Full-time year-round — men	12,729	2,252	14,981
Full-time year-round — women	3,657	570	4,227
Total	16,386	2,822	19,208
Part-time or seasonal — men	54,595	5,468	60,063
Part-time or seasonal — women	36,622	3,622	40,244
Total	91,217	9,090	100,307
All professional personnel	107,603	11,912	119,515
Activity leaders (volunteers)	373,353	47,239	420,592
Other volunteers	60,814	13,001	73,815
Total volunteers	434,167	60,240	494,407

* From *Recreation and Park Yearbook 1966*, NRPA, pp. 50-51.

TABLE 7
Outdoor Playgrounds and Indoor Centers under Leadership*

Facility	Cities	Counties	Total
Playgrounds			
Open year-round	6,076	350	6,426
Open summer only	16,142	1,558	17,700
Total	22,304	1,994	24,298
Recreational buildings			
Large	1,945	156	2,101
Other	3,774	611	4,385
Total	5,719	767	6,486
Indoor recreation centers			
School	12,905	1,389	14,294
Other	1,542	205	1,747
Total	14,447	1,594	16,041
Total buildings and indoor centers	20,166	2,361	22,527

* From *Recreation and Park Yearbook 1966*, NRPA, pp. 50-51.

TABLE 8

Municipal and County Park and Recreation Areas: Number, Acreage, Professional Personnel, and Selected Facilities 1965 and 1970*

Item	1965	1970
Park and other recreation areas		
Number	30,509	31,235
Acreage	1,496,378	965,785
Professional personnel, total		
Full time, year-around	19,208	17,287
Playgrounds under leadership	24,298	11,691
Selected facilities		
Ball diamonds, 90 foot	3,335	4,486
Bathing beaches	1,261	760
Golf courses, 9- and 18-hole	1,005	518
Outdoor swimming pools	4,277	4,435
Tennis courts	19,926	12,343
Recreation buildings	6,486	9,212
Indoor recreation centers	16,041	14,237
Softball diamonds, 60-foot	17,467	14,808

* Source: National Recreation and Park Association, *Recreation and Park Year-book*, in U. S. Department of Commerce, *Statistical Abstract* (Washington, D. C.: Government Printing Office, 1970, Table No. 312, p. 197. (Represents only park and recreation systems which returned questionnaires. In 1965, 2,784 municipal and 358 county agencies and in 1970, 1,119 local agencies submitted reports. See *Historical Statistics, Colonial Times to 1957,* series H 488-499, for related data.)

APPENDIX C

TABLE 1
Participation in Outdoor Activities Apart from Vacation by Race*

Outdoor Activity	White	Negro
Driving	73%	57%
Picnicking	65	54
Hiking/walking	49	34
Outdoor swimming	44	14
Boating/canoeing	30	8
Fishing	30	22
Skiing	17	3
Golfing	14	3
Camping	8	4

* From John B. Lansing and Gary Hendricks, *Living Patterns and Attitudes in the Detroit Region* (Detroit Metropolitan Area Regional Planning Commission, 1967), p. 27.

TABLE 2

Proportion Who Participated in Selected Outdoor Activities by Income and Race*

Activity	Detroit				Outside City of Detroit			
	Under $6000		$6000+		Under $6000		$6000+	
	Negro	White	Negro	White	Negro	White	Negro	White
Swimming	10	24	20	53	a	31	a	63
Boating	9	24	10	42	a	28	a	45
Fishing	20	24	26	41	a	28	a	41
Skiing, winter sports	2	2	3	17	a	14	a	23
Hiking, walking	33	41	35	51	a	56	a	60
Driving	50	51	68	83	a	71	a	81
Picnicking	58	57	68	72	a	63	a	73
Camping	1	6	9	12	a	12	a	19
Golfing	2	2	6	15	a	6	a	18
Number of interviews	86	83	78	156	10	125	5	449

a Too few interviews to tabulate.

* From John B. Lansing and Gary Hendricks, *Living Patterns and Attitudes in the Detroit Region* (Detroit Metropolitan Area Regional Planning Commission, 1967), p. 194. Participation at any time during last 12 months, includes vacation.

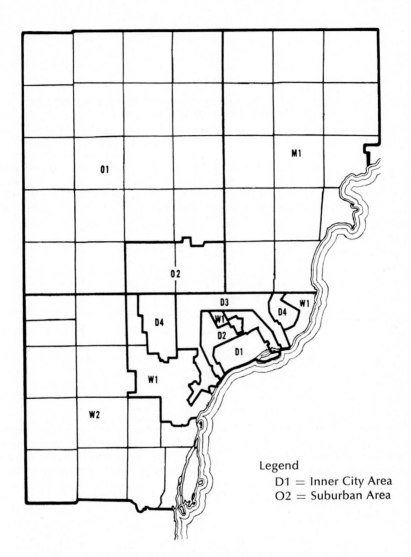

Fig. 5.   Sub-regional statistical areas: the Detroit region.

TABLE 3

Percentage Who Rate Each Publc Service Unsatisfactory by Detailed Location of Residence*

Public Service	Location of Residence[a]									
	Detroit				Rest of Wayne		Oak-land		Macomb	Washtenaw, St. Clair, Monroe, Livingston
	D1	D2	D3	D4	W1	W2	O1	O2		
Parks and playgrounds	19	17	16	16	20	28	12	18	24	27
Residential streets	25	13	10	13	14	23	12	34	22	30
Major streets	12	16	12	18	19	15	8	17	21	28
Schools	11	10	9	5	8	13	1	4	8	12
Police	17	8	12	6	7	23	5	16	9	10
Garbage collection	29	22	28	16	10	16	4	9	9	9
Storm sewers	17	17	18	9	18	33	9	10	25	18
Number of interviews	101	112	103	103	113	97	96	93	105	119

[a] In general the areas are arranged in order of their distance from downtown Detroit. In interpreting this table it should be kept in mind that percentages such as those shown may be expected to vary substantially due to sampling variability.

* From John B. Lansing and Gary Hendricks, *Living Patterns and Attitudes in the Detroit Region* (Detroit Metropolitan Area Regional Planning Commission, 1967), p. 202.

TABLE 4

Income, Race, and Index of Satisfaction with Public Services by Detailed Location of Residence*
(in Percent)

| | Location of Residence | | | | | | | | | | |
| | Detroit | | | | Rest of Wayne | | Oakland | | Macomb | Washtenaw, St. Clair, Monroe, Livingston | All Areas |
	D1	D2	D3	D4	W1	W2	O1	O2			
Family Income											
Under $2000	20	10	7	8	2	5	a	3	3	6	7
$2000-3999	15	24	7	6	1	11	7	11	7	10	10
$4000-5999	20	18	19	10	13	11	12	9	11	16	14
$6000-7999	21	20	17	17	22	28	13	19	22	19	20
$8000-9999	9	16	27	15	16	14	17	15	21	18	16
$10,000-$14,999	10	9	15	27	26	21	27	29	31	19	21
$15,000+	5	3	8	17	20	10	24	14	5	12	12
Total	100	100	100	100	100	100	100	100	100	100	100
Median	$5500	$5800	$7700	$9400	$9600	$7600	$10,300	$9100	$8700	$7900	$6900
Race											
White	29	34	81	100	98	100	94	96	97	98	82
Non-white	71	66	19	*	2	*	6	4	3	2	18
Total	100	100	100	100	100	100	100	100	100	100	100

TABLE 4—Continued

| | Location of Residence | | | | | | | | | | |
| | Detroit | | | | Rest of Wayne | | Oakland | | Macomb | Washtenaw, St. Clair, Monroe, Livingston | All Areas |
	D1	D2	D3	D4	W1	W2	O1	O2			
Indices of satisfaction with public services[b]											
Parks and playgrounds	86	84	90	96	105	75	99	91	79	83	89
Residential streets	80	88	96	92	107	83	93	71	86	75	87
Major streets	95	91	97	93	101	92	100	88	88	81	93
Schools	107	100	115	112	131	100	129	118	110	116	114
Police	102	103	117	123	121	87	131	106	111	112	111
Garbage collection	83	84	87	102	122	94	117	106	115	109	102
Storm sewers	89	81	94	106	97	69	104	97	88	81	90
Number of interviews	101	112	103	96	113	97	96	93	105	119	1042

a Less than 0.5 percent.
b This index was computed as follows:

$$\frac{\text{Percent excellent} - \text{percent unsatisfactory}}{\text{Percent excellent} + \text{percent satisfactory} + \text{percent unsatisfactory}} + 100.$$

For example, assume that 100 people in an area rated a service. If 10 rate the service excellent and 10, unsatisfactory, the percent excellent minus the percent unsatisfactory is 0, the fraction is zero, and the index is 100. The index exceeds 100 whenever there are more excellent ratings than unsatisfactory ratings; it equals 100 whenever the number of excellent ratings equals the number of unsatisfactory ratings; it is less than 100 whenever the number of unsatisfactory ratings exceeds the number of excellent ratings.

* From Lansing and Hendricks, *Living Patterns and Attitudes in the Detroit Region*, pp. 203-204.

TABLE 5

Selected Neighborhood Variables by Detailed Location of Residence*
(in Percent)

Variable	Detroit				Rest of Wayne		Oakland		Macomb	Washtenaw, St. Clair, Monroe, Livingston	All Areas
	D1	D2	D3	D4	W1	W2	O1	O2			
Attractiveness of neighborhood											
Attractive 1	22	35	33	49	48	28	40	49	43	35	37
2	11	17	15	15	19	26	19	19	22	17	18
3	26	43	36	27	27	33	35	23	22	36	31
4	6	4	9	1	2	3	2	5	5	6	4
Unattractive 5	32	10	7	8	1	8	3	4	6	6	9
Not ascertained	3	1	a	a	3	2	1	a	2	a	1
Total	100	100	100	100	100	100	100	100	100	100	100
Whether neighborhood is well kept up											
Well kept up 1	27	37	39	58	55	34	45	47	52	40	43
2	17	20	25	17	21	23	32	25	23	18	22
3	14	31	25	16	15	27	15	20	15	34	21
4	5	2	6	1	2	8	4	4	4	5	4
Poorly kept up 5	33	9	5	6	2	6	3	3	6	3	8
Not ascertained	4	1	a	2	5	2	1	a	a	a	2
Total	100	100	100	100	100	100	100	100	100	100	100

TABLE 5—Continued

Variable	Detroit				Rest of Wayne		Oakland		Macomb	Washtenaw, St. Clair, Monroe, Livingston	All Areas
	D1	D2	D3	D4	W1	W2	O1	O2			
Overall neighborhood satisfaction											
Like it very much	38	37	45	52	67	52	57	63	48	50	51
Like it moderately well	50	53	43	42	31	44	38	33	48	44	43
Dislike it	11	9	12	5	2	2	4	3	4	4	6
Not ascertained	1	1	a	1	a	2	1	a	a	2	a
Total	100	100	100	100	100	100	100	100	100	100	100
Number of interviews	101	112	103	103	113	97	96	93	105	119	1042

a Less than 0.5 percent.

* From Lansing and Hendricks, *Living Patterns and Attitudes in the Detroit Region*, pp. 205-206.

TABLE 6

Variables Related to Children's Outdoor Recreation by Detailed Location of Residence*

(in Percent)

	Location of Residence										
	Detroit				Rest of Wayne		Oakland		Macomb	Washtenaw, St. Clair, Monroe, Livingston	All Areas
Variable	D1	D2	D3	D4	W1	W2	O1	O2			
Availability											
Have children under 16	44	37	45	41	65	62	44	60	73	56	53
Public play space within walking distance	35	35	42	38	62	48	41	35	48	32	42
No play space within walking distance	6	1	3	a	3	12	2	24	23	23	10
Not ascertained	3	1	a	3	a	2	1	1	2	1	1
No children under 16	56	63	55	59	35	38	56	40	27	44	47
Total	100	100	100	100	100	100	100	100	100	100	100
Use of nearest public space											
Have children under 16	44	37	45	41	65	62	44	60	73	56	53
Use public play space	18	16	20	26	38	28	32	22	25	18	24
Do not use the public play space within walking distance, there is no such space	26	21	25	15	27	34	12	38	48	38	29
No children under 16	56	63	55	59	35	38	56	40	27	44	47
Total	100	100	100	100	100	100	100	100	100	100	100

TABLE 6—Continued

	Location of Residence										
Variable	Detroit				Rest of Wayne		Oakland		Macomb	Washtenaw, St. Clair, Monroe, Livingston	All Areas
	D1	D2	D3	D4	W1	W2	O1	O2			
Satisfaction of users of play space											
Have children under 16 who use nearby space	18	16	20	26	38	28	32	22	25	18	24
Very satisfactory	a	4	7	7	8	9	12	11	11	4	7
Satisfactory	11	5	7	11	12	8	14	5	9	4	9
Neutral	1	2	3	2	7	7	2	3	1	5	3
Unsatisfactory	5	5	3	6	10	3	3	2	3	4	5
Very unsatisfactory	a	a	a	a	a	a	a	a	a	a	a
Have no children who are users	82	84	80	74	62	72	68	78	75	82	76
Total	100	100	100	100	100	100	100	100	100	100	100
Where children play											
Have children under 16	44	37	45	41	65	62	44	60	73	56	53
School yard	3	2	7	4	10	8	12	8	11	4	7
Public playground, park	6	7	7	16	15	6	11	2	2	11	9
Yard	29	22	28	24	48	42	27	42	56	39	36
Vacant lot	2	a	a	1	2	4	a	3	3	2	2
Alley	a	a	1	1	a	a	a	a	a	a	a
Street	2	4	4	2	2	a	2	2	7	1	3
Sidewalk	11	7	8	a	8	2	1	1	2	a	4
Number of interviews	101	112	103	103	113	97	96	93	105	119	1042

a Less than 0.5 percent.

* From Lansing and Hendricks, *Living Patterns and Attitudes in the Detroit Region*, pp. 207-209.

APPENDIX D

TABLE 1
Summary of Analysis of Recreation Area Plans*

A study of the 26 playground plans indicated that they varied widely in a number of respects, although, in general, the school-related playgrounds and the separate playgrounds were quite comparable. Playground sizes, for example, varied from 2.43 acres to 12 acres and the area served from 0.43 square mile to 4 square miles. The population served varied from 1,336 to 24,724 and the population per playground acre from 111 to 7,064. The following list indicates the median figures for the two types of playgrounds:

Criteria	School-Related Playgrounds (13)[a]	Separate Playgrounds (13)[a]
Size	6.75 acres	6.10 acres
Population served	5,362	6,372
Population per acre	1 per 778	1 per 984
Area served	1.00 sq. mile	1.00 sq. mile

[a] If five school-related and seven separate playgrounds were enlarged, as recommended by the authorities reporting, their acreage would be 8.07 acres and 8 acres respectively.

With few exceptions, the areas had the following units: apparatus area, paved area for court games and/or multiple use, a field for sports, a shelter house or recreation building, landscaped area or areas (some with picnic facilities). Other units were reported at the number of areas indicated:

Area	Units
Preschool unit	15
Open area for free play	13
Parking area	12
Shaded area for quiet activities	6
Wading or spray pool	6
Area for older adults	1

Analysis of the plans for the 14 areas classified as community playfields likewise revealed wide variation. For example, the size ranged from 8.54 to 22.42 acres; the area served from 1.1 to 26.1 square miles. The population served varied from 5,000 to 61,000, and the population per acre of playfield from 1 acre per 342 to 1 acre per 7,143. The median figures for the 14 areas were:

* Table 1 is excerpted from *Recreation Magazine*, January, 1963. Reprinted in *Outdoor Recreation Space Standards*, 1967, by NRPA, pp. 46-49.

TABLE 1—Continued

Criteria	Median
Size	18 acres
Population served	27,684
Area served	4.0 square miles
Population per acre of playfield	1 acre per 1,475

All the playfield plans provided for one or more landscaped sections and areas for field sports. A majority included the following units: areas for court and lawn games, children's playground, parking area (one or more), recreation building, and picnic area (one or more). The lack of diversity in the activities made available at the playfields is illustrated by the fact that the following facilities were indicated on only *one* plan: boccie or roque court, bowling green, craft area, fire circle, pitch-and-putt course, putting green, running track, theater, and garden (wildflowers).

The wide variations in the size, service area, population, and development of the areas that supposedly approximated standard conditions were surprising. However, in most respects, the median areas did not vary widely from the NRA standards. In the case of the playgrounds, their size was between 6 and 8 acres, their maximum radius ½ mile, the population served under 6,000, and the population per playground acre well under 1 acre per 1,000. As for the playfields, the median size was 18 acres and the median area served, 4 square miles, or a radius of about 1 mile. The population served and the population per acre of playfield, on the other hand, were much higher than proposed by the standard.

The following lists indicate the median space recommended for each unit in a recreation area serving a community of 20,000 and the total space required for these units. In contrast with the similarity in the total space requirements for the neighborhood recreation area, as previously indicated, the median space proposed for the sum of the units in the community recreation area, 28.4 acres, is much greater than the median of 18 acres for the plans submitted in the first phase of the study. A still larger median area, 34.52, was proposed in the recommendations for total space in the latter phase. The increase over the NRA playfield space standard is due in part to the fact that it did not provide for a separate park unit.

TABLE 1—Continued

Unit or Facility	Space Recommended in Square Feet
Children's playground	
Playlot for preschool children and mothers	10,000
Apparatus area for older children	12,000
Open area for group games and informal play	41,500
Wading or spray pool	3,000
Paved multiple-use area for games and activities	10,000
Quiet activity area	5,000
Field for children's team sports	60,000
Total	**141,500**

Unit or Facility	Space Recommended in Square Feet
Community recreation area	
Field house or recreation building	12,000
Older adults area	13,000
Special game courts	43,560
Paved multiple-use area for games, etc.	15,000
Lawn game area for croquet, bowling, etc.	20,000
Field for sportsmen	217,800
Field for sportswomen	90,720
Running track and field events	75,000
Archery range	20,000
Swiming pool	21,780
Theater or bandshell	11,890
Ice-skating rink (artificial)	22,500
Picnic area for families and large groups	87,120
Nature center	43,560
Separate landscape park unit	94,450
Other landscape areas, such as border and buffer strips	75,670
Parking areas and/or service road	87,060
Paths and walks	32,000
Undesignated space (10 percent)	112,461
Total area	**1,237,071**
	28.40 acres

The table that follows indicates the median space recommended for each unit in a recreation area serving a neighborhood of 6,000 and the total space required. The median total of unit spaces, 8.17 acres, is only slightly more than the median of 6.57 acres for the plans of neighborhood recreation areas submitted in the first phase of the study; it is less than the 10.15 acres, which was the median amount of total acreage recommended in the second phase.

TABLE 1—Continued

Unit or Facility	Space Recommended in Square Feet
Playlot for preschool children and mothers	10,000
Apparatus area for older children	10,000
Shelter house or recreation building	3,000
Open area for group games and informal play	21,890
Wading or spray pool	1,600
Quiet activity area for crafts, storytelling, etc.	2,800
Paved multiple-use area for games, roller skating, etc.	10,000
Special game courts	18,400
Lawn games area for croquet, clock golf, etc.	10,000
Field for team games and sports	130,680
Older adults area	10,000
Picnic area for family and small groups	20,890
Swimming pool — instructional	6,000
Landscaped areas, such as border and buffer strips, etc.	43,000
Parking area and/or service drive	17,424
Paths and walks	8,000
Undesignated space (10 percent)	32,368
Total	356,052 (8.17 acres)

TABLE 2
Recreation Land Area Statistics for the 50 Largest Cities*

Cities	Recreation Area 1960			Population Statistics 1960		
	Ac./1000	% of Area[a]	Total Acres	Total Pop.	Change 1950-60	Per Sq. Mile
Phoenix, Ariz.	51.8	19.0	22,757	439,170	311.1	2,343
Denver, Colo.	32.2	35.1	15,927	493,887	18.8	6,956
Fort Worth, Texas	26.9	10.7	9,586	356,268	27.8	2,536
Portland, Oregon	19.1	16.5	7,109	372,676	-0.3	5,546
San Diego, Calif.	14.1	6.5	8,054	573,224	71.4	2,979
Tulsa, Okla.	13.9	11.9	3,634	261,685	43.2	5,475
Dallas, Texas	13.0	4.9	8,808	679,684	56.4	2,428
Omaha, Nebr.	11.7	10.8	3,540	301,598	20.1	5,891
Minneapolis, Minn.	11.5	15.3	5,533	482,872	-7.4	8,546
Louisville, Ky.	10.5	11.2	4,100	390,639	5.8	6,841
Cincinnati, Ohio	10.1	10.2	5,059	502,550	-0.3	6,501
Washington, D.C.	9.9	19.2	7,531	763,956	-4.8	12,442
Honolulu, Hawaii	9.9	5.4	2,914	294,194	18.6	3,506
Columbus, Ohio	9.9	7.4	4,242	471,316	25.4	5,296
Oklahoma City, Okla.	8.9	1.4	2,882	324,253	33.2	1,009
Kansas City, Mo.	8.6	4.9	4,100	475,539	4.1	3,664
Los Angeles, Calif.	8.0	7.7	19,856	2,479,015	25.8	5,451
Oakland, Calif.	8.0	8.6	2,928	367,548	-4.4	6,935
Indianapolis, Ind.	7.9	8.3	3,762	476,258	11.5	6,689
Memphis, Tenn.	7.9	4.8	3,948	497,524	25.6	3,881

TABLE 2—Continued

Cities	Recreation Area 1960			Population Statistics 1960		
	Ac./1000	% of Area[a]	Total Acres	Total Pop.	Change 1950-60	Per Sq. Mile
Baltimore, Md.	7.5	13.9	7,052	939,024	−1.1	11,886
Toledo, Ohio	7.4	7.7	2,362	318,003	4.7	6,598
Dayton, Ohio	7.3	8.8	1,903	262,332	7.6	7,808
Long Beach, Calif.	7.2	8.4	2,461	344,168	37.2	7,498
Rochester, N.Y.	6.6	9.0	2,103	318,611	−4.2	8,753
Seattle, Wash.	6.3	6.2	3,500	557,087	19.1	6,295
St. Louis, Mo.	6.3	12.0	4,692	750,026	−12.5	12,296
St. Paul, Minn.	6.1	5.7	1,907	313,411	0.7	6,004
Atlanta, Ga.	5.1	3.0	2,500	487,455	47.1	3,802
Cleveland, Ohio	5.1	8.7	4,500	876,050	−4.2	10,789
San Francisco, Calif.	5.1	12.4	3,774	740,316	−4.5	15,553
Boston, Mass.	5.0	11.3	3,455	697,197	−13.0	14,586
Houston, Texas	4.9	2.2	4,604	938,219	57.4	2,860
San Antonio, Texas	4.8	2.8	2,827	587,718	43.9	3,662
Philadelphia, Pa.	4.7	11.5	9,378	2,002,512	−3.3	15,743
New York, N.Y.	4.7	18.2	36,663	7,781,984	−1.4	24,697
Norfolk, Va.	4.7	4.5	1,427	305,872	43.3	6,117
Pittsburgh, Pa.	3.8	6.6	2,274	604,332	−10.7	11,171
Birmingham, Ala.	3.7	2.6	1,256	340,887	4.6	4,576
Detroit, Mich.	3.7	6.8	6,106	1,670,144	−9.7	11,964

TABLE 2—Continued

Cities	Recreation Area 1960			Population Statistics 1960		
	Ac./ 1000	% of Area[a]	Total Acres	Total Pop.	Change 1950-60	Per Sq. Mile
Miami, Fla.	3.1	4.1	900	291,688	17.0	8,529
New Orleans, La.	2.7	1.3	1,708	627,525	10.0	3,157
Akron, Ohio	2.1	1.7	600	290,351	5.7	5,387
Chicago, Ill.	2.1	5.3	7,627	3,550,404	-1.9	15,836
Buffalo, N.Y.	2.0	4.2	1,069	532,759	-8.2	13,522
Tampa, Fla.	0.9	0.5	249	274,970	120.5	3,235
Milwaukee, Wis.	a	a	b	741,324	16.3	8,137
Newark, N.J.	a	a	b	405,220	-7.6	17,170
El Paso, Texas	a	a	b	276,687	112.0	2,414
Jersey City, N.J.	a	a	b	276,101	-7.7	21,239
For 46 Cities	7.0	7.8	263,167	37,406,901	6.7	7,118

[a] Cities did not report whether parks were within the city limits or not, but such was assumed in making this computation.
[b] Recreation area not reported in the Recreation and Park Yearbook—1961.

*Recreation areas statistics from Recreation and Park Yearbook—1961. Populations and city areas from the U. S. Census reports. Excerpted from Recreation, National Recreation Association, Vol. LVIII, no. 1, January, 1965, p. 21. Cited in Recreation and Park Yearbook 1966 (Washington, D. C.: NRPA, 1967), pp. 50-51. Arranged in order of acres per 1,000 of the 1960 population.

TABLE 3

Population per Acre of Park 1926–1960*
(Eleven Largest Cities in the U.S.)

City	Population		Park Acreage		Population per Acre	
	1926	1960	1926	1960	1926	1960
New York	6,299,500	7,710,346	10,482	35,463	601	219
Chicago	3,048,000	3,611,648	5,865	6,665	520	532
Los Angeles	1,222,500	2,450,068	4,889	16,856	250	147
Philadelphia	2,008,000	1,971,239	7,801	9,368	257	214
Detroit	1,290,000	1,654,125	3,418	5,831	377	286
Houston	a	32,630	a	4,454	a	211
Baltimore	808,000	922,244	2,833	6,000	285	157
Cleveland	960,000	769,728	2,221	4,093	432	214
St. Louis	a	750,026	a	4,697	a	150
San Francisco	567,000	716,279	2,535	3,721	224	199
Boston	787,000	682,303	3,594	2,700	219	258
				Median	257	214

a Not listed.

* From National Recreation and Park Association, *A Study of New York Outdoor Recreation Needs* (New York: City Planning Commission, 1967), p. 41.

TABLE 4
Percent of Total Area Devoted to Parks 1926–1960*
(Eleven Largest Cities in the U.S.)[a]

City	Total City Area (Acres)		Park Area (Acres)		Percent in Parks	
	1926	1960	1926	1960	1926	1960
New York	190,161	201,664	10,482	35,463[b]	5.5	17.6
Chicago	125,430	143,488	5,865	6,665	5.5	4.7
Los Angeles	282,035	291,072	4,889	16,856	1.7	5.5
Philadelphia	83,017	81,403	7,801	9,368	9.4	11.5
Detroit	88,960	89,344	3,418	5,831	3.8	6.5
Houston	c	209,984	c	4,454	c	2.1
Baltimore	50,560	50,560	2,833	6,000	5.6	11.7
Cleveland	43,160	51,970	2,221	4,093	5.2	7.9
St. Louis	39,040	39,046	2,880	4,697	7.3	12.0
San Francisco	26,880	30,460	2,535	3,721	9.4	12.2
Boston	27,634	30,490	3,594	2,700	13.0	8.8
				Median	5.5	8.8

[a] Washington, D. C. is not included because of its unique character as a Federal District.

[b] The inventory made for this study recorded a total acreage under jurisdiction of the Department of Parks (as of June 1, 1966) of 36,913 of which 6,452 acres (17.4 percent) were undeveloped and not in use. In addition, 9,777 acres (26.5 percent) were under water and 1,288 (3.5 percent) were in wetlands.

[c] Not listed.

*From National Recreation and Park Association, A Study of New York Recreation Needs (New York: City Planning Commission, 1967), p. 40.

TABLE 5

Recreation Area Statistics for Counties*

County and Principal City	Ac./1,000 Pop.	% of Land Area for Rec.	Total Rec. Acres	County Area (Sq. Miles)	Pop. 1960
Hill (Havre), Mont.	589.8	.59	11,000	2,926	18,653
Napa (Napa), Calif.	303.5	4.12	20,000	758	65,890
Natrona (Casper), Wyo.	139.5	.20	6,920	5,342	49,623
Iron (Iron River), Mich.	100.9	.23	1,785[a]	1,197	17,692
Pima (Tucson), Ariz.	98.8	.44	26,242[a]	9,241	265,660
Kern (Bakersfield), Calif.	71.7	.40	20,926[a]	8,152	291,984
Jackson (Pascagoula), Miss.	69.1	.81	3,836	744	55,522
Larimer (Ft. Collins), Col.	56.2	.18	3,000	2,614	53,343
Mendocino (Ukiah), Calif.	40.4	.09	2,065	3,507	51,059
Weber (Ogden), Utah	40.0	1.26	4,429[a]	549	110,744
Clark (Neillsville), Wis.	39.6	.16	1,250	1,222	31,527
Marathon (Wausau), Wis.	20.5	.18	1,820	1,584	88,874
San Luis Obispo (SLO), Calif.	17.2	.07	1,397	3,316	81,044
Merced (Merced), Calif.	13.4	.10	1,212[a]	1,982	90,446
Rock Island (R.I. Moline), Ill.	13.4	.75	2,028	420	150,991
Lane (Eugene), Oreg.	13.2	.07	2,158	4,560	162,890
Westchester (Yonkers), N.Y.	12.9	3.75	10,440[a]	435	808,891
Maricopa (Phoenix), Ariz.	10.2	.11	6,785[a]	9,226	663,510
Union (Eliz.), N.J.	10.1	7.75	5,109	103	504,255
Milwaukee (Milwaukee), Wis.	10.0	6.77	10,355	239	1,036,041

Cuyahoga (Cleve. Met. Pks), Ohio	9.5	5.36	15,639	456	1,647,895
Lucas (Toledo), Ohio	9.2	1.91	4,200	343	456,931
Cook (Chicago), Ill.	9.0	7.57	46,200	954	5,129,725
Montgomery & Prince Georges, Md.	8.3	.93	5,800[a]	978	698,323
Onondaga (Syracuse), N.Y.	8.1	.68	3,439	792	423,028
Fairfax (Fairfax), Va.	8.1	.86	2,229[a]	405	275,002
Santa Clara (San Jose), Calif.	7.7	.59	4,928	1,302	642,315
Morris (Morristown), N.J.	7.6	.67	2,000	467	261,620
Baltimore (Baltimore), Md.	7.0	.88	3,442[a]	608	492,428
Summit (Akron), Ohio	7.0	1.36	3,600	413	513,569
Huron-Clinton-Wayne, Mich.	6.8	1.44	18,487	2,000	2,738,272
Winnebago (Rockford), Ill.	6.5	.41	1,360	520	209,765
Dupage (Elmhurst), Ill.	6.4	.95	2,000	331	313,459
East Baton Rouge Parish, La.	6.3	.49	1,458[a]	462	230,058
Anne Arundel (Annapolis), Md.	5.9	.46	1,214[a]	417	206,634
Jefferson (Louisville), Ky.	5.6	1.44	3,450[a]	375	610,947
Kent (Grand Rapids), Mich.	5.5	.29	1,600	862	288,292
Essex (Newark), N.J.	5.5	6.23	5,104	128	923,545
Hamilton (Cincinnati), Ohio	5.4	1.77	4,680	414	864,121
San Mateo (San Mateo), Calif.	5.2	.79	2,297	454	444,387
Monroe (Rochester), N.Y.	5.1	.70	3,000	673	586,387
Polk (Des Moines), Iowa	4.8	.34	1,284	594	266,315
Dade (Miami), Fla.	4.6	.33	4,298	2,054	935,047
Bergen (Hackensack), N.J.	4.5	2.35	3,500	233	780,255

TABLE 5—Continued

County and Principal City	Ac./1,000 Pop.	% of Land Area for Rec.	Total Rec. Acres	County Area (Sq. Miles)	Pop. 1960
Salt Lake (Salt Lake City), Utah	4.4	.34	1,679[a]	764	383,035
Riverside (Riverside), Calif.	3.9	.03	1,200	7,177	306,191
Allegheny (Pittsburgh), Pa.	2.6	.92	4,274	730	1,628,587
St. Louis (University City), Mo.	2.3	.50	1,603	497	703,532
Erie (Buffalo), N.Y.	2.2	.34	2,310	1,054	1,064,688
Los Angeles (Los Angeles), Calif.	1.7	.41	10,528	4,060	6,038,771
San Diego (San Diego), Calif.	1.6	.06	1,620	4,255	1,033,011
All 51 Counties	8.7	.52	311,180	92,889	35,694,774

[a] Includes school recreation areas.

*Excerpted from *Recreation*, National Recreation Association, Vol. LVIII, no. 2, February 1965, p. 81. Cited in National Recreation Park Association, *Outdoor Recreation Space Standards* (Washington, D. C.: NRPA, 1967), pp. 52-53. Data include only counties in the 48 states having 1200 acres or more of recreation land according to the *Recreation and Park Yearbook 1961*. List is arranged according to acres per 1,000 of 1960 population.

TABLE 6

Recreational Open Space Standards in Selected Areas in the U.S.*
(in Acres per 1,000 Population)

Planning Area	Neighborhood Parks	Urban Parks	Special Facilities	Parks	Regional Reservation	Hunting and Fishing	Total
Detroit region	...	...	1.6	12.4	10.2	...	24.2
Tulsa region	3.5	6.5	...	10.0	...	...	20.0
Baltimore region	4.0	10.0	...	10.0	...	20	44.0
Richmond	5.0	5.0	...	7.5	7.5	...	25.0
Santa Clara Co.	...	...	...	...	30.0	...	30.0
Somerset Co., N.J.	...	10.0	...	15.0	...	...	25.0
Denver region	5.0	5.0	...	15.0	...	...	25.0
Lorain Co., Ohio	4.3	10.0	...	10.0	...	...	24.3
St. Clair Co., Mich.	3.4	1.0	...	10.0	...	...	14.4
Tri-County, Ohio	3.5	6.0	Golf Course 2.0	15.0	...	...	26.5
Twin Cities, Minn. region	...	...	...	10.0	...	...	10.0
Regional Plan Association of New York	...	7.0	...	12.0	12.0	...	31.0
Harlow Whittemore	...	13.0	...	10.0	...	20	43.0

* From Philip H. Lewis, Jr., *Recreation and Open Space in Illinois*, Bureau of Community Planning, University of Illinois, Urbana, Illinois, September, 1961. Cited in *Open Space in Northeastern Illinois* (Chicago: Northeastern Illinois Metropolitan Area Planning Commission, 1962), p. 39.

TABLE 7
State Park Area Statistics*

States	Existing Park Acres		Additional Park Needed @ 65 Acres per M		Existing Forests and Other Areas	
	Per 1,000 Pop.	% State Area	Additional Acres Needed	% of State 65 Ac./ 1,000	% State Area	Acres per 1,000 Pop.
Wyoming	489.8	.26	....	.26	.39	741.5
Maine	219.2	1.07	....	1.07	1.96	401.1
New York	154.3	8.44	....	8.44	2.73	49.8
South Dakota	110.0	.15	....	.15	.03	23.1
Tennessee	70.1	.94	....	.94	2.48	185.6
California	45.0	.71	314,052	1.02	.27	17.3
Nevada	39.0	.02	7,420	.03	...	....
Idaho	38.3	.05	17,806	.08	.14	110.0
Oregon	36.6	.11	50,276	.19	1.43	498.8
Minnesota	29.5	.20	121,039	.43	29.53	4,428.9
Oklahoma	28.7	.15	84,481	.34	.64	120.4
Washington	28.0	.19	105,500	.36	9.75	1,459.0
Vermont	24.7	.16	15,711	.43	1.43	217.5
Florida	24.6	.25	200,075	.93	9.93	695.5
Michigan	24.1	.52	319,753	1.39	13.82	644.5
West Virginia	23.9	.29	76,395	.78	1.50	124.5
South Carolina	20.4	.25	106,205	.80	1.29	105.1
Kentucky	19.8	.24	137,195	.77	.58	48.7
Missouri	17.5	.17	205,406	.63	.97	99.2
Montana	15.6	.01	33,334	.05	.99	1,363.4
Pennsylvania	15.0	.59	565,966	2.55	14.85	377.9
Indiana	11.7	.24	248,561	1.31	2.63	130.5
Georgia	11.7	.12	210,184	.69	...	.1
Arkansas	11.3	.06	95,988	.35	.02	.4
Alabama	11.1	.11	176,154	.65	1.70	173.1
Iowa	10.4	.08	150,530	.50	.72	94.1
Rhode Island	9.9	1.26	47,367	8.25	1.15	9.1
Ohio	9.7	.36	536,315	2.14	2.07	55.8
Connecticut	8.8	.71	142,568	5.26	4.01	49.6
North Carolina	8.4	.12	257,723	.94	.65	44.9

TABLE 7—Continued

States	Existing Park Acres		Additional Park Needed ' @ 65 Acres per M		Existing Forests and Other Areas	
	Per 1,000 Pop.	% State Area	Additional Acres Needed	% of State 65 Ac./ 1,000	% State Area	Acres per 1,000 Pop.
Colorado	8.3	.02	99,472	.17	.35	132.6
Maryland	8.3	.41	175,881	3.19	2.55	52.0
Delaware	7.8	.28	25,514	2.29	1.74	49.2
Virginia	7.8	.12	226,962	1.01	.62	39.6
Nebraska	7.2	.02	81,641	.19	.19	67.2
North Dakota	7.0	.01	36,683	.09	.14	100.7
Texas	7.0	.04	556,063	.37	.20	35.6
Massachusetts	6.7	.68	330,315	6.65	4.22	41.3
Mississippi	6.6	.05	127,178	.47	. . .	. . . .
Wisconsin	5.6	.06	234,662	.73	9.96	882.6
New Mexico	4.8	.01	57,225	.08	1.22	997.1
Illinois	4.8	.13	607,339	2.14	.27	9.4
Arizona	4.5	.01	78.839	.12	.06	35.1
Kansas	4.4	.02	132,018	.27	.21	50.0
New Jersey	3.9	.50	370,539	8.19	5.34	42.4
Louisiana	3.8	.04	199,466	.73	3.47	307.6
New Hampshire	2.2	.02	38,114	.68	1.24	117.6
Utah	1.5	.002	58,571	.11	.48	282.7
All 48 States	32.4	.30	7,630,488	.70	2.50	268.1

* U. S. Department of the Interior, Bureau of Outdoor Recreation, *State Outdoor Recreation Statistics, 1962* (Washington, D. C.: Division of Research and Education, Report No. 1, Statistical Series, 1963). Excerpted from *Recreation*, Vol. LVIII, No. 3 (New York: National Recreation Association, March, 1965), p. 127. Cited in National Recreation and Park Association, *Outdoor Recreation Space Standards*, pp. 54-55. Includes forests, reservoir areas, fish and game areas, roadside parks, etc. List arranged according to acres per 1,000 of 1960 population.

TABLE 8

Population of 25 Largest SMSA's by Rank: 1966 and 1960*

Standard Metropolitan Statistical Areas	Population		Rank	
	July 1, 1966 (Prov.)	April 1, 1960 (Census)	1966	1960
New York, N.Y.	11,410,000	10,694,633	1	1
Los Angeles-Long Beach, Calif.	6,789,000	6,038,771	2	3
Chicago, Ill.	6,732,000	6,220,913	3	2
Philadelphia, Pa.-N.J.	4,690,000	4,342,897	4	4
Detroit, Mich.	4,060,000	3,762,360	5	5
Boston, Lawrence-Haverhill, Lowell, Mass.[a]	3,201,000	3,109,158	6	6
San Francisco-Oakland, Calif.	2,958,000	2,648,762	7	7
Washington, D.C.-Md.-Va.	2,615,000	2,064,090	8	10
Pittsburgh, Pa.	2,376,000	2,405,435	9	8
St. Louis, Mo.-Ill.	2,284,000	2,104,669	10	9
Cleveland, Ohio	2,004,000	1,909,483	11	11
Baltimore, Md.	1,980,000	1,803,745	12	12
Newark, N.J.	1,862,000	1,689,420	13	13
Houston, Tex.	1,740,000	1,418,323	14	15
Minneapolis-St. Paul, Minn.	1,629,000	1,482,030	15	14
Cincinnati, Ohio-Ky.-Ind.	1,353,000	1,268,479	16	18
Dallas, Tex.	1,352,000	1,119,410	17	20
Milwaukee, Wis.	1,331,000	1,278,850	18	17
Buffalo, N.Y.	1,323,000	1,306,957	19	16
Paterson-Clifton-Passaic, N.J.	1,318,000	1,186,873	20	19
Atlanta, Ga.	1,258,000	1,017,188	21	24
Seattle-Everett, Wash.	1,214,000	1,107,213	22	21
Kansas City, Mo.-Kans.	1,209,000	1,092,545	23	22
San Diego, Calif.	1,168,000	1,033,011	24	23
Anaheim-Santa Ana-Garden Grove, Calif.	1,164,000	703,925	25	39

[a] Metropolitan state economic area.

* From Bureau of the Budget's Population Estimates Series (P-25) Report No. 378, "Provisional Estimates of the Population of the Largest Metropolitan Areas: July 1, 1966." Cited in *ASPO Newsletter* (May, 1968), p. 48.

TABLE 9
Comparison of 1968 Population, Area and Park Acreage in 15 Selected Cities*

City[a]	Estimated Population	Area in Square Miles	Population Density per Square Mile	Park Acreage	Park Acreage as Percent of Total Area
New York	8,171,000	300	27,237	37,991	19.8
Chicago	3,587,000	222	16,158	6,888	4.8
Los Angeles	2,873,500	463	6,206	11,900	4.0
Baltimore	923,900	75	12,319	6,097	12.8
San Antonio	722,400	61	11,843	2,932	7.5
St. Louis	684,800	182	3,763	2,728	2.3
Pittsburgh	564,000	55	10,255	2,374	6.7
Atlanta	516,600	136	3,791	2,318	2.7
Minneapolis	493,100	53	9,304	5,314	15.7
Nashville[b]	457,500	527	868	4,905	1.5
Oakland	391,300	52	7,525	2,000	6.0
Tampa	324,900	85	3,822	1,123	2.1
Dayton	281,000	37	7,324	3,149	13.2
Peoria	137,900	37	3,940	6,647[c]	28.1
Portland	71,400	22	3,245	655	4.7

[a] Park data obtained from city recreation officials; area data determined by adding annexations since 1960 to area reported by U. S. Census Bureau; population figures computed by straight line extrapolation of population data obtained from city officials.

[b] Data is for Nashville-Davidson County consolidated government.

[c] Includes acreage owned by the Park District beyond the district boundaries.

* From National League of Cities, *Recreation in the Nation's Cities Problems and Approaches* (Washington, D. C.: National League of Cities, 1968), p. 4.

TABLE 10
Park Acreage per 1,000 Residents in 15 Selected Cities*

City	Estimated Population 1968	Park Acreage per 1,000 Residents[a]		
		Actual 1960	Estimated 1968	Estimated 1973
New York	8,171,000	4.5	4.6	4.8
Chicago	3,587,000	1.9	2.0	2.0
Los Angeles	2,873,500	4.8	4.5	4.2
Baltimore	923,900	6.0	6.2	6.3
San Antonio	722,400	5.0	5.8	6.0
St. Louis	684,800	3.6	4.2	4.5
Pittsburgh	564,000	3.6	4.1	NA[b]
Atlanta	516,600	NA[b]	4.9	NA[b]
Minneapolis	493,100	11.5	11.4	NA[b]
Nashville	457,500	20.5	11.5	12.0
Oakland	391,300	5.7	6.2	6.3
Tampa	324,900	NA[b]	3.7	NA[b]
Dayton	281,000	9.5	10.5	12.7
Peoria	137,900	17.0	46.0	50.0
Portland	71,400	8.2	9.8	18.0

[a] Park acreage data obtained from city recreational personnel.

[b] Not available.

* From National League of Cities, *Recreation in the Nation's Cities Problems and Approaches* (Washington, D. C.: National League of Cities, 1968), p. 5.

TABLE 11

Park Acreage by Major Classification in 15 Selected Cities*

City	Population[a] 1968	Neighborhood[b]	Community[b]	City-Wide[b]	Other[b]	Total[b]	Estimated Additional Needs[b]
New York	8,171,000	1,736	12,787	18,745	4,723	37,991	1,541
Chicago	3,587,000	—c	—c	6,808	80	6,888	NAd
Los Angeles	2,873,500	1,432	1,088	9,380	—c	11,900	1,089
Baltimore	923,900	152	1,001	4,711	233	6,097	2,505
San Antonio	722,400	87	439	1,674	732	2,932	5,068
St. Louis	684,800	453	—c	1,736	539	2,728	4,000
Pittsburgh	564,000	350	—c	2,024	—c	2,374	NAd
Atlanta	516,600	390	540	1,233	155	2,318	1,535
Minneapolis	493,100	604	—c	2,818	1,892	5,314	NAd
Nashville	457,500	81	481	4,343	—c	4,905	3,170
Oakland	391,300	—c	500	1,500	—c	2,000	717
Tampa	324,900	212	—c	911	—c	1,123	NAd
Dayton	281,000	290	—c	2,670	189	3,149	1,602
Peoria	137,900	347	584	5,716	—c	6,647	NAd
Portland	71,400	415	—c	175	65	655	1,664

a The 1968 estimated population determined by straight-line extrapolation of population data obtained from city officials.
b Data obtained from city recreation personnel.
c Not reported by this classification.
d Not available.

* From National League of Cities, Recreation in the Nation's Cities Problems and Approaches (Washington, D. C.: National League of Cities, 1968), p. 9.

TABLE 12

Park and Recreation Planning in 15 Selected Cities*

City	Type of Plan	Duration of Plan	Updating	Financing for Plan	Participants in Developing the Plan	Public Hearings	Capital Improvement Plan
Atlanta	Park and recreation master plan	15 years	Periodically	50% United Appeal, 50% Citizens Park and Advisory Commission	Board of Aldermen, Mayor, City Planning Department, Park and Recreation Department, Community Council	Yes	Yes
Baltimore	Park and recreation master plan	20 years	Periodically	City general fund	Recreation and Park Board, Planning Commission, City Council, city departments, citizen groups, private consultant	Yes	Yes
Chicago	Comprehensive plan for city	15 years	Continuous	City general fund	Planning Commission, City Council, Mayor, city departments, Park District, citizens, semi-public organizations	Yes	Yes
Dayton	Area plans for parks and recreation	Indefinite	No	City general fund	City Council, neighborhood group, private architect	No	Yes
Los Angeles	Park and recreation master plan	10 years	Annual	City Planning Department	City Council, Planning Department, citizen groups, city departments	Yes	Yes
Minneapolis	No plan	—	—	—	—	—	Yes
Nashville	Park and recreation master plan	6 years	—	City general fund	Park and Recreation Department is now in the process of developing the plan.	Yes	Yes

TABLE 12—Continued

City	Type of Plan	Duration of Plan	Updating	Financing for Plan	Participants in Developing the Plan	Public Hearings	Capital Improvement Plan
New York	Park and recreation master plan	Indefinite	Annual	State and Federal funds	City Planning Commission, city operating departments, State Department of Conservation, neighborhood groups	Yes	Yes
Oakland	General development plan for city	25 years	Annual	City Planning Commission	City Planning Commission, Mayor, City Council, city departments, community groups	Yes	Yes
Peoria	Park and recreation master plan	Indefinite	At request of staff	Park District funds	Park District, City Planning Department, School District, Tri-County Planning Commission, Recreation Advisory Committee	Yes	Yes
Pittsburgh	No Plan	—	—	—	—	—	Yes
Portland	Park and recreation master plan	Indefinite	Annual	City general fund	Park and Recreation Department, City Manager, City Council, Planning Board, city departments	Yes	Yes
St Louis	No Plan	—	—	—	1944 plan has never been updated	—	Yes
San Antonio	Park master plan	20 years	Every 5 years	City general fund	Department of Planning, Park and Recreation Advisory Board, neighborhood groups, city departments	Yes	Yes
Tampa	No Plan	—	—	—	—	—	Yes

* From National League of Cities, *Recreation in the Nation's Cities Problems and Approaches* (Washington, D. C.: National League of Cities, 1968), pp. 48-49.

TABLE 13

Summary of Major Findings and Conclusions about Recreation in 15 Selected Cities*

1. Location of parks and recreation facilities is a primary factor affecting the success of recreation programs. Consideration must be given to population density and the availability of public transportation in the location of new facilities. The acquisition of large tracts in outlying areas will not meet the recreation needs of the great majority of city residents. Emphasis must be placed on neighborhood facilities. Rather than just providing acreage for football, baseball, and basketball, and swings and slides, programs meeting cultural, artistic, and creative needs must be provided as must facilities for sports that people can participate in all their lives.

2. City expenditures for park and recreation purposes have increased substantially in recent years. Although recreation has traditionally been given a relatively low priority in relation to other city services, city officials and recreation leaders indicate that recreation is beginning to be recognized as an essential local government function. However, in spite of a virtually unanimous commitment to increase recreation programs and opportunities, cities do not have the financial capability to sustain expanded recreation programs indefinitely.

3. Cities increasingly must look to state and Federal governments for the additional financial assistance necessary to sustain the desired level of recreation programs. Generally, state financial assistance to date has been negligible. Fortunately for cities, Federal aid has been more abundant. Major Federal programs from which city park and recreation programs are benefiting include Land and Water Conservation Fund, Neighborhood Facilities, Open-Space Land, Urban Beautification, and Community Action programs.

4. Optimum utilization of potential recreation resources is not being achieved in most of the nation's cities. The substantial acreage adjacent to, underneath, and above expressways and highway interchanges has been virtually undeveloped for recreation purposes. Publicly owned facilities with existing recreation capabilities are being underused. School facilities in particular, even in jurisdictions having city-school recreation agreements, are not being utilized effectively. To meet the rising demand for recreation, in spite of the declining availability of open space, cities must expand the multiple use of facilities, establish park-school complexes, and employ imaginative designs and new construction techniques.

5. Lack of communication among city, county, and private agencies is a major problem preventing the optimum utilization of existing recreational facilities and programs. As a consequence, coordination is inadequate between city and county recreation departments and between such departments and the various semi-public organizations carrying on

TABLE 13—Continued

---

recreation activities. In addition, communication between recreation departments and the citizen is frequently inadequate. In the past, recreation officials have felt it sufficient merely to provide recreation opportunities. Today, citizens not only must be informed of the availability of the various programs, but also convinced that participation and utilization are worthwhile. However, communication alone is not enough. Recreation officials and recreation leaders must have the ability to relate departmental activities and programs to the needs of the community.

6. Cities must take into consideration the recreation needs of special segments of the population — the aged, the young, the handicapped, the economically and socially deprived — in developing priorities. In most cities surveyed, officials readily admitted that the needs of all population groups were not being adequately met. Only in recent years have cities begun to recognize an obligation to provide recreation for the handicapped and deprived.

7. Residents of deprived urban neighborhoods are almost entirely dependent upon public recreation facilities, whereas residents of more affluent neighborhoods have a wide range of recreational alternatives. Adequate recreation programs and facilities thus are considered a high priority item among the deprived.

8. Residents of urban slum neighborhoods frequently charge that too much effort is directed toward park and recreation facilities for the middle and upper income groups, and that recreation planning is being performed by persons having no real knowledge of the needs or desires of the deprived. To overcome this charge, planners should encourage the participation of a wide spectrum of the community in the planning process. To be successful, recreation programs must be what the people want, not what the recreation department believes to be best for the people. Increased emphasis on citizen participation can be an essential component for the development of meaningful programs.

---

* From National League of Cities, *Recreation in the Nation's Cities Problems and Approaches* (Washington, D. C.: National League of Cities, 1968), pp. 1-2.

APPENDIX E

TABLE 1

Recommend Standards by Classification and Population Ratio*

Classification	Acres/ 1,000 People	Size Range[b]	Population Served	Service Area
Playlots	NA[a]	2,500 sq. ft. to 1 acre	500–2,500	Sub-neighborhood
Vest-pocket parks	NA[a]	2,500 sq. ft. to 1 acre	500–2,500	Sub-neighborhood
Neighborhood parks	2.5	Min. 5 acres up to 20 acres	2,000–10,000	$1/4$–$1/2$ mile
District parks	2.5	20–100 acres	10,000–50,000	$1/2$–3 miles
Large urban parks	5.0	100+ acres	One for ea. 50,000	Within $1/2$ hr. driving time
Regional parks	20.0	250+ acres	Serves entire population in smaller communities; should be distributed throughout larger metro areas	Within 1 hr. driving time
Special areas and facilities	NA[a]	Includes parkways, beaches, plazas, historical sites, flood plains, downtown malls, and small parks, tree lawns, etc. No standard is applicable.		

[a] Not applicable.
[b] By percentage of area: The National Recreation and Park Association recommends that a minimum of 25 percent of new towns, planned unit developments, and large subdivisions be devoted to park and recreation lands and open space.

* From Robert D. Buechner (Ed.), *National Park Recreation and Open Space Standards* (Washington, D. C.: National Recreation and Park Association, 1971), p. 12.

TABLE 2
Standards for Special Facilities*

Facility (Outdoor)[a]	Standard/ 1,000 People	Comment
Baseball diamonds	1 per 6,000	Regulation 90'
Softball diamonds (and/or youth diamonds)	1 per 3,000	
Tennis courts	1 per 2,000	(Best in battery of 4)
Basketball courts	1 per 500	
Swimming pools — 25 meter	1 per 10,000	Based on 15 sq. ft. of water for each 3% of pop.
Swimming pools — 50 meter	1 per 20,000	
Skating rinks (artificial)	1 per 30,000	
Neighborhood centers	1 per 10,000	
Community centers	1 per 25,000	
Outdoor theaters (noncommercial)	1 per 20,000	
Shooting ranges	1 per 50,000	Complete complex incl. high-power, small-bore, trap and skeet, field archery, etc.
Golf courses (18-hole)	1 per 25,000	

[a] All of the facilities listed are desirable in small communities, even though their population may actually be less than the standard. Every effort should be made to light all facilities for night use, thus extending their utility.

* From Robert D. Buechner (Ed.), *National Park Recreation and Open Space Standards* (Washington, D. C.: National Recreation and Park Association, 1971), p. 13.

TABLE 3
Space Standards for Neighborhood Parks*

Facility or Unit	Area in Acres[a]	
	Park Adjoining School	Separate Park
Play apparatus area — preschool	.25	.25
Play apparatus area — older children	.25	.25
Paved multi-purpose courts	.50	.50
Recreation center building	b	.25
Sports fields	b	5.00
Senior citizens' area	.50	.50
Quiet areas and outdoor classroom	1.00	1.00
Open or "free play" area	.50	.50
Off-street parking	b	2.30[c]
Subtotal	4.00	11.55
Landscaping (buffer and special areas)	2.50	3.00
Undesignated space (10%)	.65	1.45
Total	7.15 acres	16.00 acres

[a] Suggested space standards for various units within the park. The minimum size is 5 acres.

[b] Provided by elementary school.

[c] Based on 25 cars @ 400 sq. ft. per car.

* From Robert D. Buechner (Ed.), *National Park Recreation and Open Space Standards* (Washington, D. C.: National Recreation and Park Association, 1971), p. 14.

TABLE 4
Space Standards for District Parks*

Facility or Unit	Area in Acres[a]	
	Park Adjoining School	Separate Park
Play apparatus area — preschool	.35	.35
Play apparatus — older children	.35	.35
Paved multi-purpose courts	1.25	1.75
Tennis complex	1.00	1.00
Recreation center building	b	1.00
Sports field	1.00	10.00
Senior citizens' complex	1.90	1.90
Open or "free play" area	2.00	2.00
Archery range	.75	.75
Swimming pool	1.00	1.00
Outdoor theater	.50	.50
Ice rink (artificial)	1.00	1.00
Family picnic area	2.00	2.00
Outdoor classroom area	1.00	1.00
Golf practice hole	b	.75
Off-street parking[c]	1.50	3.00
Subtotal	15.60	28.35
Landscaping (buffer and special areas)	3.00	6.00
Undesignated space (10%)	1.86	3.43
Total	20.46 acres	37.78 acres

[a] Suggested space requirements for various units within the park. The minimum size is 20 acres.

[b] Provided by Jr. or Sr. High School.

[c] Based on 330 cars @ 400 sq. ft. per car.

* From Robert D. Buechner (Ed.), *National Park Recreation and Open Space Standards* (Washington, D. C.: National Recreation and Park Association, 1971), p. 15.

TABLE 5
Principles of Recreational Planning*

---

1. Recreational experience is essential in the daily lives of people. Such experience is necessary to the balance growth and development of individuals.

2. Recreational service is a vital function of government at all levels, but its greatest manifestation is as a responsibility of local government.

3. Opportunities for participation in and appreciation of recreational experiences should be available to all of the people during whatever time they may have for such activity.

4. No artificial restriction can ever be imposed to prevent participation of people in publicly provided recreational experiences. Unjust legislative enactments, educational deficits, cultural deprivation, and other inadequacies must not be permitted to interfere with the provision of public recreational service.

5. Community organization for recreational service must include employment, coordination, and controlled development of all resources — natural, personal, artificial, public, quasi-public, and private — for the benefit of all the people of the community.

Standards for Planning Public Recreational Places

1. Land or property should be acquired in the path of a community development as forecast by a comprehensive analysis of the present community and its future outlook. A logical plan of acquisition should be initiated prior to actual need and ability of the community to develop such space.

2. Properties for recreational service use in districts already fully developed should be acquired as fortuitous circumstance permits.

3. Lands acquired for recreational purposes, such as parks, beaches, golf courses, etc., should be perpetually dedicated for such use. No other utilization should be permitted for these places, nor can they be diverted to private utilization for any reason.

4. Public recreational facilities, structures, and spaces should be situated in the most equitable manner possible so that all citizens will be provided with opportunities for engaging in the recreational experience of their choice.

5. Facilities should be situated so as to make the most efficient use of land, for the convenience of the age group or groups which utilize them, the safety of users, effectiveness of supervision, and attractive appearance.

TABLE 5—Continued

6. Public recreational places should be designed and constructed in terms of suitability for the environment and attractiveness that is in keeping with the decor of the neighborhood or community in which it is situated. Appropriate maintenance of such facilities and spaces insures their cleanliness, safety, and continued use.

7. Recreational structures, wherever situated, should provide the essential public conveniences and amenities. Whatever is suitable and necessary to the requirements of the comprehensive and well-balanced public recreational program produced therein should be an integral part of the facility.

8. Buildings and grounds of the local public school system should be designed for multipurpose utilization and made available for use by the public recreational service department, as well as other community-based groups, when such utilization does not interfere or come into conflict with the established curriculum. In return, the facilities and spaces of the public recreational service system should be made available to the public school system under reciprocal agreements.

9. Duplication of areas and facilities may be avoided by official agreements concerning the incorporation of public school plans into the total public recreational service master plan.

10. Recreational service spaces may be developed adjacent to schools.

11. If certain neighborhoods of the community do not contain schools, other recreational service places should be situated there to serve the needs of residents.

12. The plan for acquiring and developing recreational places for a given municipality should give cognizance to spaces beyond the present political borders of the city.

13. Planning for recreational places within a system should place a premium on integration and relating all recreational places in the public domain to more effectively serve the constituent population.

* From J. S. Shivers and George Hjelte, *Planning Recreational Places* (Cranbury, New Jersey; Fairleigh Dickinson University Press, 1971), pp. 47-60.

Glossary

Activity – A medium through which individuals satisfy their recreation needs and interests. Recreation activities are performed during leisure and may be of a passive or active nature.

Activity Occasion – The participation by one person in one outdoor recreational activity during all or any part of one day. One person participating in several activities during a day could account for several activity occasions.

Administration – A social process common to all areas of organized human behavior and concerned with the establishment and implementation of organizational goals.

Advocacy Planning – Planning to attain the ends of the organization or individual engaged in planning.

Aesthetic – Of or relating to the beauty in art, nature, places or things; relating to the beautiful as distinguished from merely pleasing and especially from the useful and utilitarian.

Beauty – The quality of a thing, place or experience that gives pleasure to the senses, mind or spirit.

Carrying Capacity – The number of people an outdoor recreation area can accommodate and maintain at a desirable level of landscape quality for a given recreational experience.

Central City – The largest city of an SMSA (Standard Metropolitan Statistical Area) which gives the SMSA its name.

Commitment – An action which obliges an individual or group to take certain acts or which limits future choice by foreclosing action possibilities which would otherwise exist.

Community Planning – A type of public planning in which the public is the whole community.

Comprehensive Plan – The official statement of a legislative body which sets forth its major policies concerning desirable future physical development; a unified design for a community which relates physical development policies to social and economic goals.

Computer – A device capable of employing operations that manipulate objects or symbols. It is able to take in information, perform a variety of operations on the data given, and then feed out a solution.

Condition – A feature of the situation which the planner treats as fixed either because he does not choose to change it or because he lacks the means to do so.

Conservation – The rational use of the environment to achieve the highest quality of living for mankind.

Course of Action – A sequence of prospective acts which are viewed as a unit of action, the acts which comprise the sequence are mutually related as means to the attainment of ends.

Critical Path Method (CPM) – A technique to assist management in helping to assess its progress toward an objective in terms of the time, functional responsibilities and resources needed to move from one event or action to the next.

Deviant Behavior – Leisure behavior in public parks which is not understood or accepted by other users, the suppliers, community decision-makers or general public.

End – An image of a state of affairs which is the object or goal of activity.

Environment – The aggregate of surrounding space, conditions, and influences; the totality of factors external to an organism; the sum of all the external conditions and influences affecting the life and development of an organism.

Environmental Administration – The policies, methods and processes by which man shapes his environment; the control of human action in relation to the environment.

Environmental Education – A communication process used to produce a society that is knowledgeable concerning the biophysical environment and its associated problems; aware of how to help solve these problems, and motivated to work toward their solution.

Environmental Planning – A collaboration of individuals, institutions and disciplines to improve the quality of man's life and surroundings.

Environmental Pollution – The unfavorable alteration of natural or urban surroundings.

Environmental Quality – A value orientation toward man and his surroundings; an attitude toward life, his planet and the universe.

Environmental Values – A set of attitudes or ethics dictating the nature of man's relationship with his environment, in which the good of that environment is the foremost consideration.

Expressed Demand – The expression of latent or induced needs in recreation places; or consumption of recreation opportunities by preference.

Exurb – An unincorporated, low-density, residential area outside and usually beyond the suburbs which generally ring a central city.

Facilities – Those man-made improvements in an outdoor recreation area provided to facilitate recreation use.

Gaming – A type of simulation involving the use of human decision-makers in the simulation of a real-life situation which concerns conflicting interests.

Ghetto – A residential area in which members of an ethnic or racial minority group live because of social, legal or economic pressure.

Goal – An end to which a design trends, a direction not a destination, an ideal expressed in abstract terms, a value to be sought after, not an object to be achieved.

Human Ecology – A branch of ecology which deals with the influence of human activity on the environment and the reciprocal effect of human-influenced environments on man.

Inner City – Those neighborhoods which usually surround the central business district of a metropolitan area and are considered within the geographic core of the central city.

Issue – A conflict between the objectives of different individuals or groups on a given topic.

Latent Demand – That recreation demand inherent in the population but not reflected in the use of existing facilities; additional participation could be expected to occur if adequate facilities were made available. Also see *Expressed Demand*.

Leisure – Any portion of an individual's time not occupied by gainful employment or in the pursuit of essential activities.

Limiting Condition – One which restricts the real options open to an individual, professional or institution.

M

Model – A representation of an object, process or system.

Multiple Use – Use of a resource or land area for more than one purpose at the same time.

Neighborhood – A residential area with a social and physical identity.

Objective – An aim or end of action, a point to be reached.

Open Space – All land and water in an urban area which is not covered by buildings.

Operations Research – The application of scientific and mathematical methods to the study and analysis of complex problems.

Opportunity – Those acts or courses of action which are not precluded because of some limiting conditions.

Outdoor Recreation – Leisure-time activities which utilize an outdoor area or facility.

Park – Any public area of land set aside for aesthetic, educational, recreational or cultural use.

Plan – A course of action that can be implemented to accomplish stated objectives and which someone intends to implement.

Planning – Designing a course of action to achieve ends, or a way of defining purposes and of choosing means for attaining them; or the systematic collection, organization and processing of information to facilitate decision-making; or the anticipation of and preparation for the future; or the formulation of goals and designing means to achieve these goals.

Planning-Programming-Budgeting System (PPBS) – A system to help management make more rational decisions on alternative ways to allocate resources to attain objectives in an efficient and economical manner.

Play – The free, happy, spontaneous, natural expression of people.

Policy – Any governing principle or course of action; or a general guide to conduct which, subject to modification, does imply commitment; or a guide to consistent and rational public and private decisions.

Politics – The activity (negotiation, argument, discussion, application of force, persuasion, etc.) by which an issue is agitated or settled.

Process – Change or activity in an organism or system over time.

Program – A time-phased plan for resource allocation and specifying successive steps required to achieve stated objectives.

Program Evaluation Review Technique (PERT) – A technique which management can use to assess its progress toward an objective in terms of the time, functional responsibilities and resources needed to move from one event to the next.

Program Objective – Specific results to be attained by the planned commitment of resources.

Public Interest – The ends or values of all people in a given planning unit at a given time.

Public Policy – Prevailing decisions regarding those activities that a public body will undertake, permit, or prohibit; or a consistent way of moving between means and ends until visibly changed.

Rational Decision – A decision which considers all possible courses of action to attain desired ends, identifies and evaluates the consequences of each alternative and selects the preferred alternates in terms of most valued ends; or those actions which are in the best long-term interests of man and the environment, and which recognize the irreversible biological limits of each.

Recreation – Any leisure-time activity which is pursued for its own sake.

Recreation Area – Any public or private space oriented primarily to recreation uses.

Recreation Day – A visit by one individual to a recreation development or area for recreation purposes during a reasonable portion or all of a 24-hour period.

Recreation Need – The lands, facilities and program required to provide adequate outdoor recreation opportunities.

Recreation Program – The application of human resources and technology to improve the quantity and quality of a recreational experience.

Region – An extensive area composed of related social, political, economic and geographic elements.

Self-generated Park – A recreational space initiated, planned, designed, developed and maintained by the users.

Simulation – The representation of a system to study its component parts and their relationships in terms of variable inputs and outputs.

Slum – A highly congested residential area marked by deteriorated, unsanitary buildings, absentee landlords, poverty and social disorganization.

Social Indicator – A measure of human welfare in terms of the opportunity or accommodation for a public or private good or service.

Social Issue – A question or problem that has aroused concern within society and that requires a social or public decision for its resolution.

Standard – A measure for relating an allocation of resources to existing or potential needs as determined by stated goals, objectives and policies; or a prescribed criterion of acceptable, desirable or optimum quality or performance.

Standard Metropolitan Statistical Area (SMSA) – An integrated social and economic unit which contains at least one central city of 50,000 or more inhabitants.

Suburb – An incorporated residential area outside the existing political boundaries of the central city.

System – A set of entities that collectively perform some prescribed task.

Systems Analysis – The application of scientific disciplines to a system to determine its relative worth and/or the relationships between elements or components of that system.

User Preference – The voluntary choice of an activity or experience to fulfill a recreation desire or need.

User Satisfaction – The degree of fulfillment of a recreation desire or need that occurs during or after a recreation experience.

Utopian Scheme – A course of action which could not be carried out, which would not have the consequences intended, or which no one intends to carry out.

Vandalism – The willful or thoughtless destruction of property in park and recreation areas.

Variable – A quantity that may increase or decrease without other essential changes.

Water Pollution – Any change in water quality that impairs it for the subsequent user.

Wilderness – An area where the earth and its community of life are untrammeled by man, and where man himself is a visitor who does not remain.

Bibliography

Abrams, Charles, *The Language of Cities* (New York: The Viking Press, 1971).

Adams, Frederick J., *Urban Planning Education in the United States* (Cincinnati: Bettman Foundation, 1954).

"Age-Group Playgrounds in Kalamazoo Please Child Patrons," *News Bulletin of the Public Administration Clearing House*, Release No. 5 (October 31, 1941).

Alinsky, Saul, *Reveille for Radicals* (Chicago: University of Chicago Press, 1946).
———, "Plan of Operations, Neighborhood Urban Extension" (Pittsburgh: ACTION Housing, Inc., 1963).

Altshuler, Alan A., *The City Planning Process* (Ithaca, N. Y.: Cornell University Press, 1965).

American Institute of Planners, *Handbook and Roster* (Washington, D. C.: American Institute of Planners, 1968).

American Society of Planning Officials, *Policy Statements: Guides to Decision Making*, Report #152 (Chicago: American Society of Planning Officials, November, 1961).
———, "What Is Expected of a Planning Program," *ASPO Newsletter* (May, 1964), p. 42.
———, "HUD's Guide to Model Neighborhoods in Demonstration Cities," *ASPO Newsletter*, XXXIII, No. 2 (February-March, 1967), p. 24.

Amherst Wilder Foundation, *Participation in Leisure-Time Activities*, 1955-56 (St. Paul: The Foundation, October, 1956).

Appleyard, Donald, and Lintell, Mark, *Environmental Quality of City Streets* (Berkeley: Center for Planning and Development Research, University of California, 1970).

Aschman, Frederick T., *The ABC's of Community Planning* (Chicago: Community Planning Division of Sears, Roebuck and Co., 1962).

Bagdikian, Ben H., "It Has Come to This," *Saturday Evening Post* (August 10, 1968), pp. 20-21.

Balk, Alfred, "Progress and Parks," *National Civic Review* (October, 1960). Cited in *Current* (March, 1961), p. 57.

Bangs, H. P., and Mahler, S., "Users of Local Parks," *Journal of the American Institute of Planners*, XXXVI, No. 5 (September, 1970), pp. 330-334.

323

Bauer, Raymond A., Ed., *Social Indicators* (Cambridge: M.I.T. Press, 1966).

Bellush, Jewel, and Hansknecht, Murray, "Planning Participation and Urban Renewal," *Urban Renewal: People, Politics and Planning,* edited by Bellush and Hansknecht (Garden City, N. Y.: Anchor Books, 1967).

Boulding, Kenneth E., *The Meaning of the Twentieth Century* (New York: Harper & Row, 1964).

——, "The Ethics of Rational Decision," *Management Science,* XII (February, 1966), p. 161.

Brewer, C. E., "The Influence of Zoning on the Design of Public Recreation Facilities," *Proceedings of the American Society of Civil Engineers* (Chicago, February, 1925).

Broady, Maurice R., "The Social Aspects of Town Development," *Taming Megalopolis,* edited by Wentworth Eldredge (New York: Doubleday, 1967).

Brockman, C. Frank, *Recreational Use of Wild Lands* (New York: McGraw-Hill Book Co., 1959).

Brown, Claude, *Manchild in the Promised Land* (New York: Macmillan Co., 1965).

Buechner, Robert D., Ed., *National Park, Recreation and Open Space Standards* (Washington, D. C.: National Recreation and Park Association, 1971).

Bureau of Government Research, *The Local Planning Process in New Jersey* (New Brunswick, N. J.: Rutgers University Press, 1967).

Burns, DeLisle, *Leisure in the Modern World* (New York: The Century Company, 1932).

Butler, George D., Introduction to Community Recreation (New York: McGraw-Hill Book Company, 1967).

——, *Recreation Areas* (New York: A. S. Barnes & Co., 1947).

——, "Standards for Municipal Recreation Areas," *Recreation* (July, 1948), p. 161.

——, *Standards for Municipal Recreation Areas* (New York: National Recreation Association, 1962).

——, Ed., *Playgrounds* (New York: A. S. Barnes & Co., 1936).

Cain, Stanley A., "Concluding Remarks," *Elements of Outdoor Recreation Planning,* edited by B. L. Driver (Ann Arbor: University Microfilms, 1970).

California Committee on Planning for Recreation, Park Areas and Facilities. *Guide for Planning Recreation Parks in California* (Sacramento: California Recreation Commission, 1956).

Canty, Donald, *A Single Society* (New York: Praeger Publishers, 1969).

Carlson, Reynold E., Deppe, Theodore R., and MacLean, Janet R., *Recreation in American Life* (Belmont, Calif.: Wadsworth Publishing Co., 1963).

Carmichael, Stokely, and Hamilton, Charles V., *Black Power* (New York: Vintage Books, 1967).

Carson, D. H., and Driver, B. L., *An Environmental Approach to Human Stress and Well-Being with Implications for Planning* (Ann Arbor: Mental Health Research Institute, The University of Michigan, 1967).

Catholic Youth Organization, *The Leisure-Time Problems of Puerto Rican Youth in New York City* (New York: Archdiocese of New York, 1953).

"Census Data on U. S. Population," *ASPO Newsletter* (August, 1967), p. 102.

Chapin, F. Stewart, Jr., *Urban Land Use Planning* (Urbana: University of Illinois Press, 1965).

Chicago Recreation Commission, *Principles for Chicago's Comprehensive Recreation Plan* (Chicago: The Commission, May, 1954).

Clark, Kenneth B., *Dark Ghetto* (New York: Harper & Row, 1965).

Clawson, Marion, *The Dynamics of Park Demand* (New York: Regional Plan Association, 1960).

———, "A Positive Approach to Open Space Preservation," *Journal of the American Institute of Planners*, XXVIII (May, 1962), p. 126.

———, *Land and Water for Recreation* (Chicago: Rand-McNally and Company, 1963).

———, *Economics of Outdoor Recreation* (Baltimore: Johns Hopkins Press, 1966).

———, and Knetsch, Jack, *Outdoor Recreation Research* (Washington, D. C.: Resources for the Future, Inc., Reprint #43, 1963).

Clegg, Gilbert, "Playground Planning and Layout," *Recreation* (June, 1935). Cited by Butler in *Recreation Areas*, p. 99.

Committee for Economic Development, *Budgeting for National Objectives* (New York: Committee for Economic Development, 1966).

Community Chest of San Francisco, *Recreation in San Francisco* (San Francisco: The Community Chest, 1950).

Conant, James B., *Slums and Suburbs* (New York: McGraw-Hill Book Co., 1961).

———, Commencement address at Michigan State University, June, 1967. Published in *Michigan State University Publication*, Vol. 62, No. 5 (November, 1967), p. 18.

Converse, Phillip E., and Robinson, John P., *Summary of United States Time Use Survey* (Ann Arbor: The University of Michigan, Survey Research Center, 1966).

Cooper, Clare C., *The Adventure Playground: Creative Play in an Urban Setting* (Berkeley: Center for Planning and Development Research, University of California, 1970).

———, "Adventure Playgrounds," *Landscape Architecture* (October, 1970), pp. 18-25.

Creative Playthings, Inc., *A Child's Way of Learning* (Princeton, N. J.: Creative Playthings, Inc., 1968).

Curtis, Henry, "Provisions and Responsibility for Playgrounds," *The Annals* (February, 1910), p. 125.

Cutten, George A., *The Threat of Leisure* (New Haven: Yale University Press, 1926).

Davidoff, Paul, "Advocacy and Pluralism in Planning," *Journal of the American Institute of Planners* (November 1965), p. 331.

Davis, Hugh C., "A Comprehensive Recreation Plan for the City," unpublished paper presented at the annual meeting of the American Nature Study Society, New York, December 28, 1967.

———, "Technological Change and Recreation Planning," *Elements of Outdoor Recreation Planning*, edited by B. L. Driver (Ann Arbor: University Microfilms, 1970).

Davis, Kingsley, "The Urbanization of the Human Population," *Cities*, Editors of Scientific American (New York: Alfred A. Knopf, 1966).

Davis, Robert K., "Recreation Planning as an Economic Problem," *Natural Resources Journal* (October, 1963), pp. 239-249.

DeGrazia, Sebastian, *Of Time, Work and Leisure* (Garden City, N. Y.: Anchor Books, Doubleday, 1964).

———, "Some Reflections on the History of Outdoor Recreation," paper presented at the National Short Course on Elements of Outdoor Recreation Planning, Ann Arbor: The University of Michigan, 1968.

Department of Commerce and Economic Development, *Washington Statewide Outdoor Recreation and Open Space Plan* (Spokane: Department of Commerce and Economic Development, January, 1967).

Detroit Metropolitan Area Regional Planning Commission, *Regional Recreation Lands Plan* (Detroit, Mich.: The Commission, June, 1960).

Dewhurst, James Frederick, *America's Needs and Resources* (New York: 20th Century Fund, 1955).

Dickens, Charles, *Oliver Twist* (New York: Dodd, Mead & Co., 1941).

Doell, Charles E., *A Brief History of Parks and Recreation in the United States* (Chicago: The Athletic Institute, 1954).

———, *Park and Recreation Administration* (Minneapolis: Burgess Publishing Co., 1963).

Douglass, Paul, "The Administration and Leisure for Living," *Bulletin of the American Recreation Society*, XII, No. 3 (April, 1960), p. 11.

Downs, Anthony, "The Future of American Ghettos," paper presented at the American Academy of Arts and Sciences Conference on Urbanism, Cambridge, Mass., Oct. 27-28, 1967.

Driver, B. L., Ed., *Elements of Outdoor Recreation Planning* (Ann Arbor: University Microfilms, 1970).

Dúbos, Rene Jules, "Man Adapting: His Limitations and Potentials," *Environment for Man*, edited by William R. Ewald (Bloomington, Indiana: Indiana University Press, 1967).

Editors of Fortune, *The Changing American Market* (Garden City, N. Y.: Hanover House, 1955).

Erber, Ernest, "New Directions in Planning," *The Local Planning Process* (New Brunswick, N. J.: Bureau of Government Research, Rutgers State University, 1967).

Fels Institute of Local and State Government, *Proceedings of the 1966 Graduate Colloquium*, Philadelphia, Pa., 1966.

Ford, James, *Slums and Housing: History, Conditions, Policy* (Cambridge: Harvard University Press, 1936).

Fried, Marc, and Levin, Joan, "Some Social Functions of the Urban Slum," *Urban Planning and Social Policy*, edited by Bernard J. Frieden and Robert Morris New York: Basic Books, Inc., 1968).

Friedberg, Paul M., *Play and Interplay* (New York: Macmillan Company, 1970).

Galbraith, John Kenneth, *The Affluent Society* (Boston: Houghton Mifflin Co., 1958).

Gans, Herbert, "Recreation Planning for Leisure Behavior: A Goal Oriented Approach." Unpublished Ph.D. dissertation, University of Pennsylvania, 1957.

——, *The Urban Villagers* (New York: The Free Press, 1962).

——, "City Planning and Urban Realities," *Journal of the American Institute of Planners* (January, 1962), p. 132.

——, "Social and Physical Planning for the Elimination of Urban Poverty," *Urban Planning and Social Policy*, edited by Bernard J. Frieden and Robert Morris (New York: Basic Books, Inc., 1968).

Gavin, James M., and Hadley, Arthur, "The Crisis of the Cities: The Battle We Can Win." *Saturday Review* (February 24, 1968), p. 31.

Gold, Seymour M., "A Concept for Recreation Planning in the Inner City." Unpublished Ph.D. dissertation, University of Michigan, 1969.

——, "An International Glossary for Environmental Studies," *International Journal of Environmental Studies*, Vol. 4 (September, 1972), pp. 1-6.

——, "Nonuse of Public Parks," *Leisure, Society and Politics*, Richard Harris (ed.), (Davis, Calif.: University of California Extension, 1972), pp. 1-14.

——, "Environmental Studies: An Educational Prospectus," *International Journal of Environmental Studies*, Vol. 3 (March, 1972), pp. 55-64.

——, "Environmental Planning: A Professional Challenge," *Parks and Recreation*, VII, No. 6 (June, 1972), pp. 23-26.

——, "Nonuse of Neighborhood Parks," *Journal of the American Institute of Planners*, Vol. 38, No. 5 (November, 1972), pp. 369-378.

Goodale, Thomas L., "The Fallacy of Our Programs," *Parks and Recreation* (November, 1967), p. 39.

Goodman, William I., ed., *Principles and Practice of Urban Planning* (Washington, D. C.: International City Managers Association, 1968).

Gottman, Jean, *Megalopolis* (Cambridge: The M.I.T. Preess, 1961).

Guetzkow, Harold S., *Simulation in the Social Sciences* (Englewood Cliffs, N. J.: Prentice-Hall, 1962).

Halpern, I., *The Slum and Crime* (New York: New York City Housing Authority, 1934).

Hanmer, Lee, *Regional Survey of New York and Its Environs*, Public Recreation, Vol. V. (New York: Committee on the Regional Plan, 1928).

Harrington Michael, *The Other America* (New York: The Macmillan Co., 1962).

Higbee, Edward, *The Squeeze* (New York: William Morrow and Co., 1960).

Hjelte, George, *The Administration of Public Recreation* (New York: The Macmillan Co., 1940).

——, and Shivers, Jay S., *Public Administration of Park and Recreational Services* (New York: The Macmillan Co., 1963).

——, and ——, *Planning Recreational Places* (Cranbury, N. J.: Fairleigh Dickinson University Press, 1971).

Hubbard, Henry, "The Size and Distribution of Playgrounds and Similar Recreation Facilities in American Cities," *Proceedings of the 6th National Conference on City Planning*, Boston, 1914.

Hunter, David R., *The Slums: Challenge and Response* (New York: The Free Press, 1964).

Illinois, *1967 Addenda, State Outdoor Recreation Plan* (Springfield: Illinois Department of Business and Economic Development, June, 1967).

Inter-County Regional Planning Commission, *Recreation in the Denver Region* Denver, Colo.: The Commission, July, 1958).

International City Managers' Association, *Local Planning Administration* (Chicago: The Association, 1948).

————, *Municipal Recreation Administration* (Chicago: The Association, 1960).

Jacobs, Jane, *The Life and Death of Great American Cities* (New York: Random House, 1961).

Jacobs, Paul, *Prelude to Riot* (New York: Random House, 1966).

Jensen, Clayne R., *Outdoor Recreation in America* (Minneapolis: Burgess, 1970).

Kahl, J. A., *The American Class Structure* (New York: Holt, Rinehart & Winston, 1957).

Kaplan, Max, *Leisure in America* (New York: John Wiley & Sons, Inc., 1960).

Knetsch, Jack, "Demand for Outdoor Recreation," *Elements of Outdoor Recreation Planning*, edited by B. L. Driver (Ann Arbor: University Microfilms, 1970).

Knickerbocker, Conrad, 'No One's in Charge," *Life Magazine* (December 24, 1965), p. 37.

Lady Allen of Hurtwood, *Planning for Play* (Cambridge: M.I.T. Press, 1968).

Laidles, R. W., *Criminal Activity in Selected Seattle Parks* (Seattle: Department of Parks and Recreation, 1970).

Landahl, William L., "Park Standards, Open Space and Quality," *Trends in Parks and Recreation*, XV, No. 1 (January, 1968), p. 21.

Landsberg, Hans H., *Resources in America's Future* (Baltimore: Johns Hopkins Press for Resources for the Future, Inc., 1963).

Lansing, John B., and Hendricks, Gary, *Living Patterns in the Detroit Region* (Detroit, Michigan: Detroit Regional Transportation and Land Use Study, 1967).

————, and ————, *Living Patterns and Attitudes in the Detroit Region* (Detroit, Mich.: Detroit Metropolitan Area Regional Planning Commission, 1967).

————, and Marans, Robert W., "An Approach to the Evaluation of the Quality of Neighborhoods," unpublished paper, Survey Research Center, The University of Michigan, 1967.

————, ————, and Zehner, R. B., *Planned Residential Environments* (Ann Arbor: Survey Research Center, Institute for Social Research, University of Michigan, 1970).

Leopold, Aldo, *A Sand County Almanac* (New York: Oxford University Press, 1966).

Levin, H. M., *Estimating the Municipal Demand for Public Recreation Land* (Washington, D. C.: Brookings Institution, October, 1966).

Lewis, Philip H., Jr., *Recreation and Open Space in Illinois* (Urbana, Ill.: Bureau of Community Planning, University of Illinois, September, 1961), cited in *Open Space in Northeastern Illinois* (Chicago: Northeastern Metropolitan Area Planning Commission, 1962).

Lies, Eugene T., *A Study in the Leisure-Time Problem and Recreation Facilities in Cincinnati and Vicinity* (Cincinnati: Bureau of Government Research, 1935).

Life Magazine, "The Cities Lock Up" (New York: Time-Life Publishing Company, Vol. 71, No. 21), pp. 24-33.

Lindblom, Charles E., and Braybrooke, David, *The Strategy of Decision* (New York: The Free Press, 1963).

Loftus, Joseph A., "Census Clock," *New York Times* (Oct. 29, 1967).

Lynch, Kevin, and Rivkin, M., "A Walk Around the Block," *Environmental Psychology,* edited by H. M. Prohansky et al. (New York: Holt Rinehart & Winston, 1970).

MacIver, Robert, "The Pursuit of Happiness," *Mass Leisure,* edited by Eric Larrabee and Rolf Meyersohn (Glencoe, Ill., The Free Press, 1958).

Madge, John, *The Tools of Social Science* (Garden City, N. Y.: Anchor Books, 1965).

Malt, Harold L., "An Analysis of Public Safety as Related to the Incidence of Crime in Parks and Recreation Areas in Central Cities," by Harold Lewis Malt Associates for U. S. Department of Housing and Urban Development, January, 1972.

McHarg, Ian L., *Design with Nature* (Garden City, N. Y.: Natural History Press, 1969).

Meier, Richard L., and Duke, Richard D., "Gaming Simulation for Urban Planning," *Journal of the American Institute of Planners* (January, 1966), pp. 3-16.

Meyer, Harold D., and Brightbill, Charles K., *Community Recreation* (Boston: D. C. Heath & Co., 1948).

———, Brightbill, C. K., and Sessoms, H. D., *Community Recreation* (Englewood Cliffs, N. J.: Prentice-Hall, 1969).

Meyerson, Martin, and Banfield, Edward, *Politics, Planning and the Public Interest* (Glencoe, Ill.: The Free Press, 1955).

Michael, Donald, *The Next Generation* (New York: Random House, 1965).

Miller, Norman P., and Robinson, Duane M., *The Leisure Age* (Belmont, Calif.: Wadsworth Publishing Company, Inc., 1963).

Miller, Walter B., *Cultural Features of an Urban Lower Class Community* (Washington, D. C.: Community Services Branch, National Institute of Health, 1959).

Mueller, Eva, and Gurin, G., *Participation in Outdoor Recreation: Factors Affecting Demand among American Adults,* ORRRC Study Report 20 (Washington: Government Printing Office, 1962).

Municipal Recreation Commission, *1955 Annual Report* (Syracuse: City of Syracuse, 1955).

Nading, Martin M., Jr., "The Relationships of Selected Program Variables to the Playgrounds of Fort Wayne, Indiana." Unpublished M.S. thesis, Indiana University, February, 1952.

Nash, Jay, "Standards of Play and Recreation." *National Municipal Review* (July, 1931), p. 493.

National Academy of Sciences, *A Program for Outdoor Recreation* (Washington, D. C.: National Academy of Sciences, 1969).

National Advisory Commission on Civil Disorders, *Report of the National Commission on Civil Disorders* (New York: Bantam Books, 1968).

National Association of Counties, *Community Action Guides for Outdoor Recreation: Planning* (Washington, D. C.: National Association of Counties, 1968).

National League of Cities, *Recreation in the Nation's Cities Problems and Approaches* (Washington, D. C.: National League of Cities, 1968).

National Recreation and Park Association, *Recreation and Park Yearbook, 1961* (Washington, D. C.: National Recreation and Park Association, 1961).

———, *Recreation and Park Yearbook, 1966* (Washington, D. C.: National Recreation and Park Association, 1966).

———, *A Study of New York Outdoor Recreation Needs* (New York: City Planning Commission, 1967).

———, *Outdoor Recreation Space Standards* (Washington, D. C.: National Recreation and Park Association, 1967).

———, "Local Agency Survey," *Parks and Recreation*, VI, No. 8 (August, 1971), pp. 17-31.

National Recreation Association, *Park and Recreation Yearbook* (New York: National Recreation Association, 1951).

Nesbitt, John A., Brown, Paul D., and Murphy, James F., eds., *Recreation and Leisure Service for the Disadvantaged* (Philadelphia: Lea & Febiger, 1970).

Neumeyer, Martin H., and Neumeyer, Ester S., *Leisure and Recreation*, 3rd ed. (New York: The Roland Press Co., 1958).

New York Times (Oct. 29, 1967), p. 66.

Olmsted, Frederick Law, *Public Parks and the Enlargement of Towns* (Cambridge: Riverside Press, 1870).

———, "The Normal Requirements of American Towns and Cities in Respect to Public Open Space," *Charities and the Commons* (July, 1906), pp. 411-417.

Oppenheim, A. N., *Questionnaire Design and Attitude Measurement* (New York: Basic Books, Inc., 1966).

Outdoor Recreation for America, a report to the President and Congress by the Outdoor Recreation Resources Review Commission, Washington, D. C., January, 1962. Cited in *Open Space in Northeastern Illinois* (Chicago: Northeastern Metropolitan Area Planning Commission, 1962).

Outdoor Recreation Resources Review Commission, *Outdoor Recreation for America* (Washington, D. C.: Government Printing Office, 1962).

Overstreet, Harry, *A Guide to Civilized Leisure* (New York: W. W. Norton & Co., Inc., 1934).

Pack, Arthur Newton, *The Challenge of Leisure* (New York: Macmillan Co., 1936).

Partridge, Eric, *Origins, A Short Etymological Dictionary of Modern English* (New York: Macmillan Co., 1958).

Peattie, Lisa R., "Reflections on Advocacy Planning," *Journal of the American Institute of Planners*, XXXIV, No. 2 (March, 1968), p. 80.

Playground and Recreation Association, *Play Areas* (New York: Barnes, 1928).

Prohansky, H. M., et al., *Environmental Psychology* (New York: Holt, Rinehart & Winston, 1970).

Rainwater, Clarence E., *The Play Movement in the United States* (Chicago: University of Chicago Press, 1922).

Rainwater, Lee, "Fear and the House-as-Haven in the Lower Class," *Urban Planning and Social Policy*, edited by Bernard J. Frieden and Robert Morris (New York: Basic Books, Inc., 1968).

————, and Yancy, William L., *The Moynihan Report and the Politics of Controversy* (Cambridge: The M.I.T. Press, 1967).

Regional Plan Association, *The Race for Open Space* (New York: The Association, 1960).

Reid, Leslie M., *Outdoor Recreation Preferences: A Nationwide Study of User Preferences* (East Lansing, Mich.: The B/J Press, 1964).

————, "Utilizing User Preference in Predicting Outdoor Recreation Demand." Unpublished paper presented at the National Recreation Research Conference, Pennsylvania State University, Nov. 7-10, 1965.

Reisman, David, *The Lonely Crowd* (New Haven: Yale University Press, 1950).

Resources for the Future, *Resources Newsletter* (Washington, D. C.: Resources for the Future, September, 1963).

Rettie, Dwight, "Plan Implementation, Coordination and Communication," *Elements of Outdoor Recreation Planning,* edited by B. L. Driver (Ann Arbor: University Microfilms, 1970).

Revelle, Roger, "Outdoor Recreation in a Hyper-productive Society," *Daedulus: Journal of the American Academy of Arts and Sciences* (Fall, 1967), p. 172.

Richmond Regional Planning and Economic Development Commission, *Open Spaces in the Richmond Region* (Richmond, Va.: The Commission, January, 1960).

Riis, Jacob, *How the Other Half Lives* (New York: Sagamore Press, 1957).

Russell, Bertrand, "In Praise of Idleness and Other Essays," *Mass Leisure,* edited by Eric Larrabee and Rolf Meyersohn (Glencoe, Ill.: The Free Press, 1958).

Rustin, Bayard, "From Protest to Politics: The Future of the Civil Rights Movement," *Urban Planning and Social Policy,* edited by Bernard J. Frieden and Robert Morris (New York: Basic Books, Inc., 1968).

Rutledge, Albert J., *Anatomy of a Park* (New York: McGraw-Hill Book Co., 1971).

Satterthwaite, Ann, "Some Thoughts on Planning the Recreation Environment," *Elements of Outdoor Recreation Planning,* edited by B. L. Driver (Ann Arbor: University Microfilms, 1970).

Sedlin, Barbara, "Leisure Time Planning and Open Space Programming." Paper presented at the annual meeting of the Michigan Academy of Science and Arts, Cranbrook School, Bloomfield Hills, Michigan, March 19, 1961.

Seely, John R., "The Slum: Its Nature, Use and Users," *Journal of the American Institute of Planners,* Vol. XXV, No. 1 (February, 1959), p. 7.

Sessoms, H. Douglas, "New Bases for Recreation Planning," *Journal of the American Institute of Planners* (May, 1965), pp. 26-31.

Shaw, Clifford, and McKay, Henry D., *Delinquency Areas* (Chicago: University of Chicago Press, 1929).

Shivers, Jay S., and Hjelte, George, *Planning Recreational Places* (Cranbury, N. J.: Fairleigh Dickinson University Press, 1970).

Sinn, Donald F., "Encroachment Survey Findings," *Parks and Recreation* (November, 1960), p. 505.

Sommer, Robert, *Personal Space* (Englewood Cliffs, N. J.: Prentice-Hall, 1969).

————, *Environmental Awareness* (San Francisco: Rinehart Press, 1972).

Spreiregen, Paul D., *Urban Design: The Architecture of Towns and Cities* (New York: McGraw-Hill Book Co., 1965).

Stokes, Charles, "A Theory of Slums," *Land Economics*, Vol XXXXVII, No. 3 (August, 1962), pp. 187-197.

Styles, Frederick G., "Variables Which Must Be Considered in Outdoor Recreation Planning," *Elements of Outdoor Recreation Planning*, edited by B. L. Driver (Ann Arbor: University Microfilms, 1970).

Sutherland, Edwin H., *Principles of Criminology* (Philadelphia: J. B. Lippincott Co., 1924).

Svenson, Erik A., "Differential Adaptation to Change in Urban Form." Unpublished Ph.D. dissertation, Massachusetts Institute of Technology, 1967.

Time, Inc., *The Negro and the City* (New York: Time-Life Books, 1968).

Tupper, Margo, *No Place to Play* (New York: Chilton Books, 1966).

Twardzik, Louis F., "Expanding the User Approach to Recreation Area Planning." Unpublished paper presented at the Recreation Lands Conference, Detroit, Mich.: March 28, 1963.

U. S. Department of Commerce, Bureau of the Census, *1960 Census of Population* (Washington, D. C.: Government Printing Office, 1960).

———, ———, *Statistical Abstract of the United States* (Washington, D. C.: Government Printing Office, 1971).

U. S. Department of the Interior, Bureau of Outdoor Recreation, *Guidebook for State Outdoor Recreation Planning* (Washington, D. C.: Government Printing Office, 1964).

———, ———, *Manual: Nationwide Plan* (Washington, D. C.: Government Printing Office, 1964).

———, ———, *State Outdoor Recreation Statistics, 1962*, Report No. 1. Washington, D. C.: Division of Research and Education, Statistical Series, 1963. Excerpted from *Recreation*, Vol. LVIII, No. 3 (New York: National Recreation Association, March, 1965).

———, ———, *Outdoor Recreation Research: A Reference Catalog* (Washington, D. C.: Government Printing Office, 1966 and 1967).

———, ———, *Outdoor Recreation Space Standards* (Washington, D. C.: Government Printing Office, 1967).

———, ———, *Outdoor Recreation Trends* (Washington, D. C.: Government Printing Office, 1967).

———, ———, *Lake Ontario Basin Report* (Ann Arbor: Bureau of Outdoor Recreation, 1968).

———, ———, *Selected Outdoor Recreation Statistics* (Washington, D. C.: Government Printing Office, 1971).

Warner, W. L., Meeker, Marcia, and Ellis, Kenneth, *Social Class in America: The Evaluation of Status* (Chicago: Science Research Associates, 1949).

Weaver, Robert C., *The Urban Complex* (Garden City, N. J.: Doubleday, 1960).

Webb, E. J., *Unobtrusive Measures* (Chicago: Rand-McNally & Co., 1966).

Webber, Melvin M., "Comprehensive Planning and Social Responsibility," *Urban Planning and Social Policy*, edited by Bernard J. Frieden and Robert Morris (New York: Basic Books, Inc., 1968).

Webster, Donald H., *Urban Planning and Municipal Public Policy* (New York: Harper and Bros., 1958).

Webster's New World Dictionary (New York: The World Publishing Co., 1950).

Whyte, William Foote, *Street Corner Society* (Chicago: University of Chicago Press, 1955).

————, "Urban Recreation Use," Preliminary Report to the Citizens' Committee on Environmental Quality, April 1972, in *Annual Report to the President and the Council on Environmental Quality* (Washington, D. C.: Government Printing Office, 1972).

Williams, Wayne R., *Recreation Places* (New York: Reinhold Publishing Corporation, 1958).

Wilson, James Q., "Planning and Politics: Citizen Participation in Urban Renewal," *Urban Planning and Social Policy*, edited by Bernard J. Frieden and Robert Morris (New York: Basic Books, Inc., 1968).

Wise, Harold F., "The State of the Art of Comprehensive Planning," *Elements of Outdoor Recreation Planning*, edited by B. L. Driver (Ann Arbor: University Microfilms, 1970).

Wright, Louis B., *Middle Class Culture in Elizabethan England* (Chapel Hill: University of North Carolina Press, 1935).

York, Ray D., "An Analysis of Playground Attendance and Activity." Unpublished M.S. thesis, University of Southern California, 1937.

Young, Robert C., "Goals and Goal Setting," *Journal of the American Institute of Planners*, XXXII, No. 2 (March, 1966), p. 78.

————, "Establishment of Goals and Definition of Objectives," *Elements of Outdoor Recreation Planning*, edited by B. L. Driver (Ann Arbor: University Microfilms, 1970).

"Zoom in on the City," *Life Magazine* (December 24, 1965).